Edwin
Arlington
ROBINSON

a reference guide

A
Reference
Publication
in
Literature

Ronald Gottesman
Editor

Edwin
Arlington
ROBINSON

a reference guide

NANCY CAROL JOYNER

G.K.HALL&CO.

70 LINCOLN STREET, BOSTON, MASS.

Copyright © 1978 by Nancy Carol Joyner

Library of Congress Cataloging in Publication Data
Joyner, Nancy.
    Edwin Arlington Robinson: a reference guide.

    (Reference publications in literature)
    Bibliography: p.
    Includes index.
    1. Robinson, Edwin Arlington, 1869–1935 — Bibliography.
I. Series.
Z8748.37.J68   [PS3535.025]   016.811'5'2   77-25280
ISBN 0-8161-7807-0

This publication is printed on permanent/durable acid-free paper
MANUFACTURED IN THE UNITED STATES OF AMERICA

Contents

Introduction

THE SHAPE OF ROBINSON CRITICISM

Edwin Arlington Robinson, with a fine ear for words, once observed
that his name sounded like a tin can being kicked down the stairs.
Other difficulties with his name, both literal and figurative, abound.
The curious inability to get it right has persisted since his first
book was reviewed; one of his three citations for the Pulitzer Prize
was inscribed to "Edward" instead of "Edwin," and one of the numerous
silent corrections of his name in this volume is in the title of an
article published in 1969. To the reading public he is confused,
forgivably, with Robinson Jeffers, and understandably if not so forgivably, with Edgar Lee Masters. More importantly, the somewhat dis-
maying number of viewpoints about his poetry has led to a confusion
about his proper place in American letters. That Robinson was the
most significant American poet writing during the decades on either
side of the turn of the century is as incontestable as the fact that
he never published a line of free verse, but beyond that there is
little agreement among scholars. The gamut of opinions about him runs
from the view that he is a minor writer of mediocre verses to the
assertion that he is the greatest poet America has ever produced.
While the majority of critics place his work in the romantic tradition of New England transcendentalism, persuasive arguments have been
made for Robinson as a realist, a naturalist, and an existentialist.
Lyric power is sometimes claimed as the most essential quality of his
work; at other times his narrative abilities are singled out. The
fact is that, with twenty volumes of poetry in a forty-year career,
Robinson cannot be placed neatly in a single tradition, nor can his
work be fixed as representative of a single mode. His accomplishment
is both large and multifaceted.

Just as critical assessment of the nature of his work has varied,
the amount of critical attention has fluctuated. During the first
half of his career he received relatively little public notice. From
1916 onward attention from the press grew, if not steadily then con-
tinuously, reaching peaks in 1927 and 1929 and culminating with his
death in 1935. For the last fifteen years of his career it was as-
sumed that Robinson was the most important living American poet, and
each of the fourteen volumes he issued received mandatory notices in

vii

leading newspapers and journals. After his death this high acclaim was given over to the other giants of modern American poetry, Eliot and Frost, and scholarly attention to Robinson quickly waned. This book lists eighty-one articles for 1935; in 1945 there were six; in 1955 the number had shrunk to four. In the sixties, however, interest in him was renewed, coming again to a peak in 1969, the centennial of his birth, with fifty-three articles.

Not only the number but also the kinds of articles written about Robinson have changed over the years. Many of the essays and books written during his lifetime and continuing through the next two decades are of the "gee whiz" school of criticism. His work was subjected to laudatory effusions rather than real analysis, giving credence to the suggestion of Robert Hillyer in 1930 that he was "more praised than read." With a few important exceptions, serious study of his work did not appear until the late fifties, when appreciations and reminiscences were replaced by close readings, source studies, and examinations of his intellectual background.

Even with the resurgence of critical analysis of his work, Robinson's reputation still suffers from inadequate attention. As the creator of Richard Cory, Miniver Cheevy, and Mr. Flood, he is known throughout the English-speaking world, but his major work, the book-length narratives, is known principally to literary historians, whose knowledge all too often comes from secondary rather than primary sources. The difficulty in anthologizing the long poems is one reason for this lack of attention. Another is the sanguine acceptance of the critical cliché that the long poems are of less intrinsic worth than the Tilbury pieces. Furthermore, critics have been possibly unwilling to study him because his poetry, with its Jamesian subtlety and quiet precision, lacks shock value. ("Richard Cory," a poem Robinson claimed that he did not like and complained that it was "pickled in anthological brine," shocks.) In 1940 a Sister Mary Catherine wrote approvingly of Robinson's work, "One never finds revolting passages or language better left unsaid" (1940.B5). True as the statement may be, its prim tone reflects one widespread attitude about his work that ultimately leads to a distortion of it. Nevertheless, this notion has served as a deterrent to critical interest.

The more than 1400 bibliographical entries in this book indicate that the body of Robinson criticism is considerable, but there are many avenues left to explore in the Robinson canon. Although six biographies and numerous other lesser reminiscences exist, a thorough, documented biography is yet to be written. A disproportionate number of explications of the best known poems have appeared while scores of poems, especially those of medium length, have never been analyzed. Of the dozen book-length poems, the Arthurian trilogy, Captain Craig, and Amaranth have been carefully examined, but the rest are relatively untouched by the critics' scrutiny. Discussions of Robinson's world view and the importance of his New England background to his thought are abundant, but stylistic analysis is scanty.

Introduction

In spite of the unusually large number of manuscripts housed in several libraries, little textual study has been done. Someday someone will prepare a variorum edition of Robinson's poetry; the material is on hand. A primary purpose of this work is to help future scholars avoid redundancy and to identify those areas of Robinson scholarship that merit further attention.

SCOPE AND METHOD OF THE BIBLIOGRAPHY

Richard Cary, in his Early Reception of Edwin Arlington Robinson: The First Twenty Years (1974.A1), has reprinted and meticulously annotated some 160 known reviews of Robinson's poetry from 1896 to 1916. For that reason, I have made representative selections from Cary's book and included annotations of them in the first part of this book. The bibliography proper covers the years 1916–1976, and in it I have attempted to provide comprehensive listing of all known reviews, critical assessments, and works of biographical interest about Robinson written during that period. I have deliberately omitted reviews of criticism, with a few significant exceptions. (William Carlos Williams' review of Emery Neff's biography, the only written opinion of Robinson's work by Williams, is a case in point.) According to that principle, I have not included the essays about Robinson criticism appearing annually in American Literary Scholarship, although I call the reader's attention to them here. Unless introductory material in anthologies and textbooks seemed of particular importance, I have also excluded those books. Unpublished doctoral dissertations have been included but not master's theses.

My two principal sources have been the bibliographies compiled by Charles Beecher Hogan (1936.A1) and William White (1971.A2), supplemented by the standard bibliographies in the field, such as those in PMLA and American Literature, to bring the listings up to date. A few entries have been added that do not appear in either of the major bibliographies, but I am painfully aware that numerous other reviews, especially those in newspapers, must exist and have not been located. Jacob Blanck has made the apt remark, "Sooner or later all must know that completion is not to be attained; bibliographers discover that fact earlier than most."

The bibliographic form and the format of the book follow the stipulations of the publisher. It is organized chronologically, with each year being divided into two sections. Section A lists books devoted exclusively to Robinson and includes books by Robinson if there is prefatory material by another writer. Section B lists serial articles and parts of books. Within the annotations, brackets indicate description rather than summary. Asterisks indicate articles I was unable to find and thus was unable to annotate.

Acknowledgments

In gathering material for this book I used many libraries, the most important being the Colby College Library in Waterville, Maine, where any serious Robinson scholar must start. I also found material at the Boston Public Library, the Yale University Library, the New York Public Library, the Library of Congress, the Duke University Library, and the University of North Carolina Library. I made one foray to the midwest to use the resources of the University of Chicago Library and the Center for Research Libraries. I wish to thank each of these institutions and their staffs for making their holdings available to me. While Hunter Library at my home school, Western Carolina University, is not equipped to handle research of this kind, Naja Williamson and Anita Oser of the Interlibrary Loan Department were of invaluable assistance in producing with startling speed items I had overlooked in my visits to the research libraries. Western Carolina University also provided some financial assistance for clerical help.

Numbers of scholars and friends have helped me with the preparation of this book. Richard Cary must be acknowledged first, not only for the advice he gave me personally but also for the monumental contribution he has made to Robinson scholarship as a writer and editor of books on Robinson, as the former editor of the Colby Library Quarterly, and as former curator of the collection of Robinsoniana at Colby College. My thanks are extended to three professors at the University of North Carolina at Chapel Hill: Daniel W. Patterson, my dissertation director, who guided me through my first project on Robinson; C. Hugh Holman, who gave me advice on bibliographical matters and strategies of research; and Lewis Leary, who gave me advice as well as access to his files while he was preparing the third edition of Articles in American Literature. Cynthia Swan, a graduate student at Chapel Hill, helped me with preliminary research and translated most of the articles in French.

It is impossible to name all the friends who provided the material assistance of helping me prepare the index, but I wish to thank everyone who attended Rita Byrnes' going-away party, where I introduced the parlor game called "Alphabetize the Index Cards." Also, Professors Connie Eble and Margaret Anne O'Connor, of the University of North

Acknowledgments

Carolina at Chapel Hill, and Professor Martha Jane K. Zachert, of the School of Library Science at Florida State University, spent long hours helping me with the index when there was no party. Finally, special thanks go to Jeanne Nienhuis, my typist, who has not only been patient and efficient through the long process of preparing the manuscript, but has also become a Robinson enthusiast.

List of Abbreviations

"Ben Jonson"   "Ben Jonson Entertains a Gentleman
from Stratford"

Cary   See 1974.A1 for bibliographical listing

DA and DAI   Dissertation Abstracts and Dissertation
Abstracts International

Hogan   See 1936.A4 for bibliographical listing

Lippincott   See 1937.A1 for bibliographical listing

White   See 1971.A2 for bibliographical listing

Books by Edwin Arlington Robinson

Selected Articles about Robinson, 1894-1915

from Richard Cary's *Early Reception of Edwin Arlington Robinson:
The First Twenty Years*

1894 A BOOKS - NONE

1894 B SHORTER WRITINGS

1   THORNE, W. H. "Wreck of the Mayflower." The Globe, 4 (Sep-
     tember), 801.
          "Mr. Robinson...bids fair to outshine all competitors in
     his native state." [First notice in print. Cary, p. 61.]

1896 A BOOKS - NONE

1896 B SHORTER WRITINGS

1   CHAMBERLIN, JOSEPH E. Review of The Torrent and the Night Be-
     fore. Boston Evening Transcript, December 16, p. 5.
          This pamphlet contains clearly original thought, "But it
     is desirable that one who puts out verses, even at his own
     expense, should be able to write verse. Can this man do
     it?" ["Aaron Stark" quoted. Cary, p. 31.]

1897 A BOOKS - NONE

1897 B SHORTER WRITINGS

1   ANON. "The Christmas Bookstalls." Boston Evening Transcript,
     December 18, p. 13.
          [Review of The Children of the Night, noting Robinson's
     grave manner and sympathetic attitude. "Richard Cory,"
     "George Crabbe," and "Octave I" quoted. Cary, pp. 73-74.]

2   ANON. "Edward Eggleston: An Interview." The Outlook, 60
     (February 6), 436.
          [Eggleston remarks that The Torrent and the Night Before
     has "some delightfully original little bits of poetry."

He had never heard of Robinson until he sent him the book. "They send me books of poetry until I cannot get around for them, but he has sent me a book that I cannot help reading." Cary, p. 52.]

3   B., R. H. Review of The Torrent and the Night Before. Denver Times, January 16, p. 11.
        The somberness of this volume is perhaps a fault, but the writer has great skill and has accomplished something that no more than a half dozen current poets can match. "The House on the Hill" is the best in the book. [Cary, pp. 39-41.]

4   BROWER, EDITH. "Edwin Arlington Robinson." Wilkes Barre (Penn.) Times, December 20, p. 15.
        [Lengthy review of The Children of the Night, emphasizing Robinson's spiritual depth and idealistic outlook. Copious quotes, paying particular attention to the Octaves, the sonnets, "Luke Havergal," and "The Night Before." Cary, pp. 79-84.]

5   DOLE, NATHAN HASKELL. "Correspondence." Bookseller, News-dealer and Stationer, 5 (January 1), 491.
        [Letter to the editor calling attention to The Torrent and the Night Before, quoting four poems and describing others as "vital, virile expressions of a wholly modern spirit." Suggests that although the book is small, readers in the future will "pay high prices for the little trea-sure." Cary, p. 36.]

6   GARDINER, JOHN HAYS. "A New Poet." Boston Evening Transcript, December 24, p. 5.
        [Review of The Children of the Night, noting its modesty, modernity, and emphasizing evidence of Robinson's faith in God. Cary, pp. 87-90.]

7   PECK, HARRY THURSTON. Review of The Torrent and the Night Be-fore. The Bookman, 4 (February), 509-10.
        "There is true fire in his verse...but his limitations are vital. His humour is of a grim sort, and the world is not beautiful to him, but a prison-house." [Cary, pp. 49-50.]

8   T[RENT], W[ILLIAM] P[ETERFIELD]. "A New Poetic Venture." The Sewanee Review, 5 (April), 243-46.
        [Review of The Torrent and the Night Before, noting par-ticularly Robinson's technical competence. Suggestion that "The House on the Hill," "A Poem for Max Nordau," and "The

Wilderness" are unsatisfactory, but that the sonnets, "The
Children of the Night," and "the Browning-like verse of the
last poem" are praiseworthy. Cary, pp. 54-56.]

1898 A BOOKS - NONE

1898 B SHORTER WRITINGS

1   ANON. "The Promise of Fame." The Chap-Book, 8 (January 15),
219.
[Review of The Children of the Night, observing that Robinson's most characteristic trait is "his complete appreciation of the music in a proper name." Cary, pp. 93-94.]

2   HIGGINSON, THOMAS WENTWORTH. Review of The Children of the
Night. The Nation, 66 (June 2), 426.
"While the variety of Mr. Robinson's measure is as yet
small, he does his work deftly and thoroughly within that
plot of ground." ["George Crabbe," "The Clerks," and "Luke
Havergal" quoted. Cary, pp. 100-101.]

3   THORNE, WILLIAM HENRY. "Shakespeare, Foss and Co." The Globe,
7 (March), 29-33.
Although "The Children of the Night" is one of the best
poems in English since Tennyson, its "abominable" philosophy is reminiscent of that of Thomas Paine. "A pox upon
such everlasting duplicity and ignorance as our modern
poets of atheism and boyish conceit everywhere manifest."
[Cary, pp. 96-98.]

1902 A BOOKS - NONE

1902 B SHORTER WRITINGS

1   ANON. Review of Captain Craig. New York Evening Sun, October
17, p. 10.
This volume has some strengths, but it is far too imita-
tive of Browning and Yeats, and the lines don't scan in the
title poem. [Cary, pp. 117-18.]

2   CARMAN, BLISS. Review of Captain Craig. The Reader, 1 (December), 193-94.
"'Captain Craig' is worse than Browning," but it is "a
mistake rather than a failure." The verse is boring and an
obstruction. The story is so interesting, however, that it
should have been written in prose. [Cary, pp. 132-33.]

3

1902

3   MACY, JOHN A. "Poet Robinson Receiving Recognition." Chicago
    Evening Post, October 25, p. 9.
        [Review of Captain Craig.] This is a book "of genuine
    distinction": as good as Stephen Phillips's Marpessa and
    superior to the work of William Vaughan Moody. The shorter
    poems in the volume are to be preferred to "the rough,
    bathetic prose passages" of the title poem. [Cary, pp. 119-
    20.]

4   TRAUBEL, HORACE. Review of Captain Craig. The Conservator,
    13 (October), 125.
        "He did so well in his first book he compelled us to ex-
    pect him to do better in this." [Cary, p. 116.]

1903 A BOOKS - NONE

1903 B SHORTER WRITINGS

1   BOYNTON, H. W. Review of Captain Craig. Atlantic Monthly,
    91 (April), 566-67.
        The title poem has "the mental ingenuity of Browning and
    the bare diction of Wordsworth." Though original, the poem
    is unsatisfactorily prosaic and obscure. [Cary, p. 152.]

2   PAYNE, WILLIAM MORTON. Review of Captain Craig. The Dial, 34
    (January 1), 18-19.
        This book helps to fulfill the promise made in Robinson's
    earlier work. The title poem, reminiscent of Whitman and
    Browning, is more interesting than the shorter poems, prin-
    cipally because of the quality of the philosophy it mani-
    fests. [Cary, pp. 141-42.]

3   SCOLLARD, CLINTON. Review of Captain Craig. The Critic, 42
    (March), 232.
        "Blank verse that is little more than inverted prose
    chopped up into lines is continually elbowing passages that
    are shot through with real poetic fire in this disturbing
    volume." [Cary, pp. 148-49.]

4   STICKNEY, TRUMBULL. Review of Captain Craig. The Harvard
    Monthly, 37 (December), 99-102.
        The volume is remarkable in that it demonstrates the
    honesty, kindness, and humor of Robinson. Though he chooses
    to write in "plain Saxon" rather than with an elevated
    style, his poetry is nevertheless meritorious. [Cary,
    pp. 154-56.]

1904 A BOOKS - NONE

1904 B SHORTER WRITINGS

1   FRENCH, JOSEPH LEWIS. "A Poet in the Subway." New York World
    Magazine, May 15, p. 10.
        [Biographical sketch with numerous factual errors, em-
    phasizing the extreme poverty and reclusiveness of this
    "dawning literary genius." Cary, pp. 158-60.]

1905 A BOOKS - NONE

1905 B SHORTER WRITINGS

1   ANON. "An Apology for Overlooking Mr. Robinson." The Bookman,
    22 (October), 104-105.
        Whatever a man's office, he has a right to proclaim what
    he thinks to be real poetry. "There are, of course, many
    poets of the Robinson degree, but the President [Roosevelt]
    is not to blame if he has encountered only one of them. It
    is well known that he has had a number of other matters on
    his hands of fully equal importance." [Cary, pp. 184-85.]

2   ANON. "Criticism by Ukase." New York Evening Post, August 14,
    p. 6.
        "What will be the consequence if our Presidents usurp the
    authority of critics?" The volume Roosevelt endorses is
    "mediocre in character and little distinguished from scores
    of similar volumes put out by a busy press." [Cary,
    pp. 174-75.]

3   CHASE, A. G. "Touch of Genius." Boston Sunday Globe, August
    20, p. 32.
        [Biographical sketch of the Gardiner boy Roosevelt
    praised. Cary, pp. 180-81.]

4   ROOSEVELT, THEODORE. Review of The Children of the Night.
    The Outlook, 80 (August 12), 913-14.
        This extraordinary book should have attracted more atten-
    tion. Notable are "The House on the Hill" and "The Wilder-
    ness," among others. "I am not sure that I understand
    'Luke Havergal'; but I am entirely sure that I like it."
    [Cary, pp. 170-71.]

5   SABEN, MOWRY. "The Poems of Edwin Arlington Robinson." Den-
    ver Republican, December 3, p. 14.

1905

> [Commentary on Robinson's three volumes, emphasizing his
> humanitarianism and his ability to find poetry in ordinary
> people and events. Cary, pp. 193-94.]

1906 A BOOKS - NONE

1906 B SHORTER WRITINGS

   1   SINCLAIR, MAY. "Three American Poets." Atlantic Monthly, 98
      (September), 330-33; Fortnightly Review, n.s. 80 (September 1), 429-34.
      Robinson's three kinds of poetry--lyrics, character
sketches, and psychological dramas--are all distinctive.
"Captain Craig," in spite of its apparent severity, is his
most impressive poem so far. It is "one prolonged and glorious wantoning and wallowing in truth." [Cary, pp. 200-203.]

1909 A BOOKS - NONE

1909 B SHORTER WRITINGS

   1   MARKHAM, EDWIN. "Robinson, My Hand to You." New York American, February 13, p. 13.
      "The Man Who Came" is one of the "noble remembrances" of
Lincoln. Only Emily Dickinson can compare with Robinson in
style. [Cary, p. 206.]

1910 A BOOKS - NONE

1910 B SHORTER WRITINGS

   1   BRAITHWAITE, WILLIAM STANLEY. "Down the River." Boston Evening Transcript, October 29, Section III, p. 6.
      [Review of The Town Down the River, emphasizing Robinson's originality, simplicity in diction, restraint, and
psychological perception. Cary, pp. 216-17.]

1912 A BOOKS - NONE

1912 B SHORTER WRITINGS

   1   KILMER, JOYCE. "A Classic Poet." The New York Times Review
of Books, September 8, p. 487.

Robinson is to be distinguished from his contemporaries
in that his purpose is aesthetic rather than didactic. His
realism, mastery of fixed forms, ability at writing character sketches, and sympathetic attitude are notable. [Cary,
pp. 237-39.]

2 LEDOUX, LOUIS V. "A Discussion of the Exact Value of Robinson's Poetry." The New York Times Review of Books, Section
VI, September 29, p. 533.
[Letter to the editor asserting that Robinson's chief
characteristics are humor, sympathy, and optimism. Cary,
pp. 240-42.]

1913 A BOOKS - NONE

1913 B SHORTER WRITINGS

1 BRAITHWAITE, WILLIAM STANLEY. "America's Foremost Poet."
Boston Evening Transcript, May 28, p. 21.
[Essay reminding readers of the high praise Robinson has
received and his insistence on staying in the background,
along with an interview with Robinson, who says that his
purpose is to make people understand each other better and
that he feels that public notice is useless unless the
poetry has intrinsic worth. Cary, pp. 253-55.]

2 PULSIFER, HAROLD TROWBRIDGE. "Edwin Arlington Robinson." The
Outlook, 110 (December 6), 736.
Robinson's method is similar to that of Francis Thomp-
sons. He deserves more recognition than he has received
because of the combination of depth of thought and simplicity of diction. [Cary, pp. 261-62.]

3 RANCK, EDWIN CARTY. "An American Poet With a Message." Boston Evening Transcript, May 12, p. 10.
Robinson's work should be better known because of its individuality, optimism, and sincerity. "He seems to be a
truly great poet." [Cary, pp. 248-51.]

4 THOMPSON, FRED W. "Alfred Noyes Sees American Poets Leading
World Movement." Boston Sunday Post, March 2, p. 37.
[Interview with Noyes, who considers Robinson "the second
greatest living American poet," following only Brian Hooker.
Cary, pp. 247-48.]

1914 A BOOKS - NONE

1914

1914 B SHORTER WRITINGS

1   THEIS, OTTO FREDERICK. "Edwin Arlington Robinson." The Forum,
     60 (February), 305-12.
          Robinson is one of the most distinguished and original
     American poets. Notable characteristics are objectivity,
     simplicity, and lyricism. His development has been progres-
     sive: The Town Down the River contains passages superior
     to anything in his earlier books. [Cary, pp. 262-68.]

1915 A BOOKS - NONE

1915 B SHORTER WRITINGS

1   ANON. "Mr. Robinson's Captain Craig." Rochester Herald,
     March 4, p. 6.
          [Article reporting the new edition of Captain Craig and
     noting that the title poem was inspired by an English Jew
     whom Robinson had met.] "If Mr. Robinson had never written
     anything but 'Captain Craig,' he would have written enough
     to stamp him as a man of genius." [Cary, pp. 276-77.]

2   FIRKINS, OSCAR W. Review of Captain Craig. The Nation, 100
     (May 20), 562.
          "Isaac and Archibald" and other short poems in this vol-
     ume are well done, but the title poem is hard to follow.
     "Mr. Robinson has two grave faults: a talkativeness, not
     to say glibness...and a frequent baldness...of rhythm and
     diction.... His evident wish to be a psychologist has re-
     ceived...but moderate encouragement from nature." [Cary,
     pp. 287-88.]

3   MacVEAGH, LINCOLN. "Edwin Arlington Robinson." The New Re-
     public, 2 (April 10), 267-68.
          Robinson is a symbolist, but is superior to Mallarmé's
     definition of symbolism. His Calverly poems best exemplify
     this quality. Because he evokes character from a single
     trait, his long poems are not so successful as his short
     ones. "Captain Craig" is an "interminable poem," which
     shows only "the poet's inability to handle so large and
     sustained an expression." [Cary, pp. 281-83.]

4   UNTERMEYER, LOUIS. "--And Other Poems." Chicago Evening
     Post, August 27, p. 9.
          [Review of Captain Craig, noting that the reissue is im-
     portant because "it is a sign that Robinson is at last
     coming into his own." Cary, p. 295.]

Writings about Edwin Arlington Robinson, 1916-1976

1916 A BOOKS - NONE

1916 B SHORTER WRITINGS

1   ALDEN, RAYMOND M. "The Man Against the Sky." The Dial, 61
(July 15), 62-63.
    [Review, noting particularly "Ben Jonson."] New book by
Robinson will do two things: "furnish us real creations in
characters, like those of a dramatist or novelist; and...
represent diction at once colloquial and poetical."

2   ANON. "Edwin A. Robinson's New Book of Poems." The New York
Times Review of Books, April 2, p. 121.
    [Review of The Man Against the Sky, noting particularly
the title poem and "Ben Jonson."] Robinson's "attitude toward life is the Russian attitude--the attitude of Dostoev-
sky." This book is colder and less sympathetic than earlier
ones, but "the penetrative power of the vision has grown,
and with added practice in his art the author exhibits a
greater mastery of compression and of interpretative con-
ciseness."

3   ANON. Review of The Man Against the Sky. American Review of
Reviews, 53 (May), 632.
    This book is remarkable for its intellectuality. The
title poem is the best Robinson has done so far.

4   ANON. Review of The Man Against the Sky. The Literary Digest, 52 (March 18), 738.
    Robinson has been called a realistic poet, but more im-
portantly he is "a creative artist, whose unsentimental and
yet sympathetic portraits of mankind are illuminated with
that magic glow which the world associates with what it
calls genius."

5   ANON. Review of The Man Against the Sky. The North American
Review, 203 (April), 633.

1916

Robinson is better than most contemporary poets in that
he is more intellectual and more musical. The title poem
is a bit obscure, but justifiably so. Robinson "does not
quite attain to greatness...but he unquestionably attains
to distinction."

6 ANON. "Mr. Robinson's New Poems." The Outlook, 112 (April 5),
786-87.
[Review of The Man Against the Sky, noting particularly
"Ben Jonson" and "Another Dark Lady."] Robinson treats his
characters with objectivity but the force of his personality is clear in his poetry. He is becoming more and more
influential on American poetry, but followers who copy his
"habit of thought" neglect to follow his metrical pattern.

7 ANON. Review of The Man Against the Sky. Springfield (Mass.)
Republican, May 28, p. 13.
This book is not worth the re-reading it requires. "For
all the ease of his song, Mr. Robinson's language discloses
a preponderance of abstract terms."

8 BRAITHWAITE, WILLIAM STANLEY. Review of The Man Against the
Sky. Boston Evening Transcript, February 26, Section III,
p. 9.
"In this man American poetry has its profoundest voice,
its deepest vision, its most enduring utterance."

9 BROWN, EDMUND R. "A Master of Thought and Speech." The Poetry
Journal, 5 (March), 82-89.
[Review of The Man Against the Sky, commenting particularly on "Ben Jonson."] Robinson's poetry is notable for
its simplicity of speech and its complexity of ideas. His
mastery of rhyme is also praiseworthy. His reputation is
slowly gaining, deservedly so.

10 COLUM, PADRIAC. "Edwin Arlington Robinson." The Poetry Review of America, 1 (May), 15-16.
[Review of The Man Against the Sky.] "The poem that gives
the title to the present volume is sure to become known as
one of the great American poems." It is comparable to "The
City of Dreadful Night" and Wordsworth's Intimations Ode.
The best poem in the volume is "The Poor Relation." Robinson "is the poet of suspended drama: all his people are
characters in a drama of which the climax or anti-climax
has not yet been reached."

11 E[DDY], A. K. "The Printed Play." The Drama, 6 (February),
156-67.

[Review of The Porcupine, commenting particularly on quality of dialogue and economy.] "Mr. Robinson's tragi-comedy
is a notable piece of work."

12 FIRKINS, O. W. "American Verse." The Nation, 103 (August 17),
    150-51.
    [Review of The Man Against the Sky, noting particularly
    "Ben Jonson" and "Old King Cole."] Robinson "has a way of
    giving out mysticism with the effect of its being merely a
    memorandum." The "mixture of sauciness and shyness" in
    "Old King Cole" is appealing, but not its "famished intel-
    lectualism." Robinson is similar to Browning, but "in this
    volume the power sleeps."

13 KILMER, JOYCE. "Edwin Arlington Robinson Defines Poetry."
    The New York Times Magazine Section, April 9, p. 12.
    [Interview with Robinson, which includes his frequently
    quoted definition of poetry, critical judgments about Kip-
    ling, Emerson, Housman, vers libristes, and opinions on the
    effect of war and poverty on poetry. Reprinted in 1917.B7.]

14 LOWELL, AMY. "E. A. Robinson's Verse." The New Republic, 7
    (May 27), 96-97.
    [Review of The Man Against the Sky, reprinted in 1917.B8.]
    Robinson's poetry is "undeniably, magnificently, noble."
    It is marked by reticence, astringency, and high serious-
    ness. Instead of being in the mainstream of poetic cur-
    rents, he has achieved universality. "Ben Jonson" is bet-
    ter than the title poem. Robinson says he is optimistic,
    but "a profound melancholy...pervades the whole book."

15 MacKAYE, PERCY. "To 'E. A.' [Edwin Arlington Robinson] With
    Cake and Candles," in Poems and Plays, Vol. 1. New York:
    Macmillan, p. 124.
    [Eighteen-line poem in rhyming couplets. Reprinted in
    Cary, pp. 302-303.]

16 M[ONROE], H[ARRIET]. "A Pioneer." Poetry, 8 (April), 46-48.
    [Review of The Man Against the Sky.] Robinson is not an
    influence on Masters or Frost, as has been claimed. He is
    not as moving and is more aloof and independent. This vol-
    ume is his best so far; "Ben Jonson" is "a masterpiece."

17 SCHUMANN, ALANSON TUCKER. "To Edwin Arlington Robinson (On
    Reading His Poem, 'Calverly's')." Boston Evening Tran-
    script, February 29, p. 13.
    [Twelve-line poem in ballad stanza with feminine rhyme.
    Reprinted in Cary, p. 301.]

1916

18 T[OWSE], J. R. "Drama." The Nation, 102 (June 29), 717.
    [Review of The Porcupine.] Robinson has promise as a
    dramatist because he is good in dialogue and characteriza-
    tion. In this unfortunately named play, however, the plot
    is weak. He unnecessarily mystifies the audience with the
    question of paternity in a triangular situation.

19 UNTERMEYER, LOUIS. "--and Other Poems." Chicago Evening Post,
    March 10, p. 11.
    [Review of The Man Against the Sky, commenting particu-
    larly on "The Gift of God" and "Ben Jonson."] In this com-
    mendable volume Robinson's individuality is marked by his
    diction, which is simple if not always clear. He is so
    economic in his use of words that he "sometimes throws away
    everything but the meaning--and keeps that to himself."
    Re-reading is rewarding, however.

20 _____. "Edwin Arlington Robinson Tells What He Knew of Simple
    Simon," in "-------- and Other Poets." New York: Henry
    Holt, p. 19.
    [Parody of Robinson's manner of sonnet writing.] Re-
    printed in 1969.B49 and Cary, pp. 303-304.]

1917 A BOOKS - NONE

1917 B SHORTER WRITINGS

1 ANON. Review of Merlin. The Catholic World, 106 (November),
    255.
    Robinson's treatment is "arrestingly modern in method" in
    that it is realistic and non-conventional. It is not wholly
    successful in that fate is too important for such realism
    to work. "On the whole...we prefer the terrors of 'mid-
    Victorian morality' and the symbolism of Idylls of the
    King."

2 ANON. Review of Merlin. The New York Times Book Review,
    August 26, p. 313.
    "It is not a great poem, though its failure is not in-
    trinsic in its subject.... Mr. Robinson has been widely
    praised, and he has praiseworthy qualities, but we have
    never been able, personally, to feel his greatness to the
    extent to which it has been lauded. The seriousness with
    which he takes himself has imposed a like gravity on the
    minds of many of his critics.... He is a respectable poet,
    but he is heavy."

3   ANON. "Recent Poetry: Poets Who Adhere to Rhyme." The Amer-
      ican Review of Reviews, 55 (June), 660.
         [Brief review of Merlin.] This "fine poem...has amazing
      beauty of texture and ventures a new philosophy."

4   BRAITHWAITE, WILLIAM STANLEY. The Poetic Year for 1916. Bos-
      ton: Small, Maynard, pp. 101-114.
         [Interpretations of "Flammonde," "The Man Against the
      Sky," "Bokardo," "Fragment," "The Dark House," and "Ben
      Jonson."]

5   _____. "The Year in Poetry." The Bookman, 45 (June), 429-39.
         [Review of The Man Against the Sky, stressing that Rob-
      inson is the most important poet currently writing.] "The
      notable distinction in this volume compared with Mr. Rob-
      inson's previous book is in the advance he has made from
      presenting the character of the individual to interpreting
      the destinies of mankind."

6   HENDERSON, W. B. "Edwin Arlington Robinson," in The Warner
      Library, Vol. 20. New York: Knickerbocker Press,
      pp. 1231a-1231b.
         [Introduction to three poems: "Cassandra," "Veteran
      Sirens," and "The Poor Relation."] Robinson "stands now
      the assured 'dean' among our poets" because of catholic
      understanding of men and excellence of art.

7   KILMER, JOYCE. Literature in the Making. New York: Harper
      and Brothers, pp. 265-73.
         [Reprint of 1916.B13.]

8   LOWELL, AMY. Tendencies in Modern American Poetry. New York:
      Macmillan, pp. 3-75.
         [First lengthy critical assessment in book form, empha-
      sizing the importance of Robinson's Puritan background and
      praising his technique. Commentaries on several poems,
      notably "Isaac and Archibald," "Captain Craig," "Ben Jon-
      son," and "Flammonde." Author expresses disappointment in
      Merlin and the two plays, however. Includes reprint of
      1916.B14.]

9   M[ANN], D[OROTHEA] L. "The Arthurian Legend in New Guise."
      Boston Evening Transcript, March 31, Section III, p. 9.
         [Review of Merlin.] In the United States only Richard
      Hovey has heretofore used the Arthurian legend for serious
      work. Robinson presents it in a new light, differing from
      the Tennysonian treatment in that Robinson's is essentially

realistic. His principal strength is characterization.
Critics have given him a place "among the few of our really
great poets."

10   M[ONROE], H[ARRIET]. "Mr Robinson in Camelot." Poetry, 10
     (July), 211-13.
        [Review of Merlin.] It is hard to understand why Robin-
     son tries to revive "the over-worked and much over-poetized
     Camelot crowd." The many long speeches are neither con-
     temporary nor ancient in tone. "It is Robinson experiment-
     ing à la Tennyson, and the fusion is not complete."

11   REED, EDWARD BLISS. Review of The Man Against the Sky. The
     Yale Review, 6 (January), 421-22.
        This book is difficult to read, but it is worthwhile. It
     is chiefly a series of character sketches treated with
     "gentle irony, but never cynicism." "Ben Jonson" and the
     title poem are best.

12   _____. Review of Merlin. The Yale Review, 6 (July), 863-64.
        This allegory of war is unlike other Arthurian poems, but
     it deserves to be ranked with the best. Robinson demon-
     strates again his similarity to Meredith in intellectual
     force. He is "our foremost American poet."

13   SANBORN, ROBERT ALDEN. "Mr. Robinson's Merlin." Poetry Jour-
     nal, 7 (June), 104-109.
        Merlin, compared to "Captain Craig," is found wanting.
     It is a bad subject and a bad execution. Merlin is a humor-
     less Captain Craig.

14   SHEPARD, ODELL. "Versified Henry James." The Dial, 63 (Oc-
     tober 11), 339-41.
        [Review of Merlin.] This poem is insufficiently dramatic
     and unnecessarily obscure. It is too long and a poor sub-
     ject for Robinson. Knights indicate, in the style of Henry
     James, that "they are sicklied o'er with the pale cast of
     thought." It does contain "supple, vigorous, often daring,
     blank verse."

15   Y[OUNG], S[TARK]. Review of Merlin. The New Republic, 12
     (September 29), 250-51.
        Robinson is not involved in current poetic conflict; his
     books "show originality without challenging theories."
     Comparison with Tennyson, as opposed to other Victorians,
     is inevitable. Vivian is better drawn here than anywhere
     else in literature. The poem only partially succeeds as an
     allegory.

1918 A BOOKS - NONE

1918 B SHORTER WRITINGS

1   COOK, HOWARD WILLARD. <u>Our Poets of Today</u>. New York: Moffat,
      Yard, pp. 34-40.
        [Overview of career, reprinted in 1923.B12 and 1926.B2.]
      Robinson has been accused of writing only about sad things,
      but he is a versatile poet. He is particularly adept at
      portraying women. His "unerring aim at Truth" is his chief
      quality.

2   DEUTSCH, BABETTE. "A Sophisticated Mystic." <u>Reedy's Mirror</u>,
      27 (March 22), 166-67.
        Robinson is a "traditionalist," whose poems are marked by
      tenderness and lyricism. "The Man Against the Sky" is the
      best statement of his "sophisticated mysticism." "His
      flashes of ironic wit, and...esoteric vocabulary, make him
      a kind of male Emily Dickinson."

3   PHELPS, WILLIAM LYON. <u>The Advance of English Poetry in the</u>
      <u>Twentieth Century</u>. New York: Dodd, Mead, pp. 209-12.
        Robinson is one of the leading poets. "Children of the
      Night" is noteworthy. "Isaac and Archibald" is his master-
      piece. <u>Merlin</u> may be neglected safely. [Reprinted in
      1918.B4.]

4   _____. "The Advance of English Poetry in the Twentieth Cen-
      tury." <u>The Bookman</u>, 47 (July), 551-52.
        [Reprint of 1918.B3.]

1919 A BOOKS - NONE

1919 B SHORTER WRITINGS

1   ANON. "A Poet's Birthday." <u>The New York Times</u>, December 21,
      Section III, p. 1.
        [Announcement of 1919.B4.]

2   ANON. "A Poet's Birthday." <u>The Outlook</u>, 23 (December), 535.
        Theodore Roosevelt wrote a complimentary review in <u>The</u>
      <u>Outlook</u> of <u>Children of the Night</u> some fifteen years ago.
      Robinson's achievement since then has vindicated the Presi-
      dent's opinion. His influence on the form and content of
      contemporary verse is constantly widening.

1919

3   BOYNTON, PERCY H. A History of American Literature. New York:
        Ginn, pp. 462-66.
            Recognition has been late in coming to Robinson. "Simple,
        direct realism" is his distinctive characteristic. It is
        not true, as some critics have suggested, that Captain Craig
        is insignificant.

4   PERRY, BLISS. "Poets Celebrate E. A. Robinson's Birthday."
        The New York Times Review of Books, December 21, pp. 765-66.
            [A tribute to Robinson on his fiftieth birthday, compiled
        by one who recommended Captain Craig to the publisher twenty
        years earlier. Perry compares Robinson to Donne, Whitman,
        and Browning. Other tributes by Anna Hempstead Branch,
        Witter Bynner, Arthur Davison Ficke, Hermann Hagedorn,
        Louis V. Ledoux, Vachel Lindsay, Amy Lowell, Percy MacKaye,
        Edwin Markham, Edgar Lee Masters, John G. Neihardt, Joseph-
        ine Preston Peabody, Corinne Roosevelt Robinson, George
        Sterling, Sara Teasdale, and Ridgely Torrence. Excerpt re-
        printed in 1920.B3.]

5   RANCK, CARTY. "Edwin Arlington Robinson: An Interpretation,"
        in Anthology of Magazine Verse for 1919. Edited by William
        Stanley Braithwaite. Boston: Small, Maynard, p. 140.
            [Reprint of 1919.B6.]

6   ____. "Edwin Arlington Robinson: An Interpretation." New
        York Evening Sun, June 14, p. 6.
            [Italian sonnet. Reprinted in 1919.B5.]

7   [ROOSEVELT, KERMIT]. "An Appreciation of the Poetry of Edwin
        Arlington Robinson." Scribner's Magazine, 66 (December),
        763-64.
            [Comments on Robinson's timelessness, the regard Theodore
        Roosevelt had for him, his sound philosophy, his humor, and
        the care with which he used the language.]

8   UNTERMEYER, LOUIS. The New Era in American Poetry. New York:
        Henry Holt, pp. 111-35.
            [Survey of Robinson's career from Children of the Night
        to Merlin. The Man Against the Sky is singled out as the
        best volume. Robinson's devotion to metrical form is
        praised. Reprinted and expanded in 1923.B31.]

9   WILKINSON, MARGUERITE. New Voices. New York: Macmillan,
        pp. 354-57.
            If Robinson is not great he is at least brilliant. He
        has no peer in character analysis. Merlin is his least

16

successful poem; "Ben Jonson" is his masterpiece. [Inter-
pretations of "Richard Cory," "Flammonde," and "Miniver
Cheevy."]

1920 A BOOKS - NONE

1920 B SHORTER WRITINGS

1   ANON. <u>Harvard College Class of 1895: Twenty-Fifth Anniver-
     sary Report</u>. Cambridge: The University Press, pp. 410-13.
       [Letter from Robinson with quotations from 1919.B4.]
     Robinson "is the 'favorite poet' of a number of Ninety-five
     men."

2   ANON. Review of <u>Lancelot</u>. <u>The Dial</u>, 69 (July), 103.
       Readers of <u>Idylls of the King</u> will find the characters
     unfamiliar here, especially in their halting and intro-
     spective speech. "The verse moves with dignity and attains
     at times even a detachable beauty, and yet the memorable
     lines are comparatively few--for this author."

3   ANON. Review of <u>Lancelot</u>. <u>The Open Shelf</u> (Cleveland Public
     Library), No. 10 (October), p. 86.
       This is a new and timely interpretation of an old sub-
     ject.

4   ANON. "A Poet's Birthday." <u>The Literary Digest</u>, 64 (January
     10), 32-33.
       [Commentary and quotations from 1919.B4 and 1919.B7.]

5   ANON. "Robinson's 'Lancelot' an Allegory of Today." <u>The Sun
     and the New York Herald</u>, April 18, Section VII, p. 8.
       The publication of <u>Lancelot</u> is "the poetical event of
     the year." The final meeting of Guinevere and Lancelot is
     perhaps "the zenith of Mr. Robinson's art."

6   ANON. "Mr. Robinson's Poems." <u>Springfield</u> (Mass.) <u>Republi-
     can</u>, October 7, p. 10.
       [Review of <u>The Three Taverns</u>.] Robinson is likely to
     get the reputation of "the Henry James among poets" because
     of his obliqueness, complexity, and innuendos. He is also
     like Browning, except for his lack of robustness. His
     humor makes up for his emotional thinness.

7   BRAITHWAITE, WILLIAM STANLEY. "A Bay for E. A. Robinson."
     <u>Brooklyn Daily Eagle</u>, March 27, Section II, p. 3.
       [Addition to the fiftieth birthday tribute.] Robinson

has written five of the most important contemporary books
of poetry. His knowledge of character, his humor, and his
simplicity are remarkable.

8   B[RAITHWAITE], W. S. "The Arthurian Legend in Poetry." Boston Evening Transcript, June 12, Section III, p. 9.
      [Review of Lancelot.] The critics wronged Robinson when
they failed to appreciate Merlin, but Lancelot is even better. Both poems are symbolic of the Great War. "There are
passages here that are as near pure magic as anything in
modern poetry."

9   _____. "A Poet Approaches Human Mystery." Boston Evening
Transcript, September 11, Section IV, p. 9.
      [Review of The Three Taverns, noting particularly the
title poem, "John Brown," and "The Mill."] New philosophic
quality is apparent in this volume.

10 DEUTSCH, BABETTE. "A New Light on Lancelot." Poetry, 16
(July), 217-19.
      [Review of Lancelot.] "The chief distinction of Edwin
Arlington Robinson...among the many astonishments of his
genius, is his mingling of two strains: a Puritan austerity, and a discerning tenderness.... Lancelot is finer
than Merlin by as much as it is closer to Robinson."

11 FLETCHER, JOHN GOULD. "Some Contemporary American Poets."
The Chapbook, 2 (May), 1-4.
      "Robinson is not only first in point of date among modern
American poets, but in many respects he is first in sheer
intellectual abilities." He has affinities with Browning,
Hardy, and Crabbe. The Man Against the Sky is his best
book; Merlin is inferior.

12 GORMAN, HERBERT S. "Authentic Poetry." The Freeman, 2 (November 3), 186-87.
      [Review of The Three Taverns, emphasizing fatalism, wist-
fulness, and irony.] Robinson is now at the height of his
powers. This book is "the final vindication" of his work.
"Beautiful images, compact with thought, the surest test of
true poetry, are plentiful."

13 _____. "Edwin Arlington Robinson, and a Talk with Him." New
York Sun Books and the Book World, January 4, p. 7.
      [Assessment of Robinson's work and an interview, with
Robinson giving opinions on his influences, his philosophy,
an interpretation of Lancelot, free verse, and diction as
his contribution to poetry.]

14   _____. Review of Lancelot. The New Republic, 23 (July 28),
        259-60.
            The Arthurian poems are "their own vindication." Notable
        are the symbolism and fatalism evident.

15   _____. "Robinson's 'Lancelot.'" New York Evening Post Book
        Review, April 17, p. 5.
            This poem is probably the finest of the year. Although
        Lancelot is more somber than Merlin, it should be better
        reviewed since the public now knows Robinson's approach to
        the Arthurian materials.

16   _____. "Robinson's New Poems." The Literary Review of the
        New York Evening Post, October 2, p. 5.
            [Review of The Three Taverns, with particular emphasis on
        "The Valley of the Shadow," "The False Gods," "John Brown,"
        "Tasker Norcross," and the title poem.]

17   JONES, LLEWELLYN. "E. A. Robinson's Fine 'Lancelot.'" The
        Chicago Evening Post, May 21, p. 9.
            Not many people will read this poem because it is long
        and not modern. It is not a comment on the war but "the
        tragedy of personal lives in a mutable world." While there
        are fewer "purple passages" than in Merlin, it reaches
        greater emotional heights.

18   MacKAYE, PERCY. "'E. A.'--A Milestone for America." The
        North American Review, 211 (January), 121-27.
            [Article expressing appreciation for Robinson on the oc-
        casion of his fiftieth birthday, with particular comments
        on "Isaac and Archibald" and "Cassandra."]

19   MINOT, JOHN CLAIR. "Maine's Contribution to Literature."
        Maine Library Bulletin, 9 (January), 58-59.
            [Brief sketch of career of one of the most intellectual
        poets. Quotations from "Children of the Night" and "A Gift
        of God."]

20   M[ONROE], H[ARRIET]. "Mr. Robinson's Jubilee." Poetry, 15
        (February), 265-67.
            [Article congratulating Robinson on the occasion of his
        fiftieth birthday, emphasizing his integrity and influ-
        ence.] "He struck his own path, and found, no doubt with
        surprise, that he had blazed a trail for others."

21   REED, EDWARD BLISS. "Anthologists and Poets." The Yale Re-
        view, 10 (October), 205-206.
            [Review of Lancelot.] It is superior to Merlin because

of its greater variety of characters. "Splendidly imagined and unerringly wrought, this book reaffirms the conviction that Mr. Robinson is today the most significant figure in American verse."

22 RIDGE, LOLA. "To E. A. R." in Sun-Up and Other Poems. New York: B. W. Huebsch, p. 73.
    [Twelve-line poem in free verse. Reprinted in 1923.B28.]

23 ROTH, SAMUEL. "Edwin Arlington Robinson." The Bookman, 50 (January), 507-11.
    [An appreciative but factually inaccurate article written by the editor of Thomas Seltzer, the company that published Lancelot.] "None of the reviewers quite understand ['Merlin'], but there will be a better appreciation of it, and a sounder knowledge of its value, when its sequel, 'Lancelot,' is issued."

24 _____. "Robinson--Bridges--Noyes." The Bookman, 52 (December), 361-62.
    [Review of The Three Taverns, with particular attention to "Tasker Norcross."] This book, with The Man Against the Sky, establishes the poet.

25 ROURKE, CONSTANCE MAYFIELD. "Mr. Robinson's 'Lancelot.'" The Freeman, 2 (October 27), 164.
    In Lancelot Robinson, the novelist turned poet, writes a distinguished poem. It is subtle, low-keyed tragedy. "Camelot becomes the symbol for all outworn civilizations."

26 V[AN] D[OREN], C[ARL]. "Tragedy in Camelot." The Nation, 110 (May 8), 622-23.
    [Review of Lancelot.] "Since Browning there has been no finer dramatic dialogue in verse than that spoken by Lancelot and Guinevere and no apter characterization than in the ironical talk of Gawaine. One must go out of verse, to George Meredith and Henry James, to find its match."

27 _____. "Wisdom and Irony." The Nation, 111 (October 20), 453-54.
    [Review of The Three Taverns, commending especially "Tasker Norcross."] Every poem is perfect. The short poems complement each other. The unifying theme is that of change.

28 WEAVER, RAYMOND M. "Some Currents and Backwaters of Contemporary Poetry." The Bookman, 51 (June), 457-58.
    [Review of Lancelot, comparing Robinson's matter-of-fact

tone with Tennyson's treatment of the Arthurian material.]
"The analysis is subtle, unsentimental, and contagiously
sympathetic."

29 WILKINSON, MARGUERITE. "Mr. Robinson's New Arthurian Poem."
The New York Times Review of Books, April 11, p. 170.
Lancelot is a "penetrative study of the interplay of per-
sonalities," but it isn't as colorful as Tennyson's Camelot.
Robinson would do better writing about modern subjects.

30 WOOD, CLEMENT. "Robinson's 'Lancelot.'" New York Call Magazine, May 16, p. 11.
When Lancelot "is measured against the lollypop sweetness
and stickiness of Tennyson's 'Idylls,' the great step for-
ward that our poetry has taken is at once visible."

1921 A BOOKS - NONE

1921 B SHORTER WRITINGS

1 AIKEN, CONRAD. "The Poetry of Mr. E. A. Robinson." The Freeman, 4 (September 21), 43-46.
Avons' Harvest is to Robinson's work what The Turn of the
Screw is to James's work. The knife is a cheap supernatu-
ral trick. The tone of the narrator, "midway between the
elegaic and the ironic," is typical of Robinson. He is
more a dramatist than a poet, but, like Browning, he is not
good at actual drama. Merlin is his best poem. Lancelot
does not equal it because it has too many voices. [Re-
printed in 1958.B2.]

2 ANON. "American Poetry." The Nation and the Athenaeum, 30
(November 12), 278.
[Review of Untermeyer's Modern American Poetry: An An-
thology.] Robinson is "duller than Frost, as dull as
Wordsworth in his most uninspired moments."

3 ANON. Review of Avon's Harvest. The Dial, 71 (August), 243.
"Mr. Robinson has written far better poems than Avon's
Harvest." The style is too circumlocutious.

4 ANON. Review of Avon's Harvest. Grinnel Review, 16 (June),
455.
This poem combines American directness with Greek "fate-
drama." "This is not an easy book to read, and it will not
be popular."

1921

5   ANON. Review of Collected Poems. The Literary Digest, 71
         (December 24), 38.
            "All lovers of poetry will be pleased to own all [Robin-
         son's] poetry, so conveniently bound."

6   ANON. "From Lancelot to Steeplechasing." The Outlook, 127
         (January 12), 67-68.
            [Review of Lancelot and The Three Taverns.] Since Robin-
         son follows Malory closely, his poem is better than Tenny-
         son's portrayal of Lancelot. The Three Taverns, which is
         comparable to Browning's Dramatic Lyrics, is "rather too
         obscure."

7   BRAITHWAITE, WILLIAM STANLEY. "A Poetic Tale of Consuming
         Mystery." Boston Evening Transcript, April 2, Section IV,
         p. 6.
            [Review of Avon's Harvest.] To say that this poem is
         psychological does not do its profundity justice.

8   COOPER, FREDERIC TABER. "A Golden Gargoyle." Publisher's
         Weekly, 99 (April 16), 1236.
            [Review of Avon's Harvest.] The poem is open to many in-
         terpretations, among them that it is "the allegory of an
         evil habit" or that "hatred is itself a poison." Whatever
         the interpretation, Robinson does an impressive job.

9   FARRAR, JOHN. "E. A. Robinson's Dime Novel." The Bookman,
         53 (May), 248.
            [Review of Avon's Harvest.] This poem "is less difficult
         than much of Robinson, and it is more moving.... In Ameri-
         can literature, surely there is no more powerful dramatic
         poem."

10   FIRKINS, O. W. Review of Avon's Harvest. The Weekly Review,
         5 (July 9), 39.
            This poem "will not fortify Mr. Robinson's reputation."

11   FLETCHER, JOHN GOULD. "Mr. Robinson's Poems." The Nation and
         the Athenaeum, 30 (November 19), 307-308.
            [Letter to the editor countering disparaging remarks
         about Robinson (1921.B2).] There are four reasons why The
         Man Against the Sky is a good book: "The Gift of God,"
         "Cassandra," "Ben Jonson," and the title poem. These are
         superior to Wordsworth's odes. Is anyone other than Hardy
         and Doughty any better than Robinson? [Reprinted in
         1921.B12.]

22

12   ____. "Mr. Edwin Arlington Robinson Abroad." The Living
      Age, 311 (December 17), 744.
      [Reprint of 1921.B11.]

13   G., C. F. "Somber as the Time." Grinnell Review, 16 (Jan-
      uary), 332.
         [Review of The Three Taverns.] This book is "a more
      various Man Against the Sky." Aside from monologues show-
      ing psychological insight, which are powerful if stilted,
      are "some deeply-etched short lyrics and exquisite sonnets."
      Robinson has a command of polysyllabic language. "The Dark
      Hills" is the most cheerful poem in the volume.

14   GORMAN, HERBERT S. "Destiny's Hooded Face." Literary Review
      of the New York Evening Post, April 2, p. 6.
         [Review of Avon's Harvest.] This poem illustrates Robin-
      son's skill at drawing realistic characters. It is "melo-
      drama raised to tragedy."

15   ____. "E. A. Robinson, E. L. Masters, Typical Poets of To-
      day." The New York Times Book Review and Magazine, Jan-
      uary 16, p. 18.
         [Review of The Three Taverns, with particular attention
      to "The Valley of the Shadow" and "Tact."] The book falls
      into three parts: historical figures, imaginary figures,
      and comments on the times. "Within its 120 pages is crys-
      tallized the best of modern American poetry."

16   ____. "Edwin Arlington Robinson's Poetry." The New York
      Times Book Review and Magazine, October 30, p. 6.
         [Review of Collected Poems, with particular attention to
      "Isaac and Archibald," "John Evereldown," "Ben Jonson,"
      "The Man Against the Sky," "The Valley of the Shadow," Mer-
      lin, and Lancelot.] This collection of eight volumes does
      not show Robinson's development because "he sprang full-
      grown from The Children of the Night." One of his dis-
      tinguishing characteristics is his "art of intimation." He
      may be compared favorably with Tennyson and Hardy.

17   MITCHELL, STEWART. "Edwin Arlington Robinson." The Dial, 70
      (May), 569-71.
         [Review of The Three Taverns.] Robinson has eschewed
      popularity for precision. His subject matter and depen-
      dence on "the silhouettes" will not impress the casual
      reader. "The outline of the idea seems to be his passion."

18   M[ONROE], H[ARRIET]. "Robinson's Double Harvest." Poetry,
      18 (August), 273-76.

1921

[Review of The Three Taverns and Avon's Harvest.] These poems are superior to the Arthurian ones. Avon's Harvest is a powerful psychological drama, similar to Poe in its depiction of insanity. The dramatic narratives in The Three Taverns are more interesting intellectually than emotionally. Lindsay's poem on John Brown is better than Robinson's.

19   NICHOLL, LOUISE TOWNSEND. "Robinson's New Book." The Measure, No. 4 (June), pp. 21-22.
      [Review of Avon's Harvest, principally a plot summary.] The poem is "as psychologically powerful, dramatically sound, and organically beautiful a piece of blank verse as Robinson has done."

20   RANCK, EDWIN CARTY. "Blank Verse Tale of Hate and Fear." New York Herald Magazine and Books, June 5, p. 12.
      [Review of Avon's Harvest.] This poem has "poetic punch" --the poetry does not intrude on the drama.

21   _____. "Edwin Arlington Robinson Defines and Illustrates Poetry." New York Herald Magazine and Books, January 2, p. 10.
      [Review of The Three Taverns, with particular attention to "The Valley of the Shadow" and "Souvenir." Robinson's definition of poetry, first quoted by Kilmer (1916.B13), is repeated.

22   VAN DOREN, CARL. "Greek Dignity and Yankee Ease." The Nation, 113 (November 16), 570-71.
      [Review of Collected Poems, reprinted in 1923.B32.] Perhaps Robinson is not a popular poet because he insists upon intellectualizing experience. "His characters cannot rave." But his poems contain much worldly wisdom and he is sometimes comic, as in "Uncle Ananias."

23   V[AN] D[OREN], C[ARL]. "In a Style of Steel." The Nation, 112 (April 20), 596.
      [Review of Avon's Harvest.] This poem is sometimes obscure but it is worth the effort. "The interest lies not in the little war between Avon and a spook but in the vaster war within Avon himself."

24   W., W. "Insight and Epithet." John O'London's Weekly, 6 (December 17), 364-65.
      "Richard Cory" is characteristic of American poetry. "Its vocabulary is the vocabulary of every day speech, and its outlook has the quiet ruthlessness which so often creeps into the expression, 'Such is life.'"

24

25   WALDO, FULLERTON. "The Earlier E. A. R.: Some Memories of a
     Poet in the Making." The Outlook, 129 (November 30), 531-
     32, 534.
          [Interview with Robinson emphasizing his confidence at
     making a living writing poetry. Suggests that "Old Trails"
     is autobiographical since Robinson was living in Yonkers at
     the time.]

26   WILKINSON, MARGUERITE. "A Poet Tells a Story." The New York
     Times Book Review and Magazine, June 26, p. 27.
          [Review of Avon's Harvest.] This poem is of middling
     quality, saved from melodrama by intellectuality. Avon's
     tragedy is inevitable since he does not take the recourse
     of a primitive, rational, or religious man; i.e. he does
     not fight, sue, or pray.

1922 A BOOKS - NONE

1922 B SHORTER WRITINGS

1   AIKEN, CONRAD. "A Letter From America." The London Mercury,
     6 (June), 196-98.
          [Review of Collected Poems.] This book is the most im-
     portant book of poetry in the United States this year.
     Robinson bears resemblances to Wordsworth, Browning, and
     Crabbe, but he is most like James. Merlin, superior to
     Lancelot, is "as delicate and subtle as The Wings of the
     Dove."

2   _____. "The New Elizabethans." The Yale Review, 11 (April),
     635-36.
          [Review of Collected Poems.] American contemporary
     poetry is more forceful than British. No contemporary
     British poet can be compared to Robinson in "his insight
     into character, his intellectual beauty, his exquisite
     sense of form."

3   ANON. "An American Bard and the British Reviewers." The
     Living Age, 315 (October 28), 244.
          Most British critics have dismissed Robinson without
     giving him due attention, but Drinkwater has come to his
     defense by a lecture and the preface to the British edition
     of Collected Poems.

4   ANON. "An American Poet." The Outlook (London), 50 (August
     26), 175-76.
          [Review of Collected Poems.] "Mr. Robinson's poems will

1922

be as alive two thousand years hence as they are today."
He is the conscience of his generation. The Children of
the Night is his best book.

5   ANON. "An American Poet." Times Literary Supplement, No.
    1082 (October 12), p. 639.
        [Review of Collected Poems.] Robinson is in the American
    transcendental tradition, which emphasizes ethical values.
    His work is marked by melancholy, by a "man who probes too
    deeply to hope greatly." His short poems are best. [Re-
    printed in 1957.B1.]

6   ANON. "American Poet's Verse Most Enduring in English Litera-
    ture the Past Year." National Magazine, 51 (November), 285.
        [News story on Pulitzer Prize, with sketch of Robinson's
    career and generalizations about his poetry.] "He seems to
    hear the voice of the heart."

7   ANON. "Author's Club Hails Poet: E. A. Robinson's Poems
    Voted Most Notable 1921 American Publication." The New
    York Times, January 27, Section I, p. 13.
        Collected Poems has been voted "book of most enduring
    value to American literature in 1921" by most of the 260
    members of the Author's Club.

8   ANON. Review of Collected Poems. The Magnificat, 29 (March),
    306.
        "Mr. Robinson is an Englishman living in America" [sic].
    His poems, which are entirely too cynical, are sometimes
    similar to Browning's erotic studies.

9   ANON. Review of Collected Poems. The Open Shelf (Cleveland
    Public Library), No. 5 (May), p. 35.
        "Proportion, restraint, refinement of spiritual analysis
    and a simplicity, so condensed as to be almost cryptic,
    mark the work of this poet."

10 ANON. "Edwin Arlington Robinson." Christian Science Monitor,
    April 19, p. 16.
        [Biographical sketch.] Robinson is at the peak of his
    career. He is "the Merlin of modern poetry."

11 ANON. "Robinson as a Poet Born Ahead of His Time." Current
    Opinion, 72 (April), 525-27.
        [Summary of 1922.B23.]

12 ANON. "Yale Bestows Academic Honors." The New York Times,
    June 22, Section I, p. 6.

William Lyon Phelps read the citation when Yale University conferred upon Robinson the title, Doctor of Letters.

13   BENÉT, WILLIAM ROSE. "Robinson in Retrospect." Literary Review of the New York Evening Post, February 11, pp. 409-10.
        [Essay-review of Collected Poems.] Robinson is "the Merlin of our modern poetry." His poems are often difficult to interpret, since he has a habit of avoiding the obvious, but once you do understand his work "your delight in your own perspicacity is like to make you a Robinsonian forever." His great strength is his portrayal of character, especially failures, as in Captain Craig. Lancelot shows his ability at understatement. He probably will not be remembered for Arthurian poems but "Ben Jonson" and "Isaac and Archibald" will surely endure.

14   BOYNTON, PERCY H. "American Authors of Today: Edwin Arlington Robinson." The English Journal, 11 (September), 383-91.
        [Biographical sketch and assessment of career. Reprinted in 1924.B8.] Robinson is modern without being faddish. His principal topic is "the Spirit of Man." His disembodied characters are four parts intellect and one part emotion. "Captain Craig," which is a positive poem, is "the key to Mr. Robinson's Philosophy."

15   CONVERSE, FLORENCE. Review of Collected Poems. Atlantic Monthly, 129 (February), 1.
        Robinson's poetry is notable for its impeccable form and "deep and genuine melancholy."

16   DALY, S.J., JAMES J. "Literature: Edwin Arlington Robinson." America, 55 (September 9), 496-98.
        [Essay-review of Collected Poems.] Robinson is intellectually superior to poets like Sandburg and Masters, but he has a great flaw: his faith sounds like "morose agnosticism," which makes truly great poetry impossible. Also, he is "too conscious of his own virtues" and is "cynically superior." It is a cheap shot for him to call Uncle Ananias a liar. He shares with Browning the fault of obscurity.

17   DRINKWATER, JOHN. "Edwin Arlington Robinson." The Fortnightly Review, 111 (April 1), 649-60.
        Robinson, who has been neglected, differs from other American poets in that while they "see man beset by society, which is circumstance, he sees man beset by his own character, which is fate." His use of traditional verse forms distinguishes him from other Americans. He has affinities with Milton, Arnold, and Wordsworth in that he recognizes

moral purpose as an artistic principle. "Flammonde" is a
representative poem. [Reprinted in 1922.B18, 1922.B19,
and 1925.B15.]

18 ____. "Edwin Arlington Robinson." The Yale Review, 11
(April), 467-76.
[Reprint of 1922.B17.]

19 ____. "Introduction," in Collected Poems, by Edwin Arlington
Robinson. London: Cecil Palmer, pp. vii-xvi.
[Reprint of 1922.B17.]

20 GORMAN, HERBERT S. "Edwin Arlington Robinson." The New Republic, 29 (February 8), 311-13.
[Review of Collected Poems, including survey of Robinson's
career and kinds of writing. Reprinted in 1923.B18.] Robinson has long since reached maturity as a poet.

21 LOWELL, AMY. A Critical Fable. Boston: Houghton Mifflin,
pp. 26-29.
[Ninety-four lines of satirical verse on Robinson, emphasizing his reclusive personality, his sensitive and
technically strong poetry, and the probability of his last-
ing fame.]

22 ____. "A Bird's-Eye View of Edwin Arlington Robinson." The
Dial, 72 (February), 130-42.
[Essay-review of Collected Poems.] Placing The Man
Against the Sky first corroborates the critics' view that
it is his best volume. "Children of the Night," with its
"creedless religion," suggests the difficulties Robinson
must have endured in Gardiner. He is best in contemporary
scenes with only two people talking. Habits that need correction are his indulging in melodrama and cryptic style.
His work will probably not improve much, but "he has won a
high and permanent place in American literature." [Re-
printed in 1930.B20 and 1963.B9.]

23 McCLURE, JOHN. Review of Collected Poems. The Double Dealer,
3 (April), 217-19.
Robinson is second only to Whitman in American verse because of the size and scope of his collected poems. In
"The Mill" and elsewhere "the poet looms before us as a
compelling and original genius."

24 McCORMICK, VIRGINIA TAYLOR. "Collected Poems of Edwin Arlington Robinson." Norfolk (Va.) Ledger-Dispatch, March 18,
p. 12.

[Review of Collected Poems.] This book is remarkable for
the number of portraits like "Miniver Cheevy" and "Richard
Cory." Robinson is "an aristocrat among writers...while
his subjects are general and of the proletariat, his treatment is exclusive and fastidious."

25 MAYNARD, THEODORE. "Edwin Arlington Robinson." The Catholic
    World, 115 (June), 371–81.
       Robinson is among the best American poets ever. Laughter
    is at the root of everything he writes. Captain Craig, a
    comparative failure, exemplifies his ironic voice. He is
    obscure in the lack of explicitness of the narratives. He
    excels in the lyric, sonnet, and blank verse forms. If he
    "could abandon himself" he would be among the half dozen
    great poets of the world. [Reprinted in 1922.B26.]

26 ____. Our Best Poets. New York: Henry Holt, pp. 153–168.
       [Reprint of 1922.B25.]

27 MURRY, J. MIDDLETON. "Edwin Arlington Robinson." The Nation
    and the Athenaeum, 32 (November 18), 286–87.
       [Review of Collected Poems.] Robinson is spiritually a
    New Englander who writes in the tradition of Emerson, Haw-
    thorne, and James. His long poems fail to hold the reader's
    attention because "technical perfection" is essential to
    his work; he is a verse technician rather than a poet.
    "The Man Against the Sky" is noteworthy.

*28 OSBORN, E[DWARD] B. "An American Master-Poet." London Morn-
    ing Post, November 3, p. 6.
       [Cited in White, p. 90, as a review of Collected Poems.]

29 RANCK, EDWIN CARTY. "Robinson's Poems Reveal His Greatness."
    New York Herald Books, January 29, p. 11.
       [Review of Collected Poems, noting particularly "Boston,"
    "Ben Jonson," and "Bewick Finzer."] Robinson is not only
    the greatest living American poet, but also one of the
    greatest ever in this country.

30 REILLY, JOSEPH J. "Prize-Winning Book of Poetry." Spring-
    field (Mass.) Republican, May 28, p. 7A.
       [Review of Collected Poems.] Robinson has an affinity
    to Browning. "Ben Jonson," "Rembrandt to Rembrandt," and
    "Calvary" are notable. Robinson is similar to Masters,
    but Robinson "is the finer poet and the saner mind."

31 SAPIR, EDWARD. "Poems of Experience." The Freeman, 5 (April
    19), 141–42.

29

1922

[Review of Collected Poems.] Robinson's poetry suffers from this volume because his "comment on life is too icy for bulk." He is a major poet, but he is a lyricist rather than a writer of dramatic narratives. "The core of his poetic personality is lyric and lyric alone." Although "Ben Jonson" has been highly praised, it is not representative. "John Evereldown" is the most complex poem in the volume.

32 SCHELLING, FELIX E. Appraisements and Asperities. Philadelphia: J. B. Lippincott, pp. 91-95.
    [Review of Lancelot.] Robinson's treatment of the Arthurian myth makes it significant to our age in admirably aesthetic terms.

33 WALKER, HELEN. "The Wisdom of Merlin." The Forum, 67 (February), 179-81.
    Robinson is "as wise as Merlin himself." His knowledge of the secrets of the heart is remarkable.

34 WHITE, NEWMAN I. Review of Collected Poems. The Sewanee Review, 30 (July), 365-69.
    Robinson is at last receiving the recognition he deserves. He is neither optimistic nor pessimistic enough to be popular. "The Man Against the Sky," his best poem, is an "impressive coming to grips with the central problem of human fate."

35 WINTERS, YVOR. "A Cool Master." Poetry, 19 (February), 278-88.
    [Review of Collected Poems. Reprinted in 1970.A3.] Robinson is in the tradition of Emerson and Dickinson and has influenced many contemporary poets. He is superior to Browning and is better in rhymed verse than blank verse. The way in which the material is perceived and organized is what makes a great poem. "Mr. Robinson's greatness lies not in the people of whom he has written, but in the perfect balance, the infallible precision, with which he has stated their cases."

1923 A BOOKS

1 MORRIS, LLOYD. The Poetry of Edwin Arlington Robinson: An Essay in Appreciation. Bibliography by W. Von R. Whitall. New York: George H. Doran, 116 pp.
   [An examination of Robinson's poetry divided into discussions of the dramatic narratives, the historical

subjects, the first two Arthurian poems, the plays, his
philosophy, and his influence.] Robinson's work reflects
the New England Puritan heritage and the later interest in
German idealism, which is "the fundamental intellectual
adventure of the period." [Reprinted in 1969.A7.]

1923 B SHORTER WRITINGS

1 ALLEN, HERVEY. "The Poetry of Edwin Arlington Robinson."
  The Reviewer, 4 (October), 56-58.
    [Principally a review of Morris' study (1923.A1), this
  article notes that Robinson is comparable to Hardy but ultimately more optimistic.]

2 ANON. "The Bookman's Literary Club Service. Edwin Arlington
  Robinson." The Bookman, 57 (March), 107-108.
    [Study guide for book program, including biographical
  sketch and brief bibliography of "the most important of
  living American poets."]

3 ANON. "A Dry Poet." The New Statesman, 20 (March), 664, 666.
    [Review of Collected Poems, London.] Drinkwater's in-
  troduction for this minor poet is overblown. His blank
  verse is a parody of Enoch Arden and his rhymed poems are
  like "the poorer poems of Clough." "He is a third rate
  philosopher rather than a poet."

4 ANON. "Edwin Arlington Robinson's Sombre Muse." Current
  Opinion, 74 (May), 549-50.
    It is strange that Americans should choose so pessimis-
  tic a writer as their foremost poet. In spite of Morris'
  attempt to convince the reader of Robinson's idealism, the
  despairing last lines of "The Man Against the Sky" indicate
  his skepticism.

5 ANON. "The Literary Spotlight. Edwin Arlington Robinson."
  The Bookman, 56 (January), 565-69.
    [An examination of Robinson's personality emphasizing
  his reticence and modesty and noting that his manner at
  Peterborough contrasts sharply with his manner in New York.
  Reprinted in 1924.B2.]

6 ANON. "Progress of the Philosophical Art of E. A. Robinson."
  The New York Times Book Review, March 25, p. 3.
    [Review of Roman Bartholow.] Robinson is best at long
  poems because he is able to present a group of characters.
  He is like Hardy in that these characters are always symbolic. This book can be called "a problem novel raised to
  the high plane of poetry."

1923

7 ANON. Review of Roman Bartholow. New York World, June 24,
      p. 19e.
         The characters in this poem are not well-delineated.
      They walk and talk "as if stricken with palsy."

8 ANON. Review of Roman Bartholow. The North American Review,
      217 (June), 862-63.
         No single part of this poem is very good. It is obscure,
      overblown, and non-poetic, but "the cumulative effect of
      this poem is great."

9 ANON. "Tragedy." New York Herald Books, April 8, p. 14.
      [Review of Roman Bartholow.] This is the sort of story
      Hardy might write. It is a good example of Robinson's un-
      derstatement.

10 BENÉT, WILLIAM ROSE. "Poetry Ad Lib." The Yale Review, 13
      (October), 162-63.
         [Review of Roman Bartholow (and Eliot's Waste Land).] In
      spite of the dullness of this book, Robinson is America's
      greatest living poet. Although he has been compared to
      James, he is "less embarrassed with trivialities."

11 COLTON, ARTHUR W. "Edwin Arlington Robinson." Literary Re-
      view of the New York Evening Post, June 23, pp. 781-82.
         [Essay-review of Roman Bartholow.] Robinson is "the most
      saliently original poet among us," but he is also in the
      Emersonian tradition. He is in complete control of his
      medium, and this poetry adds power to the novel of Roman
      Bartholow.

12 COOK, HOWARD WILLARD. Our Poets of Today. New York: Moffat,
      Yard, pp. 18-31.
         [Reprint of 1918.B1 and reprinted in 1926.B2.] The poems
      of Robinson omitted from Collected Poems are not to be re-
      gretted, except for "The Children of the Night."

13 CURTIS, LEWIS P. "Gabrielle Bartholow." The Yale Literary
      Magazine, 88 (May), 255-67.
         [Review of Roman Bartholow.] This poem is superior to
      Robinson's Arthurian poems because of his objectivity.
      Gabrielle is "the crowning achievement to a brilliant tier
      of characters." Through her Robinson's fatalism is ex-
      pressed positively.

14 F., M. L. Review of Roman Bartholow. The Independent, 110
      (May 12), 319.
         This poem is too obscure.

1923

15   F[ARRAR], J[OHN]. "A Circumscribed Triangle." The Bookman,
      57 (June), 450-51.
         [Review of Roman Bartholow.] This poem is "fascinating
      in all its pristine murkiness." The word "if" is Robinson's
      focal point, both in thought and the dramatic process. "He
      is the great poet of the subjunctive mood."

16   FAUSSET, HUGO I. "A Tragic Complex." The Spectator, 131 (No-
      vember 17), 759-60.
         [Review of Roman Bartholow.] This book is distinguished
      by a blend of compassion and analysis. The reader sympa-
      thizes with all three principal characters. The central
      theme is the "fatality of nature."

17   FLETCHER, JOHN GOULD. "Edwin Arlington Robinson." The Spec-
      tator, 130 (February 10), 214, 216.
         [Review of Collected Poems (London).] Robinson's work
      contrasts sharply with that of Whitman, especially in his
      innovative subject matter and prosaic diction. He is most
      like James. His chief virtue is his "power of sustained
      intellectual analysis."

18   GORMAN, HERBERT S. The Procession of Masks. Boston: B. J.
      Brimmer, pp. 15-39.
         Robinson, whose poetry is marked by sincerity, is a "pro-
      found and complex personality." He uses four "masks": the
      Tilbury characters, historical figures, Arthurian legends,
      and contemporary figures, such as Avon and Bartholow.

19   JONES, LLEWELLYN. "Edwin Arlington Robinson." American Re-
      view, 1 (March-April), 180-89.
         [Overview, emphasizing Robinson's honest portrayal of
      character and noting particularly Merlin, Lancelot, and Van
      Zorn. Reprinted in 1925.B19.]

20   JONES, RICHARD FOSTER. "Nationalism and Imagism in Modern
      American Poetry." Washington University Studies, 11 (Octo-
      ber), 97-130.
         Two schools of poetry exist emphasizing contemporary
      life: the nationalistic, which allows any form but insists
      upon American subjects, and the imagistic, which allows any
      subject but restricts the form. Robinson's poetry is an
      example of the latter.

21   LATHAM, H. F. "American First Editions, Number 25: Edwin
      Arlington Robinson." Publisher's Weekly, 103 (March 17),
      945.
         [A list of the thirteen first editions. Reprinted in
      1932.B26.]

1923

22   LE GALLIENNE, RICHARD. "Mr. Robinson's Novel in Blank Verse."
      New York Literary Digest International Book Review, 1 (May),
      23-24, 62-63.
         [Review of Roman Bartholow.] This poem is neither a
      novel nor verse. It is flawed by obscurity, a pretentious
      style, and poorly realized characters.

23   McCORMICK, VIRGINIA TAYLOR. "Edwin Arlington Robinson: Poet
      and Philosopher." Voices, 2 (June-July), 141-43.
         [Review of Roman Bartholow, suggesting that this book
      refutes the charge that Robinson lacks passion.]

24   MORRIS, LLOYD. "Mr. Robinson's Progress." The Freeman, 7
      (April 18), 140-41.
         [Review of Roman Bartholow.] This poem is like a Greek
      tragedy. It is distinguished by the emotional power of the
      narrative and its intellectual subtlety.

25   MOULT, THOMAS. "The Poetry of Edwin Arlington Robinson."
      The Bookman (London), 63 (January), 206-207.
         [Review of Collected Poems (London), encouraging readers
      for poet neglected on both sides of the Atlantic. Parti-
      cular attention to "Cliff Klingenhagen," "The Man Against
      the Sky," and "Ben Jonson."]

26   NORRIS, WILLIAM A. "The Laboratory of a Poet's Soul." Bos-
      ton Evening Transcript, April 21, Section VIII, p. 5.
         [Review of Roman Bartholow.] The story is trite and the
      poem is as unnecessarily circuitous as a book by James.
      However, this is the kind of poem Robinson does best: "an
      explanation of an unwritten drama."

27   REDMAN, BEN RAY. "Roman Bartholow." New York Tribune Maga-
      zine and Books, October 14, p. 34.
         Although some critics have denigrated this book, its ap-
      pearance confirms that Robinson is "the greatest poet that
      this country has yet produced." Particularly impressive
      is his manipulation of blank verse.

28   RIDGE, LOLA. "To E. A. R.," in The Peterborough Anthology.
      Edited by Jean Wright Gorman and Herbert S. Gorman. New
      York: Theatre Arts, p. 132.
         [Reprint of 1920.B22.]

29   ROTH, SAMUEL. "A Bookshop Night's Adventure." The Bookman,
      58 (October), 140-46.
         [A fantasy in which a bookseller praises the contempla-
      tive quality of Robinson's poetry.] Robinson "alone among

the writers of English today has an understanding of the
consciousness of modern man, with an instinctive foreboding
of his peril."

30   STARK, HAROLD. "Young Boswell Interviews E. A. Robinson."
New York Tribune, April 18, p. 13.
[Interview in which Robinson names the poems he considers
his best--"Ben Jonson," Merlin, Lancelot, and Roman Bartho-
low--and discusses the fatalism and rigor involved in the
career of a poet. Reprinted in 1924.B19.]

31   UNTERMEYER, LOUIS. American Poetry Since 1900. New York:
Henry Holt, pp. 42-66.
[Sketch of career and assessment, with copious quotations
from the poems.] Robinson shares with Frost the summit of
American poetry. His best quality is character portrayal;
his great limitation is restraint. He is just short of
greatness because he cannot give himself up "in complete
abandon to an emotion."

32   VAN DOREN, CARL. The Roving Critic. New York: Alfred A.
Knopf, pp. 231-37.
[Reprint of 1921.B22.]

33   _____. "Roman Bartholow." The Nation, 116 (June 13), 700-701.
The murkiness of Roman Bartholow is a defect. Certain
elements of the poem "unhappily suggest that Mr. Robinson
is imitating himself." However, Robinson deserves better
than Morris' book, which spends too much time on his philosophy rather than his poetry.

34   WILSON, EDMUND JR. "Mr. Robinson's Moonlight." The Dial, 74
(May), 515-17.
[Review of Roman Bartholow and Morris (1923.A1). Reprinted in 1952.B7.] Morris has written too wholesale an
appreciation, which is refuted by the lack of poetry in
Roman Bartholow. Nevertheless, Robinson is an important
poet, whose very failures are marked with originality.

1924 A BOOKS - NONE

1924 B SHORTER WRITINGS

1   ANON. "E. A. Robinson's Character Study in Blank Verse."
Springfield (Mass.) Daily Republican, September 5, p. 10.

1924

[Review of The Man Who Died Twice, noting Robinson's lack of emotional appeal but commending his diction, sound imagery, and appropriateness of style.]

2 ANON. "Edwin Arlington Robinson," in The Literary Spotlight. Edited by John Farrar. New York: George H. Doran, pp. 116-24.
   [Reprint of 1923.B5.]

3 ANON. "Look at Fernando Nash--." The New York Times Book Review, March 23, p. 10.
   [Review of The Man Who Died Twice.] This poem is superior to other long poems, although it is similar to Captain Craig. Merlin had more imagery, but there Robinson was "the artist in poetry" while here he is "the musician in poetry."

4 ANON. "Poetry: The Man Who Died Twice." Times Literary Supplement, No. 1183, September 18, p. 582.
   This poem is similar in philosophy to other works by Robinson, but "in execution it falls far short not only of his best work but of his general level."

5 ANON. "Mr. Robinson's New Poem." Times Literary Supplement, No. 1146, January 3, p. 6.
   [Review of Roman Bartholow.] This psychological drama is a characteristic development of Robinson's shorter poems. The theme is well done, but the diction is flat.

6 ARNS, KARL. "Edwin Arlington Robinson." Germanisch romanische Monatsschrift, 12 (July-August), 224-33.
   [Assessment of career, emphasizing Robinson's detachment, humanism, and irony. Commentaries on several poems and interpretation of "The Man Against the Sky."]

7 BARTLETT, ALICE HUNT. "The Dynamics of American Poetry--III." The Poetry Review, 15 (January-February), 36-38.
   [Review of Collected Poems, in which the reviewer is impressed by the number of poems but is distressed that Robinson has failed to reveal himself. Quotes letter Robinson wrote in reply to her query, saying that he did not know what his best poem was.]

8 BOYNTON, PERCY H. Some Contemporary Americans. Chicago: The University of Chicago Press, pp. 16-32.
   [Reprint of 1922.B14, with biographical sketch and bibliography updated to 1924.]

9 CESTRE, CHARLES. "L'oeuvre Poetique d'Edwin Arlington Robin-
   son." Revue Anglo-Americaine, 1 (April), 279-94.
   [Assessment of work emphasizing Robinson's debt to the
   Puritan and metaphysical traditions and stressing that he
   is a poet of the conscience. Suggests that one should read
   Robinson's work to learn about the American mentality.]

10 DUDLEY, DOROTHY. "Wires and Cross-Wires." Poetry, 24 (May),
   96-103.
   [Review of Roman Bartholow.] Robinson is best at having
   character confront character. The poem is a "cypher of
   human wires and crosswires, a journey...to the fringes of
   speculation." The theme is borrowed from Aristotle; Chekov
   is echoed.

11 GORMAN, HERBERT S. Review of The Man Who Died Twice. The
   Bookman, 59 (June), 467-68.
   This poem is "undoubtedly the best of Mr. Robinson's narratives of modern life." The form, like a symphony, is
   consistent with the content.

12 GUITERMAN, ARTHUR. "The Bloomin' Lyre." The Outlook, 126
   (April 16), 649.
   [Review of The Man Who Died Twice.] "This poem, although
   it contains fine passages, is unfortunate in its resem-
   blance to the average street parade; it is late in getting
   started and is far too long in passing a given point."

13 JONES, E[MILY] B. C. Review of The Man Who Died Twice. The
   Nation and the Athenaeum, 35 (May 24), 248, 250.
   This poem is disappointing. "Related in lines alter-
   nately grandiose and pedestrian, it seems a poor, flat, un-
   convincing little story."

14 MOORE, MARIANNE. Review of The Man Who Died Twice. The Dial,
   77 (August), 168-70.
   Robinson successfully develops in this poem his perennial
   subject of success in failure. In his "persistent tenta-
   tive credulity" he is the obverse of Hardy's "tenuous in-
   credulity." Robinson is remarkably articulate.

15 MORRISON, THEODORE. "Two Harvard Poets." Harvard Alumni Bulletin, 26 (May 29), 983-85.
   [Assessment, emphasizing Robinson's philosophic nature,
   his traditional forms, and unpoetic diction.]

16 NICHOLS, ROBERT. "The Lure of Three Favorite Poets." The
   Literary Digest International Book Review, 3 (December),
   33, 66-67.

1924

[Review of The Man Who Died Twice, naming it Robinson's "most considerable and sterling work of art."]

17 R[ICHARDS], L[AURA]. E. "The Man Who Died Twice." Gardiner
     (Me.) Journal, April 10, p. 1.
         This poem, which "will not be forgotten so long as poetry
     is read," is similar in theme to other poems by Robinson.
     Fernando Nash is especially similar to Captain Craig.

18 RYAN, KATHRYN WHITE. "The Grim Nostalgic Passion." Voices,
     3 (May-June), 89-91.
         [Review of The Man Who Died Twice.] Robinson, "the Berg-
     son of poets," is difficult to read.

19 STARK, HAROLD (YOUNG BOSWELL). People You Know. New York:
     Boni and Liveright, pp. 221-23.
         [Reprint, with minor revisions, of 1923.B30.]

20 VAN DOREN, MARK. "A Symphony of Sin." The Nation, 118
     (April 16), 445-46.
         [Review of The Man Who Died Twice.] "Mr. Robinson has
     never written any better" than in this story of unpardon-
     able sin. Someone should set it to music.

21 WEEKS, E[DWARD] A. "Lost: A Wife and a Genius." The Inde-
     pendent, 113 (July 5), 20.
         [Review of The Man Who Died Twice.] Robinson succeeds in
     what he attempts here--"sounding a note of irretrievable
     loss." The blank verse is smooth, but while there is rich
     imagery there is no music.

22 WEIRICK, BRUCE. From Whitman to Sandburg in American Poetry.
     New York: Macmillan, pp. 184-92.
         [Assessment, with particular attention to "Flammonde,"
     "Richard Cory," and "Calverly's."] Robinson is sophisti-
     cated, bookish, and dull. He is best at short poems. Even
     though his poetry "lacks opulence," it does provide a
     standard for workmanship.

23 WILLIAMS-ELLIS, A[MABEL]. "We Speak as We Can." The Specta-
     tor, 132 (June 28), 1044.
         [Review of The Man Who Died Twice.] The chief character
     and the story are good here, but the poetry is a hindrance.
     It should have been written in prose.

1925 A BOOKS - NONE

38

1925 B SHORTER WRITINGS

1   ADAMS, LEONIE. "On Properties in Sphinxes." The Measure,
        No. 52 (June), pp. 17-18.
            [Review of Dionysus in Doubt.] The short poems in this
        volume are all right, but the long poems are only "elegant
        enigma."

2   ANON. Reivew of Dionysus in Doubt. The Dial, 79 (September),
        261.
            The sonnets and "Mortmain" are superior to the title poem
        here. Robinson will be remembered for the delicacy of his
        poetry rather than his psychological and philosophical
        qualities.

3   ANON. Review of Dionysus in Doubt. The Independent, 114
        (May 16), 563.
            This book is reasonably good satire, but that is all.
        Robinson might improve himself by writing prose and not
        trying to be lyrical.

4   ANON. "Edwin Arlington Robinson." Our World Weekly, 2 (May
        4), 205.
            [Overview of Robinson's career, with emphasis on his
        short pieces.] "Robinson's poetry is 'good leather.'"

5   ANON. Harvard College Class of 1895: Thirtieth Anniversary
        Report. Cambridge: The University Press, pp. 248-49.
            [Report of the success of the double Pulitzer Prize win-
        ner, commenting on the modesty of his letter, which is
        quoted.]

6   ANON. "Precise Grotesques." Time, 5 (May 4), 12.
            [Review of Dionysus in Doubt.] This book is well-written.
        Robinson, "whose message is the curtest, the chilliest ever
        uttered by a great poet: humanity cannot succeed," has
        been given a second Pulitzer Prize.

7   AUSLANDER, JOSEPH. "Poet's Offerings: Robinson Indignant,
        Saddened." New York World, April 26, p. 7M.
            [Review of Dionysus in Doubt.] Dionysus, a persona of
        Robinson, is not in doubt but indignant. The sonnets here
        are best.

8   B[RUNCKEN], H[ERBERT] G. Review of Dionysus in Doubt. The
        Minaret, 4 (July-August), 25-26.
            Only the title poem and the sonnets in this volume can
        hold the reader's attention.

1925

9   BURTON, RICHARD. "Poetry of Edwin A. Robinson." New York
     Sun, April 18, p. 8.
        [Review of Dionysus in Doubt.] The sonnets are remark-
     ably good in this powerful volume. Robinson is, in spite
     of significant differences, "our American Browning."

10   CESTRE, C[HARLES]. "Dionysus in Doubt." Revue Anglo-
     Americaine, 2 (August), 560-62.
        [Review, criticizing the coldness and didacticism of this
     volume but maintaining that the Robinson of the great poems
     is still visible.]

*11 CESTRE, CHARLES. "Edwin Arlington Robinson's Treatment of the
     Arthurian Legend." The Bryn Mawr Alumae Bulletin, 5 (No-
     vember), 5-15.
        [Cited in Hogan, p. 123, as reprinted in 1930.A1.]

12   _____. "The Man Who Died Twice." Revue Anglo-Americaine, 2
     (June), 464-66.
        [Review, hailing Robinson as the greatest poet in the
     English language and applauding this work for its profun-
     dity and style.]

13   CONKLING, GRACE HAZARD. Review of Dionysus in Doubt. The
     North American Review, 222 (September-October-December),
     159-60.
        Robinson seems to be withholding something from the
     reader, but the sonnets are well done. Most notable are
     "The Sheaves" and "Silver Street."

14   DALY, JAMES. "The Inextinguishable God." Poetry, 27 (Octo-
     ber), 40-44.
        [Review of Dionysus in Doubt.] "Genevieve and Alexandra"
     and "Mortmain" are two well drawn psychological studies,
     and the sonnets are distinguished, but "Demos and Dionysus"
     and the title poem need not have been published.

15   DRINKWATER, JOHN. The Muse in Council. London: Sidgwick and
     Jackson, pp. 186-201, and Boston: Houghton Mifflin,
     pp. 248-62.
        [Reprint of 1922.B17.]

16   GORMAN, HERBERT S. "E. A. Robinson and Some Others." The
     Bookman, 61 (July), 595-96.
        [Review of Dionysus in Doubt.] The two Dionysus poems
     are unfortunate because they are so political, but the son-
     nets, especially "The Sheaves," are excellent.

17 GUITERMAN, ARTHUR. "Parnassus and Thereabout." The Outlook,
      140 (May 20), 112.
        [Review of Dionysus in Doubt.] Dionysus appears to dis-
      approve of the Eighteenth Amendment, but he is not very ex-
      plicit. The sonnets are well done, though.

18 HUTCHISON, PERCY A. "Unransomed Juvenile Miscalled Democracy."
      The New York Times Book Review, March 29, p. 5.
        [Review of Dionysus in Doubt. Reprinted in 1926.B4.]
      Some of Robinson's best poems are in this volume, especially
      "The Sheaves," "Silver Street," "Genevieve and Alexandra,"
      and the title poem.

19 JONES, LLEWELLYN. First Impressions. New York: Alfred A.
      Knopf, pp. 13-36.
        [Reprint of 1923.B19.]

20 M[ONROE], H[ARRIET]. "Edwin Arlington Robinson." Poetry, 25
      (January), 206-17.
        [Overview of Robinson's career, naming his recurrent
      motif as "the psychology of failure," and suggesting that
      The Man Who Died Twice is the best of the long poems. Re-
      printed in 1926.B6.]

21 MOORE, VIRGINIA. Review of Dionysus in Doubt. Atlantic
      Monthly, 135 (June), 10, 12.
        This well-written volume reveals Robinson's intellectu-
      ality and his debt to Browning.

22 NORRIS, W[ILLIAM] A. "The Dark Wood." The New Republic, 41
      (January 21), 238-39.
        [Review of The Man Who Died Twice, which the reviewer
      cannot appreciate because it is too ethereal, with insuf-
      ficient story or contact with the real world.]

23 REDMAN, BEN RAY. "Satiric Tracts in Verse." New York Herald
      Tribune Books, September 6, p. 4.
        [Review of Dionysus in Doubt.] The two Dionysus poems
      are more propaganda than poetry. The sonnets are worth-
      while, though, and "Mortmain" is "a minor masterpiece."

24 SAPIR, EDWARD. "The Tragic Chuckle." Voices, 5 (November),
      64-65.
        [Review of Dionysus in Doubt which includes praise for
      the sonnets, indifference toward the long poems, and im-
      patience with the general air of negation in Robinson's
      poetry.]

1925

*25   SHIPLEY, JOSEPH T. "Edwin Arlington Robinson." The Guardian,
         2 (October), 452-56.
         [Hogan, p. 147, lists this in reviews of Dionysus in
         Doubt.]

26   _____. "Against the Time." Literary Review of the New York
         Evening Post, April 4, p. 5.
         [Review of Dionysus in Doubt.] Robinson is best in his
         sonnets, which are reminiscent of Browning.

27   SIEGRIST, MARY. "A Poet Satirizes the Age of Prohibitions."
         The Literary Digest International Book Review, 3 (August),
         586, 589.
         [Review of Dionysus in Doubt.] This is an important vol-
         ume in spite of its didacticism. The sonnets are well
         written and "Genevieve and Alexandra" is especially nota-
         ble.

28   S[TUART], J[OHN] R. "Dionysus in Doubt." Boston Evening
         Transcript, April 4, Section VI, p. 2.
         [Review of Dionysus in Doubt.] The tone of this book is
         set by the first and last poems, which are the poet's con-
         structive criticism of society. The sonnets, however, are
         too obscure.

29   TITTLE, WALTER. "Glimpses of Interesting Americans." The
         Century Magazine, 110 (June), 189-92.
         [Interview with Robinson during sitting for a sketch.
         England, the ability of eyes to convey expression, and
         Robinson's theory of art were discussed.]

30   UNTERMEYER, LOUIS. "Demos at the Bar." The Saturday Review
         of Literature, 1 (May 9), 741.
         [Review of Dionysus in Doubt.] The first and last poems
         are not "mere political diatribe." "Genevieve and Alex-
         andra," "Llewellyn and the Tree," "Mortmain," and "The
         Sheaves" are particularly noteworthy.

31   _____. "Seven Against Realism." The Yale Review, 14 (July),
         792-93.
         [Review of The Man Who Died Twice.] This poem is "one
         of Robinson's triumphs." The description of the rats is
         memorable.

32   VAN DOREN, CARL and MARK VAN DOREN. American and British
         Literature Since 1890. New York: Century, pp. 14-18.
         [Overview of Robinson's career, with emphasis on his
         celebration of failures as a reason for his slow recognition

and the numbers of his characters as one of his distin-
guishing features. Revised and enlarged in 1939.B10.]

33   VAN DOREN, MARK. "First Glance." The Nation, 120 (April 15),
       428.
          [Review of Dionysus in Doubt.] The book is a disappoint-
       ment, especially the two Dionysus poems. "Mortmain" is
       better than "Genevieve and Alexandra." The eighteen son-
       nets "deserve all praise."

34   WALSH, THOMAS. "Dionysus in Doubt." The Commonweal, 2 (May
       13), 26.
          Robinson is "a preacher who has lost his way back to the
       pulpit" and refuses the guidance of any sect. His imagina-
       tion is thin.

35   WILSON, JAMES SOUTHHALL. "Apollo in Doubt." The Virginia
       Quarterly Review, 1 (July), 319-20.
          [Review of Dionysus in Doubt.] "If this volume does not
       contain his greatest work, it is yet a distinctive and dis-
       guished book." "Mortmain," "The Sheaves," and "New Eng-
       land" are especially noteworthy.

36   WOOD, CLEMENT. "Edwin Arlington Robinson: The Darkening
       Hill," in Poets of America. New York: E. P. Dutton,
       pp. 119-41.
          [Overview with brief comments on numerous poems.]
       Robinson's message is rare in simplicity and unity. His
       vision appears to be limited to his first twenty years of
       life in Tilbury, which gives his poetry "a narrowed inten-
       sity." Although there has been little growth since The
       Children of the Night, Robinson is entitled to "highest
       honors among our living singers."

1926 A BOOKS

1   REDMAN, BEN RAY. Edwin Arlington Robinson. Modern American
       Writers, no. 6. Edited by Ernest Boyd. New York: Robert
       M. McBride, 96 pp.
          [Overview of Robinson's career and literary milieu, with
       commentary on "Captain Craig," "The Man Against the Sky,"
       and "Ben Jonson," among others.] Robinson is "the great-
       est poet whom this country has yet produced," judged by
       "the twin measure of fecundity and excellence."

1926

1926 B SHORTER WRITINGS

1 CESTRE, CHARLES. "Amy Lowell, Robert Frost, and Edwin Arlington Robinson." The Johns Hopkins Alumni Magazine, 14
(March), 375-88.
[An analysis of Robinson's contribution to poetry, emphasizing his variety and stylistic excellence and commenting
particularly on "The Man Against the Sky."]

2 COOK, HOWARD WILLARD. Our Poets of Today. New York: Moffat,
Yard, pp. 18-30.
[Reprint of 1923.B12, expanded to include works by and
about Robinson through 1924.]

3 GUITERMAN, ARTHUR. "Edwin Arlington Robinson." The Saturday
Review of Literature, 2 (July 3), 903.
[Twelve-line poem satirizing Robinson.]

4 HUTCHISON, PERCY A. "Unransomed Juvenile Miscalled Democracy,"
in Current Reviews. Edited by Lewis Worthington Smith.
New York: Henry Holt, pp. 308-14.
[Reprint of 1925.B18.]

5 MARKHAM, EDWIN. The Book of Poetry, Vol. 1. New York: William H. Wise, p. 393.
[One-page introduction emphasizing Robinson's subtle
humor and affinity with Browning.]

6 MONROE, HARRIET. Poets and Their Art. New York: Macmillan,
pp. 1-11.
[Reprint of 1925.B20.]

7 REED, EDWARD BLISS. Review of Dionysus in Doubt. The Yale
Review, 15 (July), 811-12.
Robinson, our most intellectual poet, criticizes American
life in the two Dionysus poems.

8 RIDGE, LOLA. "Eyrie (To E. A. R.)." The New Republic, 47
(June 16), 107.
[Italian sonnet to Robinson, reprinted in 1927.B58.]

9 RITTENHOUSE, JESSIE B. "Poetry of New England," in Anthology
of Magazine Verse for 1926. Edited by William Stanley
Braithwaite. Boston: B. J. Brimmer, pp. 12-16.
Although Robinson has been given elaborate praise, most
readers do not understand him. He is a New England poet,
a man's poet, a poet "of certain aborted lives." Minor
flaws are lack of passion and monotony of characters.

10   SQUIRE, J. C.   "Edwin Arlington Robinson."   The London Mercury,
     13 (February), 401-12.
         Robinson is barely known in England because he seems dull,
     or too much trouble, but he is one of the most important
     contemporary writers because of his psychological insights
     and poetic integrity. He is comparable to Wordsworth and
     Browning. [Reprinted in 1928.B18.]

11   VAN DOORN, WILLIAM.   "How It Strikes a Contemporary."   English
     Studies, 8 (October), 135-38.
         Robinson's "sub-dramatic method" is similar to Browning.
     His Arthurian poems are better than Tennyson's because they
     are less moralistic. "Flammonde" is particularly note-
     worthy.

1927 A BOOKS

1   ANON.   Edwin Arlington Robinson.   New York: Macmillan, 34 pp.
         [Promotional booklet for Tristram, with biographical
     sketch and excerpts from essays by Cestre, Redman, Morris,
     and reviews from four British newspapers. Reprinted in
     1927.B47.]

2   BEEBE, LUCIUS.   Edwin Arlington Robinson and the Arthurian
     Legend.   Cambridge, Mass.: Dunster House Bookshop, 30 pp.
         [Brief examination of Robinson's three Arthurian poems,
     attempting a source study, textual analysis, and comparison
     with other modern poets' treatment of the legend, the the-
     sis being that Robinson gives spiritual significance to the
     Arthurian tales that other writers have failed to achieve.
     Included in 1928.A1.]

3   VAN DOREN, MARK.   Edwin Arlington Robinson.   New York: Lit-
     erary Guild of America, 90 pp.
         [Critical study written to coincide with publication of
     Tristram, divided into four chapters: an overview of Rob-
     inson's career, the short poems, the long poems, and a
     chapter on Tristram. No index or bibliography.]

1927 B SHORTER WRITINGS

1   AIKEN, CONRAD.   "Tristram."   The New Republic, 51 (May 25), 22.
         Robinson's chief gift is that of portraiture, especially
     of women characters, but Tristram is not a success because
     his characters cannot act--each is "a kind of helpless in-
     trospective Hamlet." The poem is too long and the language
     is reminiscent of James in that it is too involuted. [Re-
     printed in 1958.B2 and 1970.A3.]

1927

2   ANON. "An Ennobled Tristram." <u>Christian Science Monitor</u>,
      May 11, p. 12.
        <u>Tristram</u> is unique in that the characters are more impor-
      tant than the setting. The structure is that of a five act
      play.

*3   ANON. "Arthuriana." <u>Springfield</u> (Ohio) <u>News-Sun</u>, October 23,
      Section IV, p. 8.
        [Cited as a review of <u>Tristram</u> in Hogan, p. 150.]

4   ANON. "Into His Own." <u>Denver Rocky Mountain News</u>, June 5,
      Drama Section, p. 4.
        [Review of <u>Tristram</u> and survey of Robinson's career.]
      <u>Tristram</u> "marks the surge point in a series of great lit-
      erature by America's greatest contemporary poet and it
      brings into common knowledge the works of an artist who...
      has never been appreciated by the ordinary reader."

5   ANON. "The Merlin of Modern Poetry--Edwin Arlington Robinson."
      <u>Current Literature</u>, 3 (September 19-23), 5-7.
        [Robinson biography and synopsis of <u>Tristram</u> with ex-
      cerpts for school supplementary text.]

6   ANON. "Mr. Robinson's 'Tristram.'" <u>Times Literary Supple-
      ment</u>, No. 1338, September 22, p. 640.
        Although still somewhat prolix, Robinson is master of his
      material in <u>Tristram</u>, as he was not in the preceding Ar-
      thurian poems. He rationalizes rather than sentimentalizes
      the story.

7   ANON. "Robinson." <u>The Literary Digest</u>, 93 (May 28), 28.
        [News article about the critical success of <u>Tristram</u> and
      mention of the reading by Elinor Robeson on May 8.]

8   ANON. "Tristram." <u>The Dial</u>, 83 (August), 174.
        A good vehicle for Robinson's particular style, this poem
      is nevertheless too long and lacks emotional intensity.

9   ANON. Review of <u>Tristram</u>. <u>The Independent</u>, 117 (April 23),
      448.
        "<u>Tristram</u> surely should rank with the best of Mr. Robin-
      son's work."

10   ANON. "Verse: Heaven's Lonely Place." <u>Time</u>, 9 (May 23), 39.
        [Review of <u>Tristram</u>.] This poem is "great despite its
      faltering."

11   AUSLANDER, JOSEPH, and FRANK ERNEST HILL. The Winged Horse.
        New York: Doubleday, Page, pp. 405-407.
        [Brief overview emphasizing versatility and diction.]

12   AXSON, STOCKTON. "'Tristram,' by Edwin Arlington Robinson,
        Held as Event in American Literature." Houston Chronicle,
        June 12, Editorial-Features Section, pp. 6, 7.
        [Review of career, style, and philosophy, with summary of
        Tristram.] "This noble dome" is built for the "poetic edi-
        fice which he began to erect thirty years ago."

*13   BELLAMANN, HENRY. "The Literary Highway." Columbia (S.C.)
        Record, May 8, p. 5.
        [Cited as a review of Tristram in Hogan, p. 148.]

14   BENÉT, WILLIAM ROSE. "Escort to Leviathan." The Outlook, 146
        (June 1), 158, 160.
        [Review of Tristram.] Although Tennyson is adept in
        writing noble lines, he does not understand people, espe-
        cially women, the way Robinson does. This treatment of the
        legend is "as penetrating...as any study of it ever will
        be."

15   BRICKELL, HERSCHEL. "Edwin Arlington Robinson's Masterpiece."
        New York Evening Post, May 23, p. 10.
        [Review of Tristram.] The Literary Guild is to be com-
        mended for popularizing this poem of sustained high quality.
        It differs from Robinson's other work because of its emo-
        tional intensity.

16   [CALVERTON, V. F.] Review of Tristram. Modern Quarterly, 4
        (November-February), 310.
        "This delicate poem...is feeble as drama, but memorable
        as sheer music."

17   CESTRE, CHARLES. "Le Tristan d'Edwin Arlington Robinson."
        Revue Anglo-Americaine, 5 (December), 97-110.
        [A detailed analysis of Tristram, which the author con-
        siders Robinson's masterpiece in spite of its length.]

18   C[OOPER], M[ONTGOMERY]. "The Song of Lovers, Who Know How,
        Twitched Out of Place and Time." Memphis (Tenn.) Commer-
        cial Appeal, May 22, Section II, p. 8.
        [Review of Tristram, emphasizing its sustained beauty
        and simplicity.]

19   COTTLE, BROOKS. "Turning New Leaves." Morgantown (W. Va.)
        New Dominion, May 11, p. 6.

1927

> [Review of Tristram, suggesting that with it Robinson's
> reputation is secured and contrasting this version with
> earlier treatments of the legend.]

20   CRAWFORD, NELSON ANTRIM. "Robinson's Third Venture with the
>   Arthurian Legend." Baltimore Evening Sun, March 26, p. 6.
>   [Review of Tristram.] Robinson is "the keenest ironist
>   now writing English verse." Tristram is the best of his
>   Arthurian poems, but he would profit by sticking with mod-
>   ern subjects, such as The Man Who Died Twice.

21   CROUCH, F. M. "E. A. Robinson Revamps an Old Legend." The
>   Churchman, 136 (August 20), 20-21.
>   [Review of Tristram.] Tristram is not as good as The
>   Man Against the Sky because Robinson, a minor poet, is es-
>   sentially a lyricist. He pales beside Tennyson, Browning,
>   and Arnold.

22   DAVIDSON, DONALD. "Robinson's 'Tristram.'" Nashville Tennes-
>   sean, June 26, Magazine Section, p. 7.
>   The "literary lobbyism" of the Literary Guild is respon-
>   sible for Robinson's latest success, for Tristram is not
>   much better than his other long poems. Tristram is "a
>   weak philanderer who could not make up his mind."

23   DEUTSCH, BABETTE. "An Old Tale Retold." New York Sun, May 7,
>   p. 11.
>   [Review of Tristram.] In spite of some bits of "trivial
>   melodrama" this poem is as affecting as Wagner's Tristan und
>   Isolde. Reference to the Cornish Sea "recurs with the melo-
>   dious insistence of a musical motif."

24   D'EVELYN, CHARLOTTE. "Edwin A. Robinson's Version of Tris-
>   tram.'" Springfield (Mass.) Union and Republican, August
>   7, p. 7F.
>   [Review of Tristram, commenting on characterization,
>   simplicity, and the unusual place Gawaine has in all three
>   Arthurian poems.]

*25 DRUMMOND, ROBERT. "Tristram." Urbana Daily Illini, October
>   9, Magazine Section, p. 2.
>   [Cited in Hogan, p. 150.]

26   FAIRCLOUGH, HENRY RUSHTON. "Edwin Arlington Robinson," in The
>   Classics and Our Twentieth Century Poets. Stanford Univer-
>   sity: Stanford University Press, pp. 14-27; Stanford Uni-
>   versity Publications University Series: Language and Lit-
>   erature, 2 (1923-27), [278] - [291].

[Sources of Robinson's classical allusions traced from
The Children of the Night to Dionysus in Doubt, with particular attention to Captain Craig.]

27   F[ARRAR], J[OHN]. "A New Tristram." The Bookman, 65 (June),
465-66.
     Tristram is equal to any great narrative poem in English.
"Here is a book your great-grandchildren will read, even if
you neglect it."

28   FLANDERS, HELEN HARTNESS. "Old Themes, New Poets." The Poetry Review, 18 (September-October), 337-38.
     [Review of Tristram.] Although this poem is interesting
it is full of extraneous material. Undue attention from
the press caused it to be sold out two days after it was
announced.

29   GORDON, BAREFIELD. "A Shakespearean American." The Chicago
Defender, September 3, p. 13.
     [Review of Tristram emphasizing the verse form.]

30   GORMAN, HERBERT S. "Edwin Arlington Robinson's 'Tristram.'"
The Literary Review of the New York Evening Post, May 7,
p. 3.
     Tristram is Robinson's best poem and the best version of
the legend.

31   _____. "High Spots in Spring Books." The Bookman, 65 (July),
555.
     [Review of Tristram, calling it the best long poem ever
produced in the country.]

32   HANSEN, HARRY. "Of Love and Beauty." New York World, April
23, p. 13.
     [Review of Tristram, comparing it to Wagner's treatment
and commending the portrait of the two Isolts and the ex-
clusion of the love philtre.]

33   HARRISS, R. P. "Old Love in New Form." Asheville (N.C.)
Times, May 15, Section A, p. 13.
     [Review of Tristram, commenting on the diction and com-
paring it favorably to Dionysus in Doubt.]

34   H[ART], B. K. "A Poem as a 'Best Seller.'" Providence (R.I.)
Sunday Journal, June 26, Book Section, p. 5.
     [Review of Tristram.] This is the best long poem written
by an American and the best treatment of the legend ever.
That a poem should be a best seller is "remarkable and glorious."

1927

35 HOLMES, JOHN HAYNES. "Great Poems." Unity, 99 (August 22),
337.
[Review of Tristram.] "Mr. Robinson has glorified American literature, the world's literature, with a masterpiece
of the first order."

36 HUTCHISON, PERCY A. "American Poetry at Its Best." The New
York Times Book Review, May 8, pp. 1, 27.
[Review of Tristram, commending the shift in emphasis to
the other Isolt and analyzing the verse form. Suggests
that this masterpiece will not soon be equaled.]

37 JONES, HOWARD MUMFORD. "A More Lyric Robinson." Chicago
Daily News, May 18, p. 14.
[Review of Tristram, commenting on diction, analysis of
minor characters, and lyricism.]

38 JONES, LLEWELLYN. "That Famous Arthurian Triangle." Chicago
Evening Post Literary Review, May 13, pp. 1-2.
[Review of Tristram, commending both Robinson and the
Literary Guild for not compromising taste.]

39 JONES, W. MELVILLE. "Robinson Writes with Beauty of Tristram
Legend." Richmond News Leader, May 23, p. 13.
Tristram is a concrete example of Robinson's definition
of poetry and is superior to the versions of Tennyson and
Swinburne.

40 JUDGE, JANE. "American Poetry Reaches New Height in 'Tristram.'" Savannah (Ga.) Morning News, May 15, p. C5.
[Review emphasizing Robinson's skill at blank verse and
relative freedom from obscurity.]

41 K[ELLY], B. M. "Tristram." The Signet, 8 (November), 101-
102.
"Tristram is a great poem, but it is not Robinson's
greatest." Mark, not Andred, should have been the slayer.
Lancelot has more high points.

42 LAING, A. K. "Mr. Tristram." Voices, 7 (December), 84-88.
[Review of Tristram, comparing it to Richard Hovey's
treatment of the Arthurian legend.]

43 LOWDEN, SAMUEL MARION. "The Gift of God," in Understanding
Great Poems. Harrisburg, Pennsylvania: Handy Book Corpo-
ration, pp. 265-73.
[Background materials, outline and explication of "The
Gift of God."]

44 M[ONROE], H[ARRIET]. "On Foreign Ground." <u>Poetry</u>, 31 (December), 160-67.
   [Review of <u>Tristram</u>, suggesting that its success is due to the Literary Guild support and predicting that it will not ultimately be considered among his best works.]

45 M[OON], L. B. "Tristram." <u>The Lyric West</u>, 7 (November), 57-59.
   <u>Tristram</u> is the most important poem of the year, although Robinson is not a popular poet. The reader must like "looking around the corners of ideas."

46 MORRIS, LLOYD. "The Career of Passion." <u>The Nation</u>, 124 (May 25), 586.
   [Review of <u>Tristram</u>.] This is Robinson's best poem. The treatment is "singularly free of ethical implications," the structure has "classical austerity," and the poem is marked by "the intensity of its emotion."

47 _____. "The Rare Genius of Edwin Arlington Robinson." <u>The World Review</u>, 5 (December 12), 182-83.
   [Partial reprint of 1927.A1.]

48 MUNSON, GORHAM B. "Edwin Arlington Robinson." <u>The Saturday Review of Literature</u>, 3 (May 21), 839-40.
   Robinson has received so much praise recently that it is impossible to assess him. He uses no new forms and says simple things in a complex way. <u>Tristram</u> has been called his best work, but it may be only "a sustained conscientiousness." [Reprinted in 1928.B17.]

49 NETHERCOT, ARTHUR H. "E. A. Robinson Writes of Tristram." <u>Evanston</u> (Ill.) <u>News-Index</u>, May 18, p. 10.
   Swinburne could have written this emotional story better than Robinson, "the ironist." Robinson is wordy, and his women characters are better drawn than his men.

50 NEWELL, EMILY BLAIR. "For Those Who Love Poetry." <u>Good Housekeeping</u>, 85 (December), 208-209.
   [Review of <u>Tristram</u>, commending it but cautioning the readers about its difficulty.]

51 PATERSON, ISABEL. "A Suburban Tristram and a South Dakota Saga." <u>McNaught's Monthly</u>, 8 (July), 28.
   [Review of <u>Tristram</u>.] Mark is presented as an indignant husband; Tristram is only sulky. Robinson's "blank verse is too faultlessly blank. It scans, but it does not sing."

1927

52 PHELPS, WILLIAM LYON. "Hats Off! A Masterpiece." New York
Evening Post, June 18, p. 8.
[Essay-review of Tristram, including an overview of Robinson's career and Phelps' earlier reaction to his books.]
Robinson has beaten "the most dangerous of rivals"--his own
past reputation, for Tristram has been transfigured into
"something divine."

53 PIERCE, FREDERICK E. "Four Poets." The Yale Review, 17 (October), 177-78.
[Review of Tristram.] Although Robinson is the greatest
living American poet, his range is narrow, especially of
mood. Within the range Tristram is well done, "neither too
antiquarian nor rosily romantic."

54 POLAND, LUKE. "Tristram." The Boulevardier, 3 (September),
5, 16.
Some of Robinson's lines "are reminiscent of Shakespeare."

55 PRESTON, JOHN HYDE. "Three American Poets." The Virginia
Quarterly Review, 3 (July), 455-59.
[Review of Tristram, suggesting that Swinburne's treatment is superior to Robinson's because it has more feeling
and is not so intellectual.]

56 RANCK, CARTY. "A Poet Rewrites a Tragedy of Love." Boston
Evening Transcript, May 7, Section VI, p. 4.
[Review of Tristram, comparing the story to Wagner's
treatment and Mark's speeches to those of King Lear.]

57 REDMAN, BEN RAY. "White Fire and Red." New York Herald Tribune Books, May 8, pp. 3-4.
[Review of Tristram, noting Robinson's changes from the
Tristram legend and stating that this is the best poem ever
written by an American.]

58 RIDGE, LOLA. "Eyrie," in Red Flag. New York: Viking, p. 33.
[Reprint of 1926.B8.]

59 SALPETER, HARRY. "E. A. Robinson, Poet." New York World,
May 15, Metropolitan Section, p. 8M.
[Interview with Robinson after publication of Tristram.]
Robinson's indifference to poetic theory indicates his concern with the end instead of the means. The plethora of
inferior poeticizing might be lessened if poets did not attempt to publish until they reach their thirties. The age
is marked by more talk of poetry than previously but no
more buying and reading of it. Tennyson, Longfellow, and
Kipling are all currently under-rated.

60   SCUDDER, VIDA D. "Tristram." Atlantic Monthly, 140 (July),
         12, 14.
         Robinson's treatment is thin compared to that of the Vic-
      torians. Because Robinson writes in the old tradition he
      is superior to Eliot and the Sitwells. Here he presents
      the younger Isolt with "especial felicity."

61   SINCLAIR, UPTON. "Choose Your Poet," in Money Writes! New
         York: Albert & Charles Boni, pp. 152-55.
         [Review of Tristram, noting that Robinson has no social
      sense, mixes metaphors, forgets to finish a sentence, and
      lacks originality.]

62   SMALL, HAROLD A. "Between the Lines." San Francisco Chroni-
         cle, May 15, p. 10-D.
         [Review of Tristram, suggesting that no poem of the time
      compares with it in interest and importance and emphasizing
      both the narrative and the style.]

63   STORK, CHARLES WHARTON. "Tristram." Philadelphia Inquirer,
         May 21, p. 18.
         Tristram is very human and unheroic in this version,
      which the average reader won't like, but there is a ques-
      tion about "how much one should indulge in anachronisms of
      psychology." Nevertheless, here is Browning at his best in
      a book that contains "poetry unmistakable."

64   VAN DOREN, CARL. "The Roving Critic." The Century Magazine,
         114 (June), 255-56.
         [Review of Tristram, predicting that Robinson will be
      remembered fifty years hence because of this book.] It is
      "the greatest poem yet written...by an American."

65   _____. "Why the Editorial Board Chose This Book." Wings, 1,
         No. 4, pp. 2-3.
         [Advertisement for Tristram from the Literary Guild.]

66   VAN DOREN, MARK. "Tristram." The Forum, 78 (August), 312-13.
         It is too early to say whether Tristram is Robinson's
      masterpiece, but it certainly is most popular. His changes
      from the legend are significant.

67   WHIPPLE, LEON. "Scripts for Summer Solstice." The Survey, 58
         (July 1), 390.
         Tristram is a better love story to read for entertainment
      than "cheap and cynic things" in modern novels.

1927

68   WILKINSON, MARGUERITE.   "A Biographer of Souls."   The Woman's
     Press, 21 (May), 329-31.
          Robinson sees women as individuals, not solely in their
     relationship to men.   "Neighbors" is one of the few poems
     in the language "on the minor heroism of wearing shabby
     clothes."

69   WILSON, EDMUND.   "The Muses Out of Work."   The New Republic,
     50 (May 11), 319.
          [Review of Tristram.]   In spite of the praise given it,
     this book "is a long narrative which reads at its worse
     like a movie scenario and at its best like a romantic novel
     of adultery in the nineties."   Millay's The King's Henchman
     is far superior.

1928 A BOOKS

1   BEEBE, LUCIUS.   Aspects of the Poetry of Edwin Arlington Rob-
    inson.   Bibliography by Bradley Fisk.   Cambridge, Mass.:
    The Dunster House Bookshop, 66 pp.
         [Expansion of 1927.A2.]

1928 B SHORTER WRITINGS

1   ANON.   "American Narrative Verse."   The New Statesman, 31
    (September), 644, 646.
         [Review of Tristram, charging that praise for the poem
    has been overblown because Robinson is not innovative and
    follows Tennyson and Morris too closely.   Some lines quoted
    showing how easy it is to ridicule poem.]

2   ANON.   "Books in Brief."   The Nation, 126 (February 8), 169.
         [Announcement of five-volume edition of Collected Poems,
    pointing out its value because the Robinson canon is so
    large.]

3   ANON.   "Our Board of Editors."   The Book League Monthly, 1
    (November), 1.
         [Brief sketch of the career of "the dean of American
    poets," justifying Robinson's presence on the editorial
    staff of the Literary Guild.]

4   ANON.   "Robinson's Sonnets."   Springfield (Mass.) Republican,
    December 13, p. 10.
         [Review of Sonnets 1889-1927.]   Chronological order of
    sonnets shows Robinson's developing incisiveness.   He does
    not share with Millay the sensuous quality that Milton said

was essential, but many of the sonnets are perfect examples
of the form.

5   ANON. "Wilder Novel Wins Pulitzer Award: E. A. Robinson Also
    Three-Time Victor." The New York Times, May 8, Section I,
    p. 4.
       [News article naming winners of 1927 Pulitzer Awards.
    Tristram is described briefly.]

6   ARNS, KARL. "Amerikas Grosster Lebender Dichter im Urteil
    Seiner Zeitgenossen." Zeitschrift für franzosischen und
    englischen Unterricht, 27 (No. 7), 500-13.
       [Commentary on Robinson's attitude toward American soci-
    ety and a review of criticism, including Arns' earlier es-
    say (1924.B6).]

7   BEACH, STEWART. "Harvest of a Major Poet." The Independent,
    120 (January 21), 68.
       [Review of Collected Poems.] Fame should have come to
    Robinson sooner because his style and subject should appeal
    to the popular reader, in spite of his New England re-
    straint. A master of the sonnet, his genius lies in his
    ability "to touch an immortal beauty with the colors of a
    simple and honest mortality."

8   BEEBE, LUCIUS. "Sonnets 1889-1927." The Harvard Crimson
    Bookshelf, December 10, pp. 5-6.
       Robinson's sonnets lack the warmth of his longer poems,
    although his mastery of technique has been unquestioned
    ever since he published "Supremacy" in the Harvard Advocate
    on June 16, 1892. Publisher promised nine new titles, but
    "not more than three or four are here published for the
    first time." [Reprinted in 1929.B23.]

9   BENÉT, WILLIAM ROSE. "Sonnets 1889-1927." The Saturday Re-
    view of Literature, 5 (November 24), 412.
       There is nothing new in this collection by the "most
    notable modern American poet," but it is convenient to have
    all the sonnets in one place.

10 BOIS, JULES. "Le Poete Americain de la Conscience--Edwin Arl-
    ington Robinson." Revue Politique et Literaire, 66 (June
    16), 369-74.
       [Examination of Robinson as an explorer of the human spir-
    it continuing in the tradition of LaBruyere and the new
    world poets of the human conscience, particularly Emerson,
    using mainly the character of Fernando Nash for illustra-
    tion.]

1928

11 CESTRE, CHARLES. "Le Tristan d'Edwin Arlington Robinson."
   Revue Anglo-Americaine, 5 (February), 219-28.
   [An examination of the form of Tristram analyzing its
   "exterior beauty."]

12 CHURCH, RICHARD. "Come! Fellow Orpheus." The Spectator, 141
   (August 11), 195-96.
   [Review of Tristram, expressing surprise that the book
   has sold 40,000 copies, since it is so understated and com-
   pressed, and commending Robinson's "quiet perfection of
   tone."]

13 D[OLE], N. H. "A Collected Robinson." Boston Evening Transcript, June 23, Book Section, p. 4.
   [Review of Collected Poems in which passages from both
   Tennyson and Robinson are quoted and the reader is asked to
   tell which is which. "Morgan and Fingal" is singled out
   for praise.]

14 HICKS, GRANVILLE. "An American Poet's Services to Art."
   Springfield (Mass.) Union and Republican, February 12,
   p. 7F.
   [Essay-review of Collected Poems.] Neither Tristram nor
   The Man Against the Sky is sufficiently better than earlier
   poems to justify their reception. Robinson's poems about
   people are better than his explicitly philosophical ones.
   The long poems combine passages of majesty and those that
   are tediously prolix. His "frequently beautiful" blank
   verse is superior to Frost's. Because Robinson has sur-
   vived thirty years of changing fads, he is "as near to
   greatness as any American poet of our time."

15 HILLYER, ROBERT. "E. A. Robinson and His 'Tristram.'" The
   New Adelphi, 2 (September), 90-94.
   Although he is still neglected in England, Robinson is
   "perhaps the best poet since Tennyson." His latest poem is
   a natural development from his early work.

16 JOHNSON, EDGAR. "Edwin Robinson Sonnets Possess Elusive
   Beauty." New York Evening Post, December 1, Section III,
   p. 8M.
   Sonnets 1889-1927 represents the best and worst of Robinson since it shows the care with which he uses words as
   well as his obscurities.

17 MUNSON, GORHAM B. Destinations: A Canvass of American Literature Since 1900. New York: J. H. Sears, pp. 57-66.
   [Reprint of 1927.B48.]

18   SQUIRE, J. C. "Edwin Arlington Robinson," in Contemporary
      American Authors. New York: Henry Holt, pp. 121-48.
      [Reprint of 1926.B10.]

19   WHIPPLE, T. K. "Edwin Arlington Robinson," in Spokesman.
      New York: D. Appleton, pp. 45-69.
      [Discussion of Robinson's philosophy of "subdued tran-
      scendentalism," his melancholy, and his light and dark im-
      agery. Assessment that the long poems are major but
      "bulky," and the short character sketches positively his
      best work.]

20   WISEHART, MARION K. "'By Jove!' Said Roosevelt 'It Reads
      Like the Real Thing!'" The American Magazine, 105 (April),
      34-35, 76, 78, 80, 82, 84.
      [Interview with Robinson, who comments on Titus Coan,
      Alfred Louis, Roosevelt, and his attitudes toward writing
      and the career of poetry.]

1929 A BOOKS - NONE

1929 B SHORTER WRITINGS

1   AIKEN, CONRAD. "Poetry." The Bookman, 69 (May), 322-23.
      [Review of Cavender's House.] This poem is too much like
      previous poems and too diffuse. The subject is something
      James or Hawthorne might have picked for a short story.

2   _____. "Unpacking Hearts with Words." The Bookman, 68
      (January), 576.
      [Review of Sonnets 1889-1927.] Robinson's sonnets are
      excellent but "never glow, or become radiant, or melt into
      a sort of white-hot integrity." They are read with plea-
      sure but are quickly forgotten.

3   ANON. "An American Poet." The New York Times, December 22,
      Section III, p. 4.
      [An appreciation of Robinson on his sixtieth birthday,
      observing that he is a New Yorker as well as a New Eng-
      lander and regretting that it took Roosevelt's influence
      for him to be recognized.]

*4   ANON. "Anatomy of Suicide." Cornell Daily Sun, April 23,
      p. 4.
      [Cited as a review of Cavender's House in Hogan, p. 152.]

1929

5   ANON. "The Books of the Day. E. A. Robinson is Strangely
    Akin to Dante with a Yankee Sense of Humor." New York Sun,
    April 23, p. 27.
        [Review of Cavender's House.] This work by "our most
    vital and profound poet" puts Robinson squarely in the
    moral tradition of English poetry. It is like "The Fall of
    the House of Usher" in its evocation of brooding mystery.

6   ANON. "Cavender's House." The Book League Monthly, 2 (June),
    187.
        [Partial reprints of 1929.B30 and 1929.B43.]

7   ANON. "Cavender's House." The Book League Monthly, 2 (May),
    1.
        Copy of Cavender's House is free to new members.

8   ANON. Review of Cavender's House. The Nation, 128 (May 8),
    567.
        Robinson should stick to characters from legend or his-
    tory since this poem suffers by comparison with its imme-
    diate predecessor, Tristram.

9   ANON. Review of Cavender's House. Springfield (Mass.) Repub-
    lican, October 27, p. 7E.
        The theme is similar to Meredith's Modern Love, but the
    poem lacks immediacy and "does not fascinate as do others
    of Robinson."

10 ANON. "E. A. Robinson Gets Medal for Poetry." The New York
    Times, November 15, Section I, p. 32.
        American Academy of Arts and Letters grants Robinson a
    gold medal for "general excellence" in poetry.

11 ANON. "A House Completed." Christian Science Monitor, May 1,
    p. 14.
        [Review of Cavender's House.] Robinson has been intrigued
    with house image ever since he wrote "The House on the
    Hill." With Tristram Robinson turned a corner: "at last
    he had mastered the intricacy of his own genius."

12 ANON. "A New England Tragedy." Cincinnati Times-Star, May
    28, p. 22.
        [Review of Cavender's House.] This is "a poem of noble
    austerity, but it is as bleak as the New England moral con-
    sciousness which it expresses." Robinson is a minor poet
    because his concerns are Puritan problems, which have lit-
    tle concern today.

13   ANON. "Robinson, Poet, 60 Years Old." The New York Times, December 23, Section I, p. 9.
[News article about Robinson celebrating his sixtieth birthday at his studio on East 42nd Street.]

*14   ANON. "Robinson's Contemporary Poems Free of Miltonic Words; Reveal Feeling of Simplicity and Restraint." Canandaigua (N.Y.) Daily Messenger, June 3, p. 6.
[Cited as a review of Cavender's House in Hogan, p. 154.]

15   ANON. "Sonnets." Poetry, 34 (May), 114-115.
In Sonnets 1889-1927 there is "everywhere a dryness of tone and an overdrawn skepticism which prevents Robinson from being a great sonneteer."

16   ANON. "Sternly Tragic Mood Pervades Robinson Poem." Salt Lake Tribune, May 5, p. G 11.
[Review of Cavender's House.] This poem will not have the appeal of Tristram because it is so gloomy, but it shows Robinson's intellectual and emotional power and his mastery of the rhythmical line.

17   ANON. "Tragedy of 'Cavender's House.'" Milwaukee Journal, April 27, p. 6.
Cavender's House will probably not have the appeal of Tristram, but this poem "has greatness that transcends the meaning of greatness."

18   ARVIN, NEWTON. Review of Cavender's House. Atlantic Monthly, 144 (July), The Atlantic Bookshelf, 20.
This poem is better than preceding domestic tragedies. "No poet ever had a deeper feeling for doubtfulness than Mr. Robinson."

19   AXSON, STOCKTON. "Sorrow Blended with Beauty in 'Cavender's House.'" Houston Chronicle, June 2, Editorials--Theatres Section, p. 4.
This poem lacks the "enchantment" of previous poems because of the subject matter, but its imagery is appropriate and it demonstrates Robinson's modernity. Robinson's blank verse may be contrasted to that of Milton.

20   BANKS, T. H., JR. Review of Cavender's House. The Cardinal, 4 (June), 29-31.
"The foremost poet of America" has written another masterpiece. It is less obscure than some Robinson poems and is comparable in theme to Stevenson's Markheim.

1929

21   BEEBE, LUCIUS. "Cavender's House." The Hound and Horn, 2
         (July-September), 446.
             The theme is banal compared to the Arthurian poems, but
         the poem has "at least...an unconventional angle."

22   _____. "Robinson Sees Romantic Strain in Future Verse." New
         York Herald Tribune, December 22, Section I, p. 19.
             [Interview with Robinson, who expresses views on classi-
         cal forms, contemporary poets, and proper subjects for
         poetry.]

23   _____. "Sonnets 1889-1927." The Hound and Horn, 2 (April-
         June), 317.
             [Reprint of 1928.B8.]

24   BROWNING, ANNIE-EUNICE. "New Robinson Study Annoys This Re-
         viewer." Tulsa (Okla.) Tribune, June 16, Section C, p. 10.
             [Review of Cavender's House.] "It has all the faults and
         none of the virtues of his earlier poems." Browning is ob-
         scure from compression; Robinson from an "indefinite ex-
         pression of an idea."

25   CESTRE, C[HARLES]. "Le Dernier Poeme d'Edwin Arlington Robin-
         son." Revue Anglo-Americaine, 6 (August), 489-507.
             [Review of Cavender's House, commending Robinson's skill-
         ful use of blank verse and his unsentimental attitude.
         Suggests that Hawthorne is his literary ancestor.]

26   _____. "Edwin Arlington Robinson: Sonnets." Revue Anglo-
         Americaine, 6 (April), 377-78.
             [Review of Sonnets 1889-1927, noting particularly the
         balance of the form and the beauty of the thoughts ex-
         pressed.]

27   CLARKE, A. B. "A Poet for the Few." Richmond (Va.) Times-
         Dispatch, September 22, Section II, p. 3.
             [Review of Collected Poems.] Quantity and "richness of
         his genius" are impressive. "Admidst verse libre's amor-
         phous posturings, it is Robinson's essential correctness
         and decorum which charms us."

28   CRISP, JULIA M. "E. A. Robinson's Masterful Use of Sonnet
         Form." Fort Worth Sunday Star-Telegram, February 10,
         Magazine Section, p. 8.
             [Review of Sonnets 1889-1927, commenting on the wider
         ranging subject matter and refuting Conrad Aiken's criti-
         cism that the sonnets are colorless by noting "The
         Sheaves," "The Tree in Pamela's Garden," and "Reuben
         Bright."]

29   DAVIDSON, LEVETTE J. "Lazarus in Modern Literature." The
      English Journal, 18 (June), 457-65.
         [Robinson's "Lazarus" is compared to four other modern
      treatments of the Lazarus figure, by Tennyson, Browning,
      Andreyev, and O'Neill; Robinson's treatment is considered
      "baffling" because the question of eternity is not an-
      swered.]

30   DEUTSCH, BABETTE. "A Poet's House of Life." New York Herald
      Tribune Books, April 21, pp. 1-2.
         [Review of Cavender's House.] Robinson is extremely in-
      debted to Browning, but differs from him in his pessimism
      and adherence to verse forms. This poem reveals Robinson's
      agnosticism and versifying skill.

31   _____. "Old Truths for New." New York Sun, September 14,
      p. 7.
         [Review of Collected Poems.] Robinson's philosophy has
      not changed since his Octaves in 1897, but his poetry has
      become more complex. He differs from contemporary poets
      in his insistence upon the "desperate courage" that marked
      nineteenth century intellectuals, an attitude he shares
      with Arnold.

32   DICKINSON, EVELYN E. "Dark Places." The Minnesota Quarterly,
      6 (Spring), 105.
         [Review of Cavender's House, emphasizing the universal
      significance of the theme, praising Robinson's skill at
      blank verse, imagery, and symbolism, and noting that the
      predominant impression is that of darkness.]

33   DOLE, NATHAN HASKELL. "A Dramatic Poem by Maine's Great Poet
      and Author of 'Tristram.'" Portland (Me.) Evening News,
      July 23, p. 5.
         [Review of Cavender's House, suggesting that Robinson's
      "dark and inscrutable" tragedy is similar to that of Webster.]

34   DRINKWATER, JOHN. Twentieth Century Poetry. Boston: Hough-
      ton Mifflin, pp. 316-17.
         [One-page introduction for five poems in anthology, sug-
      gesting that Robinson is the most important of modern
      American poets.]

35   FISHER, VARDIS. "Neuroses in Poetry." The Critical Review--
      New York University Daily News Literary Supplement, 2
      (May), 6, 22.
         [Review of Cavender's House.] This poem "will add less
      to his immortality than his reputation." The theme has

1929

long preoccupied Robinson. His women are always introverts
and his men extroverts. The vogue for narrative poetry is
an "unwholesome portent."

*36 FORD, BERNICE A. "Robinson's Theme is Isolation of Spirit."
Evanston (Ill.) News-Index, May 15, p. 12.
[Cited as a review of Cavender's House in Hogan, p. 153.]

37 G., W. E. "Cavender's House." The Christian Century, 46
(May 8), 618.
"If the theme is somber, the poem itself is luminous with
insight, imagery, and terse felicity of phrase."

38 HAMMOND, JOSEPHINE. "The Man Against the Sky--Edwin Arlington
Robinson." The Personalist, 10 (July), 178-84.
This most significant American poet, whose Dionysus in
Doubt should be discounted, is frequently like his own
Rembrandt in portraying dark scenes, but in spite of cur-
rent criticism, his poetry is more positive than negative.

39 HANSEN, HARRY. "Robinson's Latest." New York World, April
23, p. 15.
[Review of Cavender's House, which is seen as similar to
Roman Bartholow but not as colorful as Tristram.]

40 H[ART], B. K. "The House of Cavender's Remorse." Providence
(R.I.) Sunday Journal Magazine, April 28, p. 26.
[Review of Cavender's House.] "It is by all odds the
greatest of Robinson's narrative poems." Laramie's pres-
ence in Cavender's mind suggests the existence of God.

41 HOLMES, JOHN HAYNES. "The Study Table." Unity, 103 (June 3),
222.
[Review of Cavender's House, noting that it is closer to
Roman Bartholow or even Captain Craig than the Arthurian
poems.] "Robinson's method is precisely that of Browning."

42 HUGHES, RICHARD. "Poetic Prestige." The Forum, 82 (July),
xvi, xviii.
[Review of Cavender's House, finding it clumsy, dull, and
simplistic and noting how it suffers from comparison with
Jeffers' Women on Point Sur.]

43 HUTCHISON, PERCY. "Tragedy of 'Cavender's House.'" The New
York Times Book Review, April 21, pp. 4, 20.
Cavender's House, which lacks the richness of Tristram,
is subtle to a fault. In theme it is reminiscent of
Othello.

44   JOHNSON, OAKLEY. "Man, Woman, and Poetry." The Book League
      Monthly, 2 (July), 183-84.
         [Review of Cavender's House, a "polished and sincere
      work."]

45   JONES, LLEWELLYN. "An Egotist's Remorse." Chicago Evening
      Post Literary Review, May 3, pp. 1, 3.
         [Review of Cavender's House.] "It is obvious that Caven-
      dar's House will not have the popular appeal of Tristram....
      This poem is really a study of the casuistry of guilt."

46   [JONES, LLEWELLYN]. "In One Volume." Chicago Evening Post
      Literary Review, August 30, p. 2.
         [Review of Collected Poems.] Robinson is "without doubt
      the greatest living American poet." "The Dark Hills" is
      an example of his lyricism. "Lost Anchors" is his most ob-
      scure poem.

47   J[ONES], W[EBSTER] A. "Cavender's House." Portland Oregonian,
      June 23, Magazine Section, p. 5.
         "Robinson has reached a new height in Cavender's House.
      It serves to establish him definitely as the greatest liv-
      ing poet." [Emphasis on his simple language and insistence
      that this poem is superior to the Arthurian poems.]

48   KNOWLTON, KENT. "Mr. Robinson Chooses a Modern Theme." Low-
      ell (Mass.) Courier-Citizen, April 27, p. 9.
         [Review of Cavender's House.] This poem, which should be
      read once for diction and once for plot, is superior to
      Tristram and can only be compared to The Ring and the Book.

49   KREYMBORG, ALFRED. "The Wise Music of Robinson," in Our Sing-
      ing Strength. New York: Coward-McCann, pp. 297-315.
         Robinson's greatest strength and weakness is his use of
      the Yankee vernacular, with its understatement and indirec-
      tion. Often autobiographical, Robinson's favorite charac-
      ter is the man who fails while on an idealistic search, but
      his women, who speak more directly than his men, are always
      his strongest characters. He is at his best in his analy-
      sis of relationships between men and women in his shorter
      poems.

50   MacAFEE, HELEN. "The Dark Hill of the Muses." The Yale Re-
      view, 18 (June), 813-14.
         [Review of Cavender's House, calling it an interesting
      narrative and regretting it was not written for the the-
      ater.]

1929

51 McWILLIAMS, RICHEBOURG G. "Forty Years of the Sonnets of
    Great American Poet." Birmingham (Ala.) News, January 20,
    Magazine Section, p. 3.
        [Review of Sonnets 1889-1927, noting that Robinson is the
    best practitioner of the Italian sonnet since Wordsworth
    and contending that of the eighty-nine good sonnets, some
    fifteen are excellent.]

52 _____. "Leading Master of Verse Shines in Latest Volume."
    Birmingham (Ala.) News, May 12, Magazine Section, p. 5.
        [Review of Cavender's House, observing that the poem suf-
    fers from two of Robinson's old faults: it is wordy and
    cryptic.] "I do not consider this book the literary event
    of the year."

53 MANLY, JOHN MATTHEWS, EDITH RICKERT, and FRED B. MILLETT.
    Contemporary American Literature. New York: Harcourt,
    Brace, pp. 47-48, 272-75.
        Robinson is currently thought to be America's greatest
    poet in spite of his role of "melancholy spectator" which
    removes him from the superficial optimism of the American
    ideal. [Biographical sketch, questions for study, and
    bibliography included.]

54 MARBLE, ANNIE RUSSELL. "Robinson's Latest Poem." Boston
    Herald, April 27, pp. 15, 16.
        [Review of Cavender's House.] Here is "a spiritual trag-
    edy with elements of mystery, intense feeling, and philo-
    sophic queries."

55 N[ORTH], J[ESSICA]. "A Classic of Indirection." Poetry, 34
    (July), 233-36.
        [Review of Cavender's House.] Robinson has maintained a
    large following through introspection rather than imagery.
    That he ignores "all sorts of virtues which modern poets
    are taught to pursue" makes his popularity the more aston-
    ishing.

56 O'NEILL, GEORGE. "Poetry From Four Men." The Outlook and
    Independent, 151 (January 16), 111.
        [Review of Sonnets 1889-1927, predicting that its publi-
    cation will attract new readers.]

57 PATERSON, ISABEL. "Edwin Arlington Robinson's New Poem." New
    York Herald Tribune, April 26, p. 19.
        [Review of Cavender's House, suggesting that the setting
    for this poem is more suitable for Robinson than that of
    the Arthurian poems.]

58 POWYS, LLEWELYN. "Discussion of Edwin Arlington Robinson's
    Cavender's House." Creative Reading, 3 (April 15), 25-30.
        Cavender's House "is sorry stuff and makes dull and dif-
    ficult reading." The Cavenders are Henry James characters
    manqué.

59 RANCK, CARTY. "Within the Walls of Cavender's House." Boston
    Evening Transcript, April 27, Book Section, p. 2.
        Cavender's House is similar to Roman Bartholow but is
    superior to it. Noteworthy are its symbolism, humor, and
    satiric attacks on materialism.

60 REDMAN, BEN RAY. "Old Wine in New Bottles." New York Herald
    Tribune Books, September 8, p. 10.
        Cavender's House, the only addition to the 1929 Collected
    Poems, is inferior to most of Robinson's work. The Arthur-
    ian characters are more life-like than Cavender.

61 REESE, LIZETTE WOODWORTH. "Recent Poetry of Robinson, Elinor
    Wylie and Others." Baltimore Evening Sun, June 1, p. 6.
        [Review of Cavender's House.] "The philosophy is often
    rich and sound, but it tends at times to obscure the story.
    A narrative should be pristine in its clarity." In spite
    of reader's confusion, the characters are real. It is a
    good subject for a poem that "has a spiritual conception of
    life."

62 _____. "Robinson's Sonnets and Other Recent Volumes of Poetry."
    Baltimore Evening Sun, March 30, p. 8.
        [Review of Sonnets 1889-1927, noting the hard quality of
    their beauty because of their compactness and remarking
    that Robinson's best poems deal with men and women.] "It
    is likely that Mr. Robinson's fame will last with his
    shorter poems, especially those portraits of his cut out of
    black irony."

63 ROBINSON, HENRY MORTON. "No Epitaph." The Commonweal, 11
    (November 13), 60-61.
        [Review of Collected Poems.] Robinson might be compared
    to the Greek playwrights and possibly Browning, but not Ten-
    nyson. "He is sometimes dull, as Milton and the ocean are
    dull."

64 ROGERS, J. W. "Dark and Illusive Poem is Robinson's 'Caven-
    der's House.'" Dallas Times Herald, May 19, Section V,
    p. 9.
        Cavender's House is suggestive rather than specific and

1929

open to many interpretations, as authentic poetry must be. Possibly the Laramie that Cavender sees is "the dramatization in his mind of his own conscience."

65   SCHMALHAUSEN, SAMUEL D. <u>Our Changing Human Nature</u>. New York: Macaulay, pp. 168-70.
      Although Robinson and Robinson Jeffers are our two most distinguished poets, <u>Cavender's House</u> is a failure because it isn't "brazen" enough. <u>Tristram</u> is a result of his wanting to get away from the "jangling of our disorderly and mechanistically disillusioning world."

66   SCHNEIDER, ISIDOR. "Collected Poems." <u>The Modern Quarterly</u>, 5 (Fall), 389-91.
      Robinson has been called profound but actually he is banal. He is unlike Frost in that he rarely uses sensory images. Critics overlooked him earlier and are over-doing it now.

67   S[CHOEN]-R[ENE], O[TTO]. "Cavender's House." <u>The Harvard Advocate</u>, 115 (June), 31-32.
      One would think that Robinson is parodying himself in <u>Cavender's House</u>, except that he lacks the sense of humor to do so.

68   SCOTT, WINFIELD. "Edwin Arlington Robinson." <u>The Brown Literary Quarterly</u>, 2 (November), 13-19.
      [Overview of Robinson's career, with thumbnail description of each of his volumes through <u>Tristram</u>, emphasizing the steady course of his idealism.]

69   S[COTT], W[INFIELD] T. "To E. A. R." <u>The Brown Literary Quarterly</u>, 2 (November), 12.
      [English sonnet dealing with King Arthur at Monadnock.]

70   SOSKIN, WILLIAM. "'Cavender's House' is a Notable Achievement in the Career of Edwin Arlington Robinson." New York <u>Evening Post</u>, April 23, p. 15.
      Robinson, more profound than Browning, demonstrates his "dignified acceptance of a poisoned universe" here. <u>Cavender's House</u> is inferior to <u>Tristram</u>, but exemplifies the "fastidious restraint" and "chisled beauty" of his verse.

71   TASKER, J. DANA. "Cavender's House." <u>The Outlook and Independent</u>, 151 (April 24), 668.
      Although <u>Cavender's House</u> is "in many ways the author's best," the style is "difficult and dull despite its technical exactness."

72 UNTERMEYER, LOUIS. "Essential Robinson." <u>The Saturday Review</u>
    <u>of Literature</u>, 5 (May 11), 995-96.
        [Essay-review of <u>Cavender's House</u>.] Similarities between
    Robinson and Browning are only superficial, as this poem
    indicates. <u>Cavender's House</u> is "one of his major crea-
    tions" and is considerably better than Masters' latest.
    Robinson's poetry exhibits a quest for moral values.

73 VAN DOREN, MARK. "Our Editors: A Series of Studies: Edwin
    Arlington Robinson." <u>The Book League Monthly</u>, 1 (January),
    271-73.
        [Brief description of Robinson's achievement, explaining
    why he is an asset to the board of editors.]

74 WHIPPLE, T. K. "Ghosts." <u>The Argonaut</u>, 105 (May 18), 4-5.
        [Review of <u>Cavender's House</u>, emphasizing the universality
    of the theme of coming to grips with ghosts.]

<u>1930 A BOOKS</u>

 1 CESTRE, CHARLES. <u>An Introduction to Edwin Arlington Robinson</u>.
    New York: Macmillan, 230 pp.
        [Following an introductory chapter which asserts Robin-
    son is "a modern classic" principally because of his blend-
    ing of form and content, the book is divided into chapters
    examining the lyric poems, the Arthurian trilogy, the dra-
    matic poems, Robinson's humor, and his psychology. Inter-
    pretations of many poems are included, especially those of
    middle length, such as "Tasker Norcross," but there is no
    index. Reprints 1925.B11. Reprinted in 1931.A1.]

*2 HUGHES, MERRITT Y. <u>Un Poeta Americano: Edwin Arlington Rob-</u>
    <u>inson</u>. Traduzione di Benvenuto Cellini. Livorno: Raf-
    faello Giusti.
        [Cited in Hogan, p. 123, as reprint of 1930.B17.]

<u>1930 B SHORTER WRITINGS</u>

 1 ANON. "Browning Without the Bounce." <u>Time</u>, 16 (September 22),
    64.
        [Review of <u>The Glory of the Nightingales</u>.] Robinson is
    perhaps a subtler psychologist but not a subtler poet than
    Browning in this low-keyed poem written "in quiet blank
    verse." There are few memorable phrases.

 2 ANON. "Cavender's House." <u>Times Literary Supplement</u>, No.
    1490, August 21, p. 666.

This is a good theme for Robinson since he is able to combine "sympathetic insight with a talent for relentless probing." Here he is the master of "bare yet concentrated statement."

3   ANON. "The Glory of the Nightingales." Among Our Books (Carnegie Library, Pittsburgh), 35 (November), 82.
    "A somber tale in blank verse, which at no time rises to the emotional heights of Tristram."

4   ANON. "Robinson is Somber in New Dramatic Narrative." Portland (Me.) Evening Express, September 20, p. 5.
    [Review of The Glory of the Nightingales.] This "work of unmistakable genius" has everything one associates with Robinson's work except humor.

5   ARGOW, ELSIE BAKER. "A Great Poet." The Christian Register, 109 (April 10), 306.
    [Review of Collected Poems.] Although Robinson is a great poet, perhaps he is tired of long poems and should return to shorter ones.

6   BAUM, PAULL F. "Collected Poems." The South Atlantic Quarterly, 29 (April), 208-210.
    Robinson's later work is not as good as his earlier, shorter pieces. He writes fluent blank verse about the mental states of people verging on the abnormal. They all should take a trip to the mountains.

7   BEEBE, LUCIUS. "Dignified Faun: A Portrait of E. A. R." The Outlook and Independent, 155 (August 27), 647-49, 677.
    [Personal reminiscence about social evenings with Robinson and an interview focusing on his transcendental attitude.]

8   BELLAMANN, HENRY. "The Literary Highway." Columbia (S.C.) State, January 19, p. 27.
    "Mr. Robinson is one of our chief glories." In spite of occasional monotony—too much Robinson is like "listening to an overlong viola recital in a darkened room"—he cannot be matched in nobility and sincerity.

9   BENÉT, WILLIAM ROSE. "Round About Parnassus." The Saturday Review of Literature, 7 (September 20), 142.
    [Review of The Glory of the Nightingales.] This is not one of his best, but it is a good example of Robinson's psychological probing. In spite of protests Robinson is similar to Browning, except that he lacks Browning's robustness and never slips into sentimentality.

10   BRENNER, RICA. "Edwin Arlington Robinson," in Ten Modern
     Poets. New York: Harcourt, Brace, pp. 85-115.
       [Overview of Robinson's career, emphasizing his single-
     mindedness and paying particular attention to the sonnets.]

11   BRUNS, FRIEDRICH. "E. A. Robinson," in Die Amerikanische
     Dichtung der Gegenwart. Leipzig and Berlin: B. G. Teubner,
     pp. 74-80.
       [Overview of career, with emphasis on the Tilbury poems.]

12   GREGORY, HORACE. "The Glory of the Nightingales." The New
     Republic, 64 (October 29), 303-304.
       Robinson brought back dignity to poetry in the first dec-
     ade of this century. This "semi-dramatic narrative" should
     be distributed through a book club since it reads like a
     detective novel and shows his "remarkable ingenuity."

13   HALL, EDWARD B. "The Glory of the Nightingales." Boston
     Evening Transcript, October 18, Book Section, p. 3.
       This poem is "not to be classed in the first order of
     Mr. Robinson's work." More than one reading is required
     to understand the plot, since he tells it backwards.

14   HICKS, GRANVILLE. "The Talents of Mr. Robinson." The Nation,
     131 (October 8), 382.
       [Review of The Glory of the Nightingales.] Although Rob-
     inson does have weaknesses, such as Jamesian mannerisms and
     limited experience, this book is another example of his
     "attitude of affirmation" that has sustained him for forty
     years.

15   HILLYER, ROBERT. "Collected Poems." The New England Quarter-
     ly, 3 (January), 148-51.
       Robinson deserves more judicious criticism than he has
     received, for he is more praised than read. He is the
     master of the five-stress line, but he is not a musical
     poet. At his best in the short poems, his artistic pur-
     pose is "the exposition of the human mind." "Mr. Robin-
     son's great virtue is the delineation of the actual."

16   HUDSON, HOYT. "Edwin Arlington Robinson." The Step Ladder,
     16 (September), 193.
       [Italian sonnet paying homage to Robinson.]

*17 HUGHES, MERRITT Y. "Un Poeta Americano: Edwin Arlington Rob-
     inson." Translated into Italian by Benvenuto Cellini. Il
     Giornale di Politica e di Letteratura, 14 (September),
     809-827.
       [Cited in Hogan, p. 123; reprinted in 1930.A2.]

1930

18 HUTCHISON, PERCY. "Robinson Returns to Modern Life in His New
    Poem." The New York Times Book Review, September 14,
    pp. 5, 18.
      [Review of The Glory of the Nightingales, in which the
    reviewer wishes it were more like Tristram, but neverthe-
    less "acknowledging the austere perfection" of the work.]

19 KRESENSKY, RAYMOND. "A Poetic Melodrama." The Christian Cen-
    tury, 47 (December 24), 1595.
      [Review of The Glory of the Nightingales, called a great
    poem because of Robinson's psychological insights.]

20 LOWELL, AMY. Poetry and Poets. Boston and New York: Hough-
    ton Mifflin, pp. 210-32.
      [Reprint of 1922.B22 and 1963.B9.]

21 MacKAYE, PERCY. "In Memoriam Twenty Years After." Boston
    Evening Transcript, October 18, Section I, p. 9.
      [Sonnet addressed to Robinson. Reprinted in 1930.B22.]

22 _____. "In Memoriam Twenty Years After." Harvard Graduates'
    Magazine, 39 (December), 140.
      [Reprint of 1930.B21.]

23 MATHER, FRANK JEWETT, JR. "E. A. Robinson: Poet." The Sat-
    urday Review of Literature, 6 (January 11), 629-30.
      [Review of Collected Poems, noting particularly Captain
    Craig, Lancelot, Tristram, and Cavender's House, but con-
    tending that the short poems are best. "Leonora" is
    quoted.]

24 M[ORRIS], G. L. K. "The Glory of the Nightingales." The Mis-
    cellany, 1 (November), 33-35.
      Robinson may be only suffering a temporary lapse, but
    this book is flawed by the encroachment of his verbal man-
    nerisms.

25 MUNSON, GORHAM B. "A Lesser Robinson." New York Sun, Septem-
    ber 19, p. 32.
      [Review of The Glory of the Nightingales.] Like Haw-
    thorne in setting and Henry Adams in attitude, this poem
    has a potentially good subject, but it is not successful
    because of mannerisms and lack of tension. It is good but
    not inspired.

26 NICHOLL, LOUISE TOWNSEND. Review of The Glory of the Nightin-
    gales. The Outlook and Independent, 156 (September 24),
    145-46.

This story is more appropriate to a newspaper account or a drama; however, "nobody but Robinson and his almost diabolical form could have piled up the terrible weariness and horror of vengeance and disgrace as he has done."

27 NUHN, FERNER. "Thoughtful, Finished." Des Moines (Ia). Sunday Register, February 9, p. 3.
    [Review of Cavender's House, suggesting that it is superior to Tristram because of its originality, but weak in that the characters are not three-dimensional.]

28 OLSON, TED. "Irony and Pity." Voices, No. 54 (March), pp. 123-25.
    [Review of Sonnets 1889-1927, noting particularly "Why He Was There" and "Many Are Called."] The sonnet form "has provided Robinson with a salutary discipline." Good examples are found throughout the book, but there is a devoloping proficiency.

29 PATTEE, FRED LEWIS. "E. A. Robinson," in The New American Literature. New York: Century, 293-98.
    [Brief assessment in literary history.] Robinson, the last of the New England traditional writers, must be viewed geographically to be understood. He is not popular because of his intellectuality and verbosity, but "he is the best of our poetic artisans."

30 PIPER, EDWIN FORD. "Importance of Edwin Arlington Robinson." Des Moines (Ia.) Sunday Register, February 9, Section XI, p. 3.
    [Review of Collected Poems.] This book demonstrates Robinson's development as a technician. His poetry, though impressive, will never be popular because of his philosophy. All of his chief characters are "intuitivists." His "humor is always delicate, usually ironic."

31 PIPKIN, EMILY EDITH. "The Arthur of Edwin Arlington Robinson." The English Journal, 19 (March), 183-95.
    The popular view of Arthurian character is still the Tennysonian one, in spite of the major shifts in Robinson's treatment. Generally the principal characters have become more human. [Reprinted in 1969.A4.]

32 RANCK, CARTY. "Edwin Arlington Robinson." The Boston Herald, December 14, Magazine Feature Section, p. 2, and New York Herald Tribune Magazine, December 14, pp. 8-9, 24.
    [Profile of Robinson by Peterborough colleague, emphasizing his modesty, his sympathy, his sense of humor, and commenting on his reading preferences.]

1930

33 REDMAN, BEN RAY. "The Way Fate Works." New York Herald Trib-
    une Books, September 21, p. 5.
        [Review of The Glory of the Nightingales.] "It is all a
    little cold and dry and labored, and as such must rank
    among the minor productions of a poet who has amply proved
    his greatness."

34 REID, DOROTHY E. "Dark House." Voices, No. 52 (January),
    pp. 33-36.
        [Review of Cavender's House, noting that egoism is the
    basis for murder as well as the motivation for Cavender's
    imaginary conversation with his wife; hence it explores the
    philosophical question of why men murder.]

35 SPEIGHT, HOWARD EDWARD BALME. "To Understand is to Forgive."
    The Christian Leader, N.S. 33 (November 8), 1412-13.
        [Review of The Glory of the Nightingales.] "A master
    like Robinson" always presents characters who "remain human
    and pitiful," but the poem is not as good as earlier ones.

36 S[TAPLES], A. G. "On 'An Adventure on Balloon Tires--Home of
    a Poet.'" Lewiston (Me.) Evening Journal, August 8, p. 4.
        [Directions on how to get to Robinson's birth place, Head
    Tide, which is coincidentally close to the home town of
    Edna St. Vincent Millay.]

37 STERNER, LEWIS G. The Sonnet in American Literature. Phila-
    delphia: University of Pennsylvania Press, pp. 75-77.
        Reticence is the strength and an enigmatic quality is the
    weakness of Robinson's sonnets. Seventy-seven of his 89
    sonnets are in Italian form. [Four sonnets here reprinted.]

38 STOVER, FRANK B. "Glory of the Nightingales." The Wesleyan
    Cardinal, 6 (November), 28-30.
        "Seldom has Robinson...handled a story of such dramatic
    possibilities in such a skillful way. He is wise, but not
    too wordy; subtle, but not to the point of confusion." It
    is the best character study Robinson has done since The Man
    Who Died Twice.

39 TATE, ALLEN. "The Ironic Mr. Robinson." New York World, Oc-
    tober 12, Editorial Section, p. 3E.
        [Review of The Glory of the Nightingales.] Of Robinson's
    five types of poems, this one follows the "tragic formula--
    a tragic situation among people too intelligent for tragic
    action." When the protagonist chooses service at the end
    Robinson is either more sentimental or more ironic than
    usual.

40   THORNTON, JAMES. "Sorts of Poets." The Nation and the Athena-
        eum, 47 (June 7), 325.
        [Review of Cavender's House, with comments on the jerky
        style.] "Mr. Robinson's great services to American litera-
        ture in first breaking down a Puritan tradition do not nec-
        essarily compel an English reader."

41   TINKER, CHAUNCEY BREWSTER. The Good Estate of Poetry. Bos-
        ton: Little, Brown, pp. 126-29.
        [Tristram cited as an example of contemporary tradition-
        alism.]

42   WALTON, EDA LOU. "Irony and Pity in Robinson's Newest Poem."
        New York Evening Post, September 13, Section III, p. 85.
        The Glory of the Nightingales continues Robinson's domi-
        nant theme, the failure of the idealist. The story is
        carried forward "by means of constant semi-circles."

1931 A BOOKS

  1   BEEBE, LUCIUS and ROBERT J. BULKLEY, JR. A Bibliography of
        the Writings of Edwin Arlington Robinson. Cambridge,
        Mass.: The Dunster House Bookshop, 110 pp.
        [Incomplete listing of book publications.]

  2   CESTRE, CHARLES. An Introduction to Edwin Arlington Robinson
        and Selected Poems by Edwin Arlington Robinson. Preface
        by Bliss Perry. New York: Macmillan, 230 pp.
        [Reprint of 1930.A1.]

1931 B SHORTER WRITINGS

  1   ANON. "Barnard Girls Vote on Pulitzer Prizes." The New York
        Times, May 13, p. 7.
        In a poll of Barnard students, Robinson was named the
        favorite American poet.

  2   ANON. "Matthias at the Door." Among Our Books (Carnegie Li-
        brary, Pittsburgh), 36 (December), 86.
        [Brief description of the plot.]

 *3   ANON. "The New Poetry." The Outlook and Independent, 159
        (October 28), 282.
        [Cited in Lippincott, p. 71, as a review of Matthias at
        the Door.]

1931

4   ANON. "Old Master." Time, 18 (October 12), 71.
    [Review of Matthias at the Door, noting its typical sub-
    tlety and psychological fine distinctions, with a person-
    ality sketch of Robinson.]

5   BERKELMAN, ROBERT G. "For Lovers of the Rhymed Word." Port-
    land (Me.) Evening News, November 3, p. 4.
    [Review of Matthias at the Door, praising its philosoph-
    ical profundity and complaining about its abstractness.]

6   BLANKENSHIP, RUSSELL. "Edwin Arlington Robinson," in Ameri-
    can Literature as an Expression of the National Mind. New
    York: Henry Holt, pp. 583-88.
    Robinson is a traditional poet whose philosophic stance
    is modern in that it tends toward naturalism. "Ben Jonson"
    is his best poem. The New England influence is strong both
    in his subject matter and "bleakly transcendental outlook."

7   BOGAN, LOUISE. "Tilbury Town and Beyond." Poetry, 37 (Jan-
    uary), 216-21.
    [Review of Collected Poems and The Glory of the Nightin-
    gales, indicating that all of Robinson's books since his
    second volume indicate a lessening of powers, although he
    is still considered a strong literary figure.]

8   CESTRE, C[HARLES]. "The Glory of the Nightingales." Revue
    Anglo-Americaine, 8 (February), 271-73.
    In spite of Robinson's splendid blank verse, this poem,
    compared to earlier ones, is disappointing because it lacks
    action and is too thin.

9   COURNOS, JOHN. "A Novelist-Poet." New York Sun, October 2,
    p. 33.
    [Review of Matthias at the Door.] Like Hardy, Robinson
    remains constant during the change of fashion. He is as
    much a novelist as a poet, and this book is "the most novel-
    like and best of his narratives."

10 DEUTSCH, BABETTE. "With no Less Wisdom." New York Herald
    Tribune Books, October 4, p. 7.
    [Review of Matthias at the Door.] This book "adds prac-
    tically nothing to what Robinson has said equally well
    elsewhere." Timberlake is better realized than the title
    character.

11 GILBERT, DOUGLAS. "Edwin Arlington Robinson--Poet." New York
    Telegram, January 3, p. 13.

74

Robinson, who "heralds the renaissance of classicism,"
has many connections with New York. His relationship with
C. E. Stedman is especially important.

12 HUTCHISON, PERCY. "Robinson's Dramatic Poem, 'Matthias at the
    Door.'" The New York Times Book Review, October 4, pp. 2,
    18.
        This book is perhaps "the crowning achievement of the
    poet's career" because it presents an ethical reading of
    life, which has been Robinson's aim.

13 KENYON, BERNICE. Review of Matthias at the Door. The Outlook
    and Independent, 159 (October 28), 282.
        This poem is better than The Glory of the Nightingales,
    but lacks "the sharp and vital poetry that appeared in
    Tristram." Robinson wrote better when his work was less
    complex.

14 PERRY, BLISS. "Preface," in Selected Poems of Edwin Arlington
    Robinson. New York: Macmillan, pp. v-viii.
        This selection is intended to provide readers with less
    forbidding amount of poetry than the Collected Poems and to
    indicate the current taste for Robinson's poetry in 1930.
    Robinson helped with the selection and provided the brief
    headnotes for the selections from the four book length
    poems. [Includes reprint of 1930.A1.]

15 PHELPS, WILLIAM LYON. "As I Like It." Scribner's Magazine,
    89 (January), 95.
        [Review of The Glory of the Nightingales, which is seen
    as inferior to Tristram. Also an account of how Theodore
    Roosevelt got a copy of The Children of the Night and ar-
    ranged to have the book reprinted.]

16 RANCK, CARTY. "Four People Caught in the Meshes of Fate."
    Boston Evening Transcript, October 3, Book Section, p. 8.
        [Review of Matthias at the Door.] "There is no poet
    writing in English today who can say so much in one line as
    Robinson." This is his best poem since Tristram.

17 RICHARDS, LAURA E. Stepping Westward. New York: D. Apple-
    ton, pp. 377-83.
        [Personal reminiscence of Robinson's association with
    this socially prominent family in Gardiner. Mrs. Richards'
    son introduced Kermit Roosevelt to Robinson's work. Par-
    tially reprinted in 1934.B25.]

18 ROOT, E. MERRILL. "Brainy Longfellow Redivivus." Voices,
     No. 60 (November), pp. 40-43.
       [Review of Collected Poems and The Glory of the Nightin-
     gales.] Robinson is cerebral while Longfellow is senti-
     mental, but both lack greatness because they parrot the
     attitudes of their age. Robinson's short poems are memo-
     rable, but his long poems "are not great or even good art."

19 ROURKE, CONSTANCE. American Humor. New York: Harcourt,
     Brace, pp. 271-74.
       Robinson was the first poet to use both American and Eng-
     lish traditions freely. His Tilbury characters reflect
     types that recur in early American comedy, and his voice is
     that of the dry Yankee ironist. "His genuine subject is
     fantasy."

20 SCHWARTZ, JACOB. 1100 Obscure Points: The Bibliographies of
     25 English and 21 American Authors. London: The Ulysses
     Bookshop, p. 83.
       [Incomplete list of Robinson's first editions.]

21 SHEPARD, ODELL. "The Glory of the Nightingales." The Book-
     man, 74 (September), 97-98.
       "This book is being praised. Perhaps it is also being
     read." The story is depressing, the philosophy dreary, the
     poetry distasteful.

22 TANTE, DILLY [STANLEY KUNITZ]. Living Authors: A Book of
     Biographies. New York: H. W. Wilson, pp. 344-46.
       [Biographical sketch, with quoted physical description
     and mention of Robinson's favorite authors.]

23 WALTON, EDA LOU. "So Wrapped in Rectitude." The Nation, 133
     (October 14), 403-404.
       [Review of Matthias at the Door.] Robinson succeeds at
     long narratives because he can fuse incident and symbol,
     and he insists upon "dramatic interaction of character."
     Natalie is "the most completely realized study of a woman
     the poet has yet given us."

24 WHITE, NEWMAN I. "America's Psychological Poet." The South
     Atlantic Quarterly, 30 (July), 334-35.
       [Review of The Glory of the Nightingales, noting that it
     is worse than earlier Robinson narratives, but it is "not
     unworthy of America's greatest psychological artist."]

25   W[HITNEY], E[MMIE] B. "Maine Poet, Edwin Arlington Robinson,
     Gives Powerful Narrative Poem to Admirers." Lewiston (Me.)
     Journal Magazine Section, November 14, p. 4.
          [Review of Matthias at the Door.] "While neither the
     story nor the philosophy may be entirely satisfactory, the
     reader cannot but admire the artistry and mentality that
     produced it."

26   WILDER, THORNTON. "Wilder Lauds Story Poem by Robinson."
     Chicago Daily Tribune, December 12, pp. 19, 20.
          [Review of Matthias at the Door, comparing Robinson's
     attitude to that of Shakespeare and his style to that of
     Frost.] Both New England poets have used blank verse and
     a colloquial manner "simultaneously and with complete in-
     dependence."

1932 A BOOKS - NONE

1932 B SHORTER WRITINGS

1   ANON. "Einstein is Terse in Rule for Success." The New York
     Times, June 20, Section I, p. 17.
          [Quotation by Robinson among those of five notables who
     give advice on how to succeed.]

2   ANON. "Matthias at the Door." Times Literary Supplement,
     No. 1599, September 22, p. 665.
          This poem is a "persuasive parable," with a style free of
     "the complicated casuistry" Robinson sometimes uses.

3   ANON. "Nicodemus." Among Our Books (Carnegie Library, Pitts-
     burgh), 37 (December), 78.
          Nicodemus "maintains the reputation of the poet but adds
     no new laurels."

4   ANON. Review of Nicodemus. The Nation, 135 (October 26),
     407.
          It is a "creditable" book, but there is nothing new here.

5   ANON. Review of Nicodemus. Time, 20 (October 10), 44.
          Robinson readers, if not Tristram readers, will want this
     new collection of eleven poems.

6   ANON. "Nicodemus." Times Literary Supplement, No. 1611, De-
     cember 15, p. 966.
          Nicodemus suffers from "too ungainly elaboration or pro-
     saic flatness of phrase."

1932

7   ANON. "Poetry That is Not Song." The Christian Century, 49
      (November 2), 1347-48.
         [Brief review of Nicodemus, with special comment on title
      poem, "Sisera," and "Toussaint L'Ouverture."]

8   BARTLETT, ALICE HUNT. "Dynamics of American Poetry: XXXV."
      The Poetry Review, 23 (January-February), 55-56.
         [Overview of the career of "America's foremost poet,"
      commenting particularly on similarity between Robinson and
      Eugene O'Neill.]

9   BEECH, JOHNSTONE. "Nicodemus." The Churchman, 146 (October
      15), 5.
         This book is far below the level of Tristram. Perhaps
      "The March of the Cameron Men" will add to the author's
      reputation.

10   B[ELLAMANN], H[ENRY]. "The Literary Highway." Columbia (S.C.)
      State, October 9, p. 24.
         [Review of Nicodemus, with analysis of the title poem
      and comparison of Robinson and Browning.] "A new book by
      Robinson is a major literary event."

11   BENÉT, WILLIAM ROSE. "Round About Parnassus: Two Veterans."
      The Saturday Review of Literature, 9 (November 5), 224.
         [Review of Nicodemus, noting that here Robinson suffers
      from comparison with himself.]

12   BUTCHER, FANNY. "E. A. Robinson Presents New Book of Poems."
      Chicago Tribune, October 22, p. 8.
         Robinson uses the same method for Nicodemus that he used
      so effectively in Tristram.

13   CALVERTON, V. F. The Liberation of American Literature. New
      York: Charles Scribner's Sons, pp. 415-16.
         Robinson is the most American poet since Whitman, al-
      though he restricts his interest to New England. His voice
      is a despairing one because he mourns the passing of "an
      individualistic culture."

14   CESTRE, CHARLES. "Recit, Drame et Symbole chez Edwin Arling-
      ton Robinson." Revue Anglo-Americaine, 9 (June), 406-12.
         [Review of Matthias at the Door, noting that it is a ve-
      hicle for character portrayal and that it restates Robin-
      son's principal theme of spirituality as a part of the
      energy and efficiency of Americans.]

15   CORNING, HOWARD McKINLEY. "Edwin Arlington Robinson."
         Voices, No. 64 (April), pp. 255-57.
            [Essay-review in series on Pulitzer Prize poets, noting
         that Robinson is a three-time winner largely because of his
         proficiency in the sonnet and dramatic monologue.]

16   DEUTSCH, BABETTE. "The Hands of Esau." The New Republic, 72
         (October 5), 213-14.
            [Review of Nicodemus.] These poems are inferior to Rob-
         inson's earlier short pieces. None can match "Ben Jonson,"
         but the best is "The Prodigal Son."

17   EVANS, NANCY. "Edwin Arlington Robinson." The Bookman, 75
         (November), 675-81.
            [Interview with Robinson emphasizing his modesty, psycho-
         logical insight, and ideological stance which is in opposi-
         tion to that of Joseph Wood Krutch's The Modern Temper.]

18   FLINT, F. CUDWORTH. "Matthias at the Door." The Symposium, 3
         (April), 237-48.
            [Essay-review with thesis that the long poems are more
         analytic than narrative or dramatic. This poem is analyzed
         for structure and imagery. Robinson's flaws of nihilism,
         narrowness of interests, and hesitancy are noted.]

19   F[OSTER], I[SABEL]. "More From Mr. Robinson." Christian
         Science Monitor, October 1, p. 6.
            [Review of Nicodemus, singling out "The March of the
         Cameron Men" as the most lyrical of the poems.]

20   FREIDBERG, SIDNEY. "A New Volume of Robinson." The Critical
         Review--New York University Daily News Literary Supplement,
         6 (November), 3-4.
            [Review of Nicodemus.] "Like Henry James in his later
         works, Robinson proposes metaphysical 'sticklers' of su-
         preme difficulty and tremendous significance."

21   FRENCH, JOSEPH LEWIS. "An Interregnum of Genius." The Com-
         monweal, 15 (February 10), 412.
            [Letter to the editor contending that Matthias at the
         Door is only a repetition of Captain Craig, parts of which
         Robinson keeps putting in later poems because he has never
         equaled it. Concludes that much of Robinson's poetry is
         "rather bald prose."]

22   GREGORY, HORACE. "E. A. Robinson Maintains His Fixed Gait."
         New York Evening Post, October 20, p. 10.
            [Review of Nicodemus noting that Robinson is not apt to
         undergo a radical change, as Yeats has recently done.]

1932

23   HAINES, HELEN E. "New Poems by Robinson." Pasadena Star-
      News, November 19, p. 24.
           [Review of Nicodemus, suggesting that these poems are
      similar to his earlier work but noting that Robinson has
      grown more mature and more obscure.]

24   [HALL-QUEST, ALFRED L.] "Nicodemus." The Kadelpian Review,
      12 (November), 94-95.
           "Ponce de Leon" best exemplifies the craftsmanship and
      sound philosophy of these poems.

25   HUTCHISON, PERCY. "Robinson's New Collection of Poems." The
      New York Times Book Review, October 2, p. 2.
           [Review of Nicodemus, noting that Robinson has returned
      to his earlier manner and saying that if he had once been
      under the influence of Browning he has now "outstripped
      his master."]

26   JOHNSON, MERLE. "Edwin Arlington Robinson," in American First
      Editions. New York: R. R. Bowker, pp. 304-307.
           [List of first editions by and about Robinson; includes
      reprint of 1923.B21.]

27   JONES, HOWARD MUMFORD. "Imagination Does But Seem." The Vir-
      ginia Quarterly Review, 8 (January), 147-48.
           [Review of Matthias at the Door.] "The blank verse is
      perpetually trembling on the verge of prose, and not very
      good prose."

28   JUDGE, JANE. "Robinson's New Poems Return to Early Manner."
      Savannah Morning News, October 16, p. A 11.
           [Review of Nicodemus, with special mention of "Hector
      Kane," "Ponce de Leon," and "The March of the Cameron Men."]

29   KNIGHT, GRANT C. American Literature and Culture. New York:
      Ray Long and Richard R. Smith, pp. 464-68.
           [Overview of Robinson's life and work, with thesis that
      he is a "spiritual orphan." Suggests that with his pol-
      ished, spare style his Arthurian poems are "less orchida-
      ceous" than Tennyson's Arthurian pieces.]

30   LEWIS, JAY. "About Books and Authors." Norfolk (Va.) Ledger
      Dispatch, September 27, p. 8.
           [Review of Nicodemus, with special attention to "Ponce
      de Leon."]

31   LEWISOHN, LUDWIG. Expression in America. New York: Harper
      and Brothers, pp. 553-60.

Robinson owes much to Naturalism in choice of subject, but
he has never gone beyond philosophic Nihilism. He lacks
"inner heat," a defect that weakens the long modern narratives. Tristram is his best poem.

32 MACY, JOHN. "The New Age of American Poetry." Current His-
      tory, 35 (January), 554-55.
        Robinson is "the oldest of the new poets, but at sixty-
      two he has not begun to yield to the youngest."

33 MASON, MADELEINE. "Music That is True." New York Sun, Octo-
      ber 15, p. 19.
        [Review of Nicodemus, suggesting that the title poem is
      superior to the other Biblical pieces but "Toussaint
      L'Ouverture" and "The March of the Cameron Men" are also
      noteworthy.]

34 MASTERS, EDGAR LEE. "The Poetry Revival of 1914." The Ameri-
      can Mercury, 26 (July), 274-75.
        "Robinson has done no more for American poetry as such
      than Thomas Bailey Aldrich." Notable is the "fastidious
      discipline" of his prosody.

35 M[ONROE], H[ARRIET]. "Robinson's Matthias." Poetry, 39
      (January), 212-217.
        Matthias at the Door, yet another triangular love story,
      is told with more directness than The Man Who Died Twice.
      Critics have overlooked Robinson's lack of children in his
      narratives. His style is notable.

36 MORRISON, THEODORE. "Nicodemus." The Bookman, 75 (November),
      750-51.
        Robinson is losing the power of creating vivid imagery
      and his poetry is marked by his dry, quibbling manner.
      His sonnets are superior to his longer poems.

*37 NADIG, HENRY DAVIS. "I'd Rather Read Poetry." New Canaan
      (Conn.) Advertiser, October 27, p. 9.
        [Listed in White, p. 93, as a review of Nicodemus.]

38 NETHERCOT, ARTHUR H. "...Ways That Make Us Ponder While We
      Praise." Voices, No. 67 (December-January), pp. 52-54.
        Robinson is like Browning in his interest in character
      and dialogue, but he is not as capable of varying them as
      Browning is. "Hector Kane" is superior to other poems in
      the volume because it is more straightforward. "The truth
      remains that Robinson is still America's most substantial
      poet."

1932

39   PAYNE, L. W., JR. "Dramatic Dialogues in Poet's Latest Book
     Prove Outstanding." Dallas Morning News, November 6, Fea-
     ture Section, p. 4.
          [Review of Nicodemus, suggesting that the first and last
     poems in the volume are the two best. Applauds his sound
     philosphical ideas and similarity to Browning.]

40   RADENZEL, EDWARD. "Man in His Own Mirror." The Wasp News
     Letter, 54 (October 8), 16.
          [Review of Nicodemus, finding title poem, "Toussaint
     L'Ouverture," and "Sisera" to be "magnificent."]

41   RANCK, CARTY. "Nicodemus and Other Robinsonian Poetry." Bos-
     ton Evening Transcript, October 1, Book Section, p. 2.
          Robinson's first book of short poems in seven years is
     well done. Most notable poems are "Nicodemus" and "Sisera."

42   REDMAN, BEN RAY. "New Poems by E. A. Robinson." New York
     Herald Tribune Books, September 25, p. 2.
          [Review of Nicodemus, finding it "a quantitative rather
     than a qualitative addition."]

43   ROMIG, EDNA DAVIS. "Tilbury Town and Camelot." The Univer-
     sity of Colorado Studies, 19 (June), 303-26.
          [Copious quotations are used to support the thesis that
     Robinson is a great poet. Emphasis is on his realistic
     outlook on life and the depth and range of his poetic vi-
     sion. Writer notes that other writers have overlooked his
     lyric beauty and "superb suggestiveness." Reprinted in
     1969.A4.]

44   ROSE, TURNER. "More Celebration [sic] and Less Emotion in
     New Robinson Book." Richmond (Va.) Times-Dispatch, Octo-
     ber 16, Pt. III, p. 5.
          [Review of Nicodemus.] This book is "more Robinsonian
     than ever, which means nearer to pure cerebration."

45   ROSENBERG, HAROLD. "Judgment and Passion." Poetry, 41 (De-
     cember), 158-61.
          [Review of Nicodemus.] Robinson's new poems are largely
     on Biblical themes, but they don't seem much different from
     others because they are so abstract.

46   ST. CLAIR, GEORGE. "Nicodemus." The New Mexico Quarterly, 2
     (November), 346-49.
          Robinson is better at blank verse than rhymed poems. It
     is not true that he has surpassed Browning. "Sisera" is
     not very interesting because Jael is a depraved woman.

47 _____. "Three Volumes Worth Reading." The New Mexico Quarterly, 2 (February), 92-93.
[Review of Matthias at the Door, noting that Robinson is
like Browning in his interest in "soul-states," which sometimes makes his poetry obscure.]

48 ST. JOHN, JESSIE. "Concerning Distinguished Poetry." Voices,
No. 61 (January), pp. 95-97.
[Review of Matthias at the Door.] "The poem does not
sparkle, but through simple phrasing it is unmistakable
poetry."

49 SHEPARD, ODELL. "Recent Verse." The Yale Review, 21 (March),
591.
Matthias at the Door, though sometimes prosaic, is a considerable improvement over The Glory of the Nightingales.

50 WARD, A. C. American Literature 1880-1930. London: Methuen,
pp. 159-62.
[Overview of career, noting that Robinson is more popular
with critics than the public and suggesting that he would
do better to write in free verse, "Llewellyn and the Tree,"
for instance, having been "murdered by metre."]

1933 A BOOKS - NONE

1933 B SHORTER WRITINGS

1 ANON. "Light Without Heat." Time, 22 (October 16), 59.
[Review of Talifer, suggesting that it neither adds nor
detracts from Robinson's reputation.]

2 BATES, ROBERT C. "Edwin Arlington Robinson's Three Poems."
The Yale University Library Gazette, 8 (October), 81-82.
[An account of Lucius Beebe's piracy of Modred, the 164
lines Robinson had deleted from Lancelot. It and two
poems published originally in the Harvard Advocate make up
Three Poems.]

3 BENÉT, WILLIAM ROSE. "Edwin Arlington Robinson," in his edi-
tion of Fifty Poets: An American Auto-Anthology. New
York: Dodd, Mead, p. 16.
When asked what his most representative short poem was,
Robinson couldn't say, but did reply that he thought the
three Arthurian poems "as likely to last as anything."

1933

4 CHAMBERLAIN, JOHN. Review of Talifer. The New York Times,
     September 27, p. 19.
       "The humorous, understated tolerance of human foibles"
     is the essence of Talifer. If Yankee wisdom and common
     sense make poetry, than Talifer is poetry.

5 COLUM, PADRIAC. "Edwin Arlington Robinson's Poetry." The
     Spectator, 151 (August 25), 256-57.
       [Review of Nicodemus.] "Ruin" is the word most frequent-
     ly used in Robinson's poetry, but it is never bare ruin.
     "Sisera" is the strongest poem in the volume. Robinson is
     more like James or Hawthorne than Browning.

6 CONRAD, LAWRENCE H. "The Critics' Poet--A Study of Edwin Arl-
     ington Robinson." The Landmark, 15 (January), 23-26.
       For years critics have hailed Robinson as the greatest
     living poet, but he does not have popular appeal. Critics
     admire but do not love his poems.

7 DEUTSCH, BABETTE. "'Talifer,' A Jamesian Novel in Verse."
     New York Herald Tribune Books, October 8, p. 8.
       Talifer is like bad James, or bad Robinson. He can do so
     much better than this "that one is impatient for a poem
     that will show him again on his native heights."

8 F[OSTER], I[SABEL]. "A New E. A. Robinson." Christian Sci-
     ence Monitor, September 30, p. 9.
       [Review of Talifer, noting its unusual happy ending and
     predicting it will be Robinson's most popular book since
     Tristram in spite of its lack of lyric passages.]

9 GROSS, GERALD. "Robinson Explains Beautifully." Washington
     Post, November 20, p. 10.
       [Review of Talifer.] In "this exceedingly amusing nar-
     rative poem" Dr. Quick has the best speeches, but Althea's
     despair after having been left by a man is "a masterful
     dissection of a woman's heart."

10 HAINES, HELEN E. "Robinson and Masefield." Pasadena Star-
     News, October 7, p. 10.
       [Review of Talifer.] This social comedy might be better
     in prose because the characters seem "somewhat detached
     from individual reality in speech and action." Neverthe-
     less, as representatives of human behavior they are "ever-
     lastingly true."

11 HASTINGS, SMITH. "Robinson in a Lighter Mood." The Argonaut,
     112 (November 17), 18.

[Review of Talifer, calling attention to the thin subject matter but suggesting that Dr. Quick is presented with brilliance and humor.]

12   HICKS, GRANVILLE. The Great Tradition. New York: Macmillan, pp. 242-45.
       Robinson has made a real contribution in creating an abstract world in which he considers success and failure, but it is hard to forgive him his long poems.

13   H[UTCHISON], P[ERCY]. "Robinson's New Narrative Poem Shows Him in a New Aspect." The New York Times Book Review, October 1, p. 2.
       [Review of Talifer, suggesting that this is a new approach because Robinson treats his characters subjectively rather than objectively, and noting the heavy use of symbolism, especially the trees.]

14   JACK, P. M. "Among Ghosts and Phrases." New York Sun, September 29, p. 25.
       [Review of Talifer.] In spite of Robinson's being canonized this poem suffers from poorly drawn characters and a silly plot. It "is a pastime rather than poetry."

15   JOHNSON, A. THEODORE. "New 'Alms for Oblivion.'" Memphis Commercial Appeal, January 8, Section I, p. 16.
       [Review of Nicodemus, applauding the skilful verse but regretting Robinson's lack of awareness with the contemporary scene. Special note of the title poem, "Hector Kane," and "The March of the Cameron Men."]

16   L[ORD], A[LICE] F. "Talifer." Lewiston (Me.) Journal Magazine Section, September 23, p. 9.
       This poem might well have been called "Dr. Quick," who is Robinson's spokesman. He probably wrote a comic poem just to show he could, and he should dramatize it.

17   LORD, ALICE FROST. "Will Head Tide Become Literary Shrine of America?" Lewiston (Me.) Journal Magazine Section, October 28, pp. 1, 4.
       [Lengthy feature story on Head Tide, where Robinson spent the first six months of his life.]

18   MILLS, CLARK. "Procession of Tableaus." Voices, No. 73 (December-January), pp. 38-41.
       [Review of Talifer, noting the improbable conversation and mechanics of plot.]

1933

19 OUTCALT, IRVING E. "Robinson Work is Challenging Aspect of
 Life." San Diego Union, October 22, Section III, p. 7.
 Robinson does not share Howells' view about the "smiling
 aspects of life." Talifer, however, is neither tragic nor
 profound.

20 RANCK, CARTY. "Edwin Arlington Robinson as Poet-Humorist."
 Boston Evening Transcript, September 30, Book Section,
 p. 1.
 [Review of Talifer.] This is the most humorous poem
 since Captain Craig, with striking imagery. Karen "is one
 of the most successful of all Mr. Robinson's feminine characters, and, by all odds, the most original."

21 SCHÖNEMANN, FRIEDRICH. "Der Lyriker der Amerikanischen Skep-
 sis (Edwin Arlington Robinson)." Die Literatur, 35 (May),
 446-49.
 [Overview of Robinson's career, emphasizing his realism
 and pessimism. Three poems translated.]

22 SCRIFTGIESSER, KARL. "An American Poet Speaks His Mind."
 Boston Evening Transcript, November 4, Book Section,
 pp. 1-2.
 [Interview with Robinson concerned primarily with the
 nature of poetry and his long poems. Comments about Frost,
 Housman, and Granville Hicks.]

23 SESSIONS, INA BETH. A Study of the Dramatic Monologue in
 American and Continental Literature. San Antonio: Alamo
 Printing Company, pp. 108-16.
 Robinson is indebted to Browning, but his dramatic mono-
 logues "lack dramatic situations, and clearly defined audi-
 ences." [Discussions of "Ben Jonson," "The Island," "Bo-
 kardo," "The Clinging Vine," and "The Three Taverns."]

24 SHEPARD, ODELL. "Poetry in a Time of Doubt." The Yale Review, 22 (March), 593.
 [Review of Nicodemus.] Robinson's "characteristic under-
 statements...frequently amount to zero."

25 S[MITH], C[HARD] P. "Talifer." American Poetry Journal (December), pp. 30-32.
 This poem answers critics who complain of Robinson's
 somberness, but it is a waste of talent. "To the old ad-
 mirers it seems like a tremendous and delicately balanced
 machine here bearing down to murder a fly."

26   TATE, ALLEN. "Again, O Ye Laurels." The New Republic, 76
      (October 25), 312-13.
         [Review of Talifer.] Robinson should not try to write
      long poems because he is unable to sustain dramatic ten-
      sion. He lacks an epos or myth to describe general pat-
      terns of conduct; thus he can't "depict action that is
      both single and complete." [Reprinted in 1936.B27,
      1948.B17, 1959.B5, and 1968.B16.]

27   TOWNE, CHARLES HANSON. "A Number of Things." New York Ameri-
      can, September 30, p. 13.
         [Review of Talifer.] This poem, with its living charac-
      ters, shows Robinson "at his passionate best."

28   UMANSKY, HARLAN. "Edwin Arlington Robinson." The Critical
      Review--New York University Daily News Literary Supplement,
      7 (November), 4.
         [Six-line poem to Robinson.]

29   UNTERMEYER, LOUIS. "Wise and Wicked." The Saturday Review
      of Literature, 10 (October 7), 161.
         [Review of Talifer.] This is Robinson's best long poem.
      He has added four memorable protraits, especially Karen,
      "whom Robinson reveals with joyful malice and leaves her
      to her own divorces in a university town."

30   WALTON, EDA LOU. "Robinson's Women." The Nation, 137 (Octo-
      ber 11), 415.
         [Review of Talifer, suggesting that Robinson is unable
      to draw women characters adequately and that his superior
      poems are those that are heavily philosophical, like Mer-
      lin and Matthias at the Door, rather than the more purely
      narrative ones, like Tristram and Talifer.]

1934 A BOOKS - NONE

1934 B SHORTER WRITINGS

1   ANON. "Amaranth." Winnipeg Free Press, December 8, p. 31.
         Some people will be bored, but they cannot deny "the in-
      tense, passionate, completely integral unity and mass of
      this poem." [Four themes are listed.]

2   ANON. "Poems: Robinson Presents His Twenty-third Book of
      Verse." News-Week, 4 (September 29), 39.
         [Review of Amaranth and survey of career.] "Amaranth
      may not rank with the poet's most famous works but it is
      one after his own heart" because Robinson likes failures
      so much.

1934

3   ANON. "Poets Old & New." Time, 24 (October 1), 62-63.
    [Review of Amaranth.] The effect of this poem by the
    most respected living American poet is "typically Robin-
    sonian: a shadow masque seen through a glass darkly, by
    a keen but puzzled eye."

4   ANON. "Two American Poets." Times Literary Supplement, No.
    167, February 1, p. 72.
    [Review of Talifer, charging that the story is insignifi-
    cant and the writing is stilted.]

5   BARNEY, VIRGINIA. "Talifer." The North American Review, 237
    (January), iv.
    This poem is "written with beauty of expression and depth
    of feeling."

6   BARTLETT, ALICE HUNT. "Dynamics of American Poetry: XLVI."
    The Poetry Review, 25 (January-February), 54-56.
    [Review of Talifer, noting that it is on the greatest of
    themes, love, but that it is written in a colloquial man-
    ner.]

7   BLACKMUR, R[ICHARD] P. "Verse That is to Easie." Poetry, 43
    (January), 221-25.
    [Review of Talifer, finding it in a "negative competence"
    in content, emotional impact, and versification, and there-
    fore not worthy of its author.]

8   BROWN, RAY C. B. "Poetic Oneirology." Voices, No. 79 (Decem-
    ber-January), pp. 41-44.
    [Review of Amaranth.] Reversing Browning's dictum of the
    reach exceeding the grasp, Robinson considers the question
    of unhappiness caused by unattainable ambition. He "has
    exchanged dramatization for ratiocination, with a result
    not wholly felicitous."

9   CESTRE, C[HARLES]. "Edwin Arlington Robinson--Artiste dans
    les Jeux de l'Humour et de la Fantasie." Revue Anglo-
    Americaine, 11 (February), 246-50.
    [Review of Talifer, praising its purity of line in
    spite of occasional heavy-handedness.]

10 C[OBLENTZ], S[TANTON] A. "Talifer." Wings, 1 (Winter), 24-26.
    "One finds nothing likely to enhance his prestige" be-
    cause the poem is too prosaic.

1934

11   DEUTSCH, BABETTE. "Robinson Not at His best in Latest Por-
     trait." New York World Telegram, October 4, p. 27.
     [Review of Amaranth, observing the lack of Robinson's
     earlier shrewdness and lyricism.]

12   FOSTER, ISABEL. "Robinsonian Avernus." Christian Science
     Monitor, September 26, p. 14.
        [Review of Amaranth.] In contrast to the "genial and
     realistic manner of Talifer," Robinson here is "somber,
     mysterious, and abstruse." The poem is not likely to at-
     tract new readers.

13   GREGORY, HORACE. "The Weapon of Irony." Poetry, 45 (Decem-
     ber), 158-61.
        [Review of Amaranth.] Robinson has two embarrassing
     characteristics for a poet: intelligence and integrity.
     Irony is the best weapon against "the hell of peculiar
     vagueness and indifference" in which his children of the
     night wander.

14   HALLECK, REUBEN POST. The Romance of American Literature.
     New York: American Book Company, pp. 269-75.
        [Brief overview of career of "the most eminent American
     poet of our time."]

*15 HAYDEN, KATHERINE SHEPARD. "E. A. Robinson Captures New Po-
     etic Laurels." Wisconsin State Journal, October 28, p. 6.
        [Listed as a review of Amaranth in Hogan, p. 162.]

16   HOLMES, JOHN HAYNES. "The Latest Robinson." Unity, 114
     (October 29), 95-96.
        [Review of Amaranth.] This poem is "as Robinsonesque as
     'Rabbi Ben Ezra' is Browningesque." He probably aimed the
     poem "directly to practitioners of free verse, modernist
     music, and cubist art."

17   HYDE, KENT GOODNOUGH. "It's All Grist." Westward, 3 (Novem-
     ber), 14-15.
        [Review of Amaranth.] "Honesty has been a characteristic
     of all the writings of Robinson and the 1934 offering makes
     a definite contribution relative to art."

18   JONES, LLEWELLYN. "Levitation by Bootstrap." The Midwest, 1
     (November), 1, 7.
        [Review of Amaranth.] This poem suffers from the com-
     bination of allegory and analysis. Robinson tried to con-
     vey deep intellectual thought through macabre images, and
     it doesn't quite work.

1934

19 LECHLITNER, RUTH. "A Page About Poets: Amaranth." The New
    Republic, 80 (October 17), 282.
        Reading the "ghoulish symbolism" of this poem is painful
    to Robinson admirers because it reveals the self-doubt of
    the poet who fears he has lost his talent.

20 LEWIS, JAY. "About Books and Authors." Norfolk (Va.) Ledger-
    Dispatch, November 28, p. 6.
        [Review of Amaranth.] This poem is intellectually im-
    pressive. The difference in Robinson and Tennyson is ap-
    parent when the opening lines here are compared to the
    opening lines of "The Brook." While Robinson's writing is
    polished, it seems more like prose than poetry.

21 LORD, ALICE FROST. "Amaranth." Lewiston (Me.) Journal Maga-
    zine Section, October 13, p. 9.
        Similar in tone to Talifer, Amaranth is difficult but
    worthwhile.

22 _____. "Gardiner Poet Was Friend of Edwin Arlington Robin-
    son." Lewiston (Me.) Journal Magazine Section, January 27,
    p. 9.
        [An account of the friendship between Robinson and Alan-
    son Tucker Schumann, along with a reprinting of Robinson's
    tribute to him and a biographical sketch of the doctor.]

23 _____. "Gardiner's One-Time 'League of Three' Dates Back to
    E. A. Robinson's Youth." Lewiston (Me.) Journal Magazine
    Section, March 3, p. 2.
        [Interview with E. G. Moore, a childhood friend who
    claims that Robinson wrote "On the Night of a Friend's
    Wedding" about his marriage in 1893.]

24 _____. "H. Dean Robinson." Lewiston (Me.) Journal, October
    27, p. 9.
        Robinson dedicated Amaranth to Dean, the brother he ad-
    mired so much. Contrary to his biographers, Robinson re-
    turned from Harvard not because of financial reverses but
    because Dean was ill.

25 _____. "Laura E. Richards Recalled Edwin Arlington Robinson."
    Lewiston (Me.) Journal Magazine Section, March 17, p. 9.
        [Excerpts of Richards-Robinson relationship recorded in
    Stepping Westward. Partial reprint of 1931.B17.].

26 MASON, MADELINE. "Wasted Lives." New York Sun, October 6,
    p. 31.

[Review of Amaranth, noting the similarity with Cavender's House in eerie atmosphere and suggesting that it might be considered Robinson's best poem someday.]

27 RANCK, CARTY. "An American Poet in a Nightmare Land." Boston Evening Transcript, September 26, Section III, p. 2.
    [Review of Amaranth.] Robinson's "finest achievement since Tristram" and one of his most original themes, this poem will be "unpopular with the self-complacent."

28 RANSOM, ELLENE. "'Amaranth' Proves Poet is a Spiritual Internist." Nashville Banner, October 7, Section III, p. 10.
    [Review of Amaranth, noting its sharp though delicate satire, its strong character delineation, and its symbolism.]

29 REICHERT, RABBI VICTOR E. "Mishandled Heritage." The American Israelite, 81 (December 27), 4.
    [Review of Amaranth, noting its lack of lyricism but praising it for psychological insight.]

30 RITTENHOUSE, JESSIE B. My House of Life: An Autobiography. Boston and New York: Houghton Mifflin, pp. 211-12, 282.
    [Personal reminiscence of Robinson during his stay at the Judson Hotel, noting particularly his dismay at Roosevelt's article about him and his inability to enjoy large crowds.]

31 ROOT, MERRILL. "The Decline of E. A. Robinson." The Christian Century, 51 (December 5), 1554.
    [Review of Amaranth.] This is "another evidence of hardening poetic arteries." "Browning's Andrea Del Sarto gives us the tragedy of an artist-failure in 270 lines; Robinson fails to give it in 105 pages."

32 ST. CLAIR, GEORGE. "E. A Robinson and Tilbury Town." The New Mexico Quarterly, 4 (May), 95-107.
    [Playlet involving Robinson at Recording Angel's Court with several Tilbury Town characters. He is charged with being untruthful and too pessimistic, but is acquitted.]

33 S[COTT], W[INFIELD] T. "E. A. Robinson's New Poem." Providence (R.I.) Sunday Journal, September 30, Section VI, p. 4.
    [Review of Amaranth.] Robinson at 65 has written a poem "which tops almost everything he has done in a productive decade." The style is characteristic, but the handling, mood, and scene are surprisingly new.

1934

34   S[MITH], C[HARD] P. "Amaranth." <u>American Poetry Journal</u> (December), pp. 18-19.
      This poem is "the greatest of Mr. Robinson's narratives in a contemporary setting." It is similar to but better than <u>The Man Who Died Twice</u>.

35   SOSKIN, WILLIAM. "Edwin Arlington Robinson's Modern Allegory." <u>New York American</u>, October 1, p. 15.
      [Review of <u>Amaranth</u>.] This is "a sort of minor American <u>Purgatorio</u>." Though the style is pleasant the theme is too minor to be treated in this heroic scale.

*36   VACADLO, OTAKAR. <u>Soucasna Literatura Spojenych Statu</u>. Prague: Vydal Jan Laichter.
      [Listed in White, p. 37.]

37   WALTON, EDA LOU. "A Compelling Theme." <u>The Nation</u>, 139 (October 17), 457-58.
      [Review of <u>Amaranth</u>.] "This is the most abstract in treatment of any of Robinson's narratives, the least dramatic, the least projected from the inner mind. But its theme is compelling."

38   _____. "Defeated Aspirations." <u>New York Herald Tribune Books</u>, October 7, p. 21.
      [Essay-review of <u>Amaranth</u>.] After recently writing a study of conscience and a study of hatred and its consequences, here Robinson "is studying the worth of men's desire to exceed themselves." In doing so he is "giving up music for thought."

39   W[ILLIAMS], M. L. "Talifer." <u>The English Journal</u>, 23 (October), 677.
      "The most optimistic of Mr. Robinson's long poems, <u>Talifer</u> shows no falling off in surgical analysis in character or in subtle, pungent dialogue."

<u>1935 A BOOKS</u>

1   FRASER, JAMES EARLE, ed. <u>In Tribute</u>. Privately printed, 90 pp.
      [Collection of fity-four newspaper and magazine articles occasioned by Robinson's death, thirteen of which are reprinted below.]

2   FROST, ROBERT. "Introduction," to <u>King Jasper</u>, by Edwin Arlington Robinson. New York: Macmillan, pp. v-xv.

"Robinson stayed content with the old-fashioned way to be new.... His theme was unhappiness itself, but his skill was as happy as it was playful." [Brief commentary on "Miniver Cheevy," "Old King Cole," "The Mill," "The Sheaves," and "Mr. Flood's Party." Reprinted in 1970.A3.]

1935 B SHORTER WRITINGS

1   ANON. Review of Amaranth. The English Journal, 24 (February), 173.
      Amaranth is "a not unworthy addition to Mr. Robinson's list."

2   ANON. "Amaranth." Springfield (Mass.) Union and Republican, January 13, p. 7E.
      "This poem is a sort of Divine Comedy with Amaranth and Fargo playing the modern replica of Virgil and Dante." It is not for the casual reader since it requires such concentration. Its big fault is irregularity of meter.

3   ANON. "Died." Time, 25 (April 15), 72.
      Robinson was a frugal, reclusive bachelor who liked billiards and Gilbert and Sullivan.

4   ANON. [E. A. Robinson.] The New York Times, April 8, Section I, p. 18.
      [Elegaic editorial with copious references to "The Man Against the Sky."]

5   ANON. "E. A. Robinson, Poet, Left $43,871 Estate." The New York Times, August 31, Section I, p. 13.
      Robinson's nieces are principal donees of his estate; his manuscripts are valued at $2250.

6   ANON. "E. A. Robinson, Pulitzer Prize Poet, Dies Here." New York Herald-Tribune, April 6, Section I, p. 19.
      [Three-column Associated Press obituary, emphasizing difficult early years. "Miniver Cheevy" and "Richard Cory" quoted.] Robinson was "a bachelor, a fatalist, and an agnostic."

7   ANON. "Edwin Arlington Robinson." The Commonweal, 21 (April 19), 708-709.
      The opinion of Robinson's achievement is varied. "The attitude of Poetry and affiliated organs was frankly hostile, but the most professional critics were enthusiastic."

1935

8   ANON. "Edwin Arlington Robinson." Modern Literature, 3 (May
      1-14), 9.
      [Obituary emphasizing his reclusiveness. Three stanzas
      of "Miniver Cheevy" quoted.]

9   ANON. "Edwin Arlington Robinson." New York Herald-Tribune,
      April 7, Pt. II, p. 8.
      Robinson's stature will increase, but he will have few
      imitators. [Reprinted in 1935.A1.]

10 ANON. "Edwin Arlington Robinson." Washington Evening Star,
      April 8, p. A-10.
      Robinson "was true to fundamental values in both the
      business of living and the art of literature." [Reprinted
      in 1935.A1.]

11 ANON. "Edwin A. Robinson, Poet, Is Dead at Sixty-six." The
      New York Times, April 6, Section I, p. 15.
      [Associated Press Obituary.]

12 ANON. "Edwin Arlington Robinson." New Haven Journal-Courier,
      April 9, p. 6.
      Robinson "became a most annoying celebrity by his lack of
      color and conviviality.... He merely wrote poetry, stead-
      ily, serenely, superbly." [Reprinted in 1935.A1.]

13 ANON. "Edwin Robinson Dies as Friends Sit at Bedside." New
      York World Telegram, April 6, Section I, p. 14.
      The friends present when Robinson died were Carty Ranck,
      George Burnham, Elizabeth Starbuck-Jones, Elizabeth Marsh,
      and Louis M. Isaacs.

14 ANON. "Edwin Robinson." The New York Times, April 7, Pt. IV,
      p. 8.
      The most widely read serious poet of his day, Robinson
      will be remembered for the range and quality of his work
      as well as its volume. [Part of "The Sheaves" quoted. Re-
      printed in 1935.A1.]

15 ANON. "The Excellent Career." The Commonweal, 21 (April 19),
      694.
      Because of Theodore Roosevelt's timely aid, Robinson will
      be remembered not only as a poet but also "as an index to
      the need for and value of literary patronage."

16 ANON. "Memorial For Poet Robinson Draws Distinguished Com-
      pany." Lewiston (Me.) Evening Journal, May 13, p. 12.

[Account of memorial service with résumés of speeches by the governor of Maine and president of Bowdoin, among others.]

17 ANON. "A Modern Allegory." Times Literary Supplement, No. 1722, January 31, p. 58.
[Review of Amaranth.] "For the most part the allegory has a Hogarthian humour, though it reflects and develops the most serious of themes."

18 ANON. "Obituaries: Edwin Arlington Robinson." Publisher's Weekly, 127 (April 13), p. 1520.
"His verse reflects his philosophy, for he was by nature a fatalist and an agnostic, but in private life he was more austere than the verse he wrote."

19 ANON. "A Poet Against the Sky." Hartford Courant, April 7, Pt. II, p. 2.
[Elegaic tribute reprinted in 1935.A1.] Robinson spent a life devoted to his art, but he never surpassed "The Man Against the Sky," which was "as dark, cryptic and powerful as anything he wrote in the next thirty years."

20 ANON. "Poet Robinson, Maine Native, Dies in New York." Lewiston (Me.) Evening Journal, April 6, p. 1.
[Associated Press Obituary.]

21 ANON. "Poet's Corner: E. A. Robinson." News-Week, 6 (November 16), p. 47.
[Review of King Jasper.] "Like other Robinson epics, this is a mixture of cerebration and sympathy, of medieval trappings and twentieth century conversation."

22 ANON. "Robinson's Contribution to Poetry in America." Birmingham (Ala.) News, April 9, p. 8.
Robinson achieved large popularity in spite of his refusal to bow to current trends. [Reprinted in 1935.A1.]

23 ANON. "Simple Rites Held for E. A. Robinson." The New York Times, April 9, Section I, p. 19.
Music for Robinson's funeral at St. George's Episcopal Church included Bach chorales, the Dead March from Saul, and the Prelude to Tristan and Isolde. Laurel wreath from the American Academy of Arts and Sciences bore the legend, "I shall have more to say when I am dead."

24 ANON. "The Splendid Character of a Great Poet." The Poetry Review, 26 (May-June), 258-59.

1935

Even ultra-modern poets, such as Sandburg and Amy Lowell, admired his craftsmanship.

25 APP, AUSTIN J. "Edwin Arlington Robinson's Arthurian Poems." Thought, 10 (December), 468-79.
Robinson does not improve on Tennyson and Malory because he spends too much time delving into character and not enough time on action. Also, since he is an agnostic he is incapable of writing inspirational verse.

26 BACON, LEONARD. "Edwin Arlington Robinson: April 7, 1935." Saturday Review of Literature, 11 (April 20), 632.
[Eight-line poetic tribute.]

27 BENÉT, WILLIAM ROSE. "E. A." The Forum and Century, 93 (June), 381.
[Obituary emphasizing Robinson's professional integrity and personal kindness.]

28 _____. "The Phoenix Nest." The Saturday Review of Literature, 11 (February 23), 508.
[Review of Amaranth.] Reviewers have not done justice to Amaranth because they are tired of Robinson and have not noticed that this poem is in an entirely new mode and is unique in narrative poetry. "It shows his fullest powers of insight, his ripest intelligence."

29 _____. "The Phoenix Nest." The Saturday Review of Literature, 11 (April 13), 628.
[Obituary emphasizing Robinson's generous nature and the justness of the praise he received during his latter years.]

30 _____. "The Phoenix Nest." The Saturday Review of Literature, 13 (November 16), 18.
[Review of King Jasper, noting its symbolism and appropriateness to our era. A speech of Zoë compared to three lines by Elinor Wylie.]

31 BERRYMAN, JOHN McALPIN. "Note on E. A. Robinson." The Nation, 141 (July 10), 38.
[Six-line poetic tribute.]

32 _____. Review of King Jasper. The Columbia Review, 17 (December), 19-20.
Robinson's posthumous poem represents a new direction in his poetry; hence his death "is seen to have been a greater loss than was at the time believed." Deeper irony is in poem because seemingly simple elements are open to a multitude of interpretations.

33   BRICKELL, HERSCHEL. "Edwin Arlington Robinson's Last Poem
     Sums up His Philosophy in Blank Verse of Great Beauty."
     New York Post, November 6, p. 13.
         [Review of King Jasper, recommending Frost's introduction
     as a good gloss and interpreting the poem as a conflict be-
     tween Capitalism and Communism.]

34   CESTRE, C[HARLES]. "Avec Edwin Arlington Robinson dans l'In-
     ferno de l'Art." Revue Anglo-Americaine, 12 (April),
     323-27.
         [Review of Amaranth, stressing Robinson's reliance on
     Emerson and indicating that his theory of art is expressed
     in the theme of the poem: creativity is associated with
     reflection, which weighs and values.]

35   COLUM, MARY M. "Poets and Their Problems." The Forum and
     Century, 93 (June), 343-44.
         America should have some provision for supporting its
     artists, as Europe does. Because Robinson could only write
     poetry he wrote more than he should to repay his backers.

36   COWLEY, MALCOLM. "The Week." The New Republic, 82 (April 17),
     268-69.
         Robinson was the most distinguished and most American
     poet of his generation. His two primary virtues, dignity
     and honesty, eventually interfered with each other. His
     later poems "are dramas of scruple, not of purpose." "Ben
     Jonson," "Luke Havergal," and "Mr. Flood's Party" will be
     remembered. [Reprinted in 1935.A1.]

37   DANIELS, MABEL. "Edwin Arlington Robinson's Ardent Enthusiasm
     for Music." The New York Times, April 21, Section IX, p. 5
     and Portland (Me.) Sunday Telegram, April 21, Section A,
     p. 7.
         Robinson most enjoyed the music of Gilbert and Sullivan,
     Brahms, Wagner, and Verdi. The Man Who Died Twice is not
     only full of musical allusions but also, as Robinson
     pointed out, the last section is an outline of a symphony.
     [Reprinted in 1935.A1 and 1938.B11.]

38   DEUTSCH, BABETTE. "E. A. Robinson," in This Modern Poetry.
     New York: W. W. Norton, pp. 103-107.
         Robinson is only partially successful. He is most effec-
     tive in dealing with the memory of things past, as in
     "Isaac and Archibald." His Arthurian and modern poems are
     "vague, verbose and romantic in the worst sense."

1935

39   DODGE, NORMAN L. "Dear Friends." The Month at Goodspeed's,
       7 (September), 10-12.
       [Notice of a copy of The Children of the Night for sale
       and comment that Robinson's Gardiner friends could not have
       foreseen his success.]

40   DOUGHTY, LEGARDE S. "King Jasper." Augusta (Ga.) Chronicle,
       December 8, p. 4.
       Although parts of it are powerful, King Jasper is too
       long, and the poetry gets lost in the prose. "Had there
       been a succession of Shakespeares, I should say Robinson
       was Shakespeare the Least, of half a dozen."

41   EMERSON, DOROTHY. "Edwin Arlington Robinson: Looking Back on
       our First Contemporary Poet." Scholastic, 27 (October 12),
       9-10.
       [Biographical sketch, emphasizing his modesty and, be-
       cause of his early interest in psychology, his modernity.
       "Ben Jonson" named as his best work.]

42   FOSTER, ISABEL. "Mr. Robinson's King Jasper." Christian
       Science Monitor Weekly Magazine Section, December 31, p. 12.
       Frost's introduction to King Jasper is notable. The
       language here is not as difficult or as mannered as in
       other poems.

43   HANDY, SARA G. "Edwin Arlington Robinson." Lewiston (Me.)
       Evening Journal, April 19, p. 4.
       [Eight-line poetic tribute.]

44   HILLYER, ROBERT. "Amaranth." The New England Quarterly, 8
       (March), 113-14.
       This poem is marred by prosaic quality and obscurity, but
       its merits outweigh its faults. Robinson "has never sur-
       passed Amaranth."

45   _____. "Edwin Arlington Robinson." Harvard Alumni Bulletin,
       37 (May), 992-94.
       [Personal reminiscence and assessment. Reprinted in
       1935.A1.] The short poems are best, although Amaranth is
       one of the best modern satires. Robinson is facilely com-
       pared to Browning, but he is more nearly like Hardy. It
       is ironic that Yale gave him an honorary degree while Har-
       vard did not.

46   HOPPER, V. FOSTER. "Robinson and Frost." The Saturday Review
       of Literature, 13 (November 2), 9.
       [Letter to editor in reply to 1935.B52.]

47   HUTCHISON, PERCY. "Robinson's Satire and Symbolism." The New
       York Times Book Review, November 10, p. 5.
           [Review of King Jasper.] This "modern satirical comedy
       of humours" is "blinding in intensity and fiercely illumi-
       nating."

48   _____. "The Poetry of E. A. Robinson." The New York Times
       Book Review, April 21, pp. 2, 11.
           [Assessment emphasizing the preeminence of the Arthurian
       poems in relation to the rest of Robinson's work, but also
       touching on his dramatic impulse, which is similar to
       Browning's, and his irony, which is reminiscent of Gals-
       worthy. Reprinted in 1935.A1.]

49   "JESSUP." "Sonnets (On the Death of Edwin Arlington Robinson)."
       Chicago Daily Tribune, April 13, p. 12.
           [Two laudatory sonnets.]

50   LARSSON, RAYMOND. Review of Amaranth. The Commonweal, 21
       (January 18), 349.
           This minor poem is a sort of "private grumbling" similar
       to Eliot's Waste Land. It is too obscure to be worthwhile.

51   LEDOUX, LOUIS V. "In Memoriam: Edwin Arlington Robinson."
       The Saturday Review of Literature, 11 (April 13), 621.
           "For though his work was to him the one thing for which
       he lived, he never lost his ability to enter into the lives
       of others,--and that, whatever he may have been as a poet,
       was a mark of greatness in the man." [Reprinted in 1935.A1
       and 1938.B17.]

52   _____. "Psychologist of New England." The Saturday Review of
       Literature, 12 (October 19), 3-4, 16, 18.
           Because Robinson was so wholeheartedly devoted to his
       work, to write about the man is to write about the poet.
       Ninety percent of his poetry is psychoanalytical; King Jas-
       per is an exception, a symbolic prophecy and dark vision.

53   L[ORD], A[LICE] F. "'King Jasper' is Last Poem From Hand of
       E. A. Robinson." Lewiston (Me.) Journal Magazine Section,
       November 9, p. 9.
           King Jasper is simpler in style than previous poems, but
       the strong symbolic content, such as the "hidden fingers"
       and the chimneys, make it subtle. The dream section is
       similar to Amaranth and "Sisera."

1935

54 LORD, ALICE FROST. "Barstow House in Gardiner Was Frequented
    by Robinson." Lewiston (Me.) Journal Magazine Section,
    March 16, p. A-8.
    [Feature story about house where three of Robinson's
    childhood friends lived.]

55 _____. "Gardiner School Authorities Sponsor Memorial to Poet,
    Robinson, Graduate of Gardiner High." Lewiston (Me.) Jour-
    nal Magazine Section, May 11, p. 9.
    Classmates and friends will gather for Robinson memorial
    on May 12, but only five of the twelve members of the class
    of 1888 are living.

56 _____. "Van Zorn: Proof That Robinson Could Write Good Com-
    edy." Lewiston (Me.) Journal Illustrated Magazine Section,
    April 13, p. A-9.
    Van Zorn should be revived not only because of its worth
    in its own right, but also because it makes an interesting
    comparison with Talifer and Amaranth.

57 MASON, MADELINE. "The Book of the Day." New York Sun, Decem-
    ber 26, p. 24.
    [Review of King Jasper, noting that it must be read on
    both the symbolic and actual levels and that it speaks of
    both the contemporary political situation and the timeless
    account of human progress.]

58 M[ONROE], H[ARRIET]. "Robinson as Man and Poet." Poetry, 46
    (June), 150-57.
    Although most of Robinson's poetry is about failures he
    invests them with dignity, and his life is a clear success.
    It is "impossible to grieve for him--the elegy should be a
    song of triumph." [Reprinted in 1969.A4.]

59 MORRISON, THEODORE. Review of Amaranth. Atlantic Monthly,
    155 (March), 10, 12.
    This unusual treatise on failed genius is a break from
    the kinds of poetry Robinson has done previously. He makes
    the subject "palatable by his irony, his quaint imagina-
    tion, and his acidulous humor."

*60 OSBORN, E. B. "America's Chief Poet." London Morning Post,
    April 8, p. 6.
    [Cited in White, p. 60.]

61 PARKER, GEORGE LAWRENCE. "Robinson Meets Nicodemus." The
    Christian Register, 113 (June 27), 425.

100

Matthias at the Door is a retelling "consciously or un-
consciously" of the third chapter of John. This interpretation was confirmed by a letter from Robinson.

62 RAMOS, JOSE ANTONIO. "E. A. Robinson," in Panorama de la
Literatura Norteamericana (1600-1935). Mexico: Ediciones
Botas, pp. 170, 173-75.
Although Robinson anticipated the next generation of
poets when he began to write, critics are now impatient for
his retreat, as is evidenced by their antagonism toward
Talifer.

63 RANCK, CARTY. "Last Work, and a Great One, From 'E.A.'" Bos-
ton Evening Transcript, November 27, Section III, p. 2.
[Review of King Jasper.] Jasper, the precious stone fan-
cied by high priests in Biblical times, is used to convey
Robinson's distaste for "the materiality the name connotes."
The poem has passionate moments similar to those in the
Arthurian trilogy, but the dream sequence is not matched in
any poem.

64 RICHARDS, LAURA E. "Recollections of 'E. A.' as a Boy in
Gardiner." New York Herald Tribune Books, May 12, pp. 10,
17.
[Reminiscence of Robinson's early years by neighbor and
early supporter. Expanded and reprinted in 1936.A5.]

65 RYAN, KATHRYN WHITE. "Tristram." Voices, No. 83 (Autumn),
pp. 32-36.
Robinson's deferential and shy manner even when he was
lionized at Peterborough summer after summer makes his description of Tristram an apt one for him: "A man stronger
than men stronger than he."

66 SABEN, MOWRY. "Edwin Arlington Robinson." The Argonaut, 113
(April 12), 4-5.
[Elegaic tribute, with a recounting of Robinson's career.]

67 SCHRIFTGIESSER, KARL. "Robinson the Poet." Washington Post,
April 14, Special Articles Section, p. 8.
[Personal reminiscence and assessment of poetry emphasizing Robinson's intellectual austerity and "weariness
which might pass for pessimism." Reprinted in 1935.A1.]

68 S[COTT], W[INFIELD] T. "Edwin Arlington Robinson." Providence (R.I.) Sunday Journal, April 14, Section VI, p. 4.
[Elegaic tribute by disciple who thinks Robinson should
be ranked at least with Emerson, Whitman, and Dickinson,
and probably above them. Reprinted in 1935.A1.]

1935

69   ____. "Robinson's Last Poem." Providence (R.I.) Sunday
        Journal, November 10, Section VI, p. 8.
            [Review of King Jasper.] After Tristram there was a
        "noticeable dimunition of power, but it has been reasserted
        in Amaranth and King Jasper, the most searing indictment of
        his own times that Robinson ever wrote."

70   SMITH, CHARD POWERS. "Final and Inclusive." The Saturday Re-
        view of Literature, 11 (April 20), 632.
            Robinson, like his character Flammonde, had uncanny per-
        ception and sympathy. His poetry, especially his long
        poems, suffered attacks from the "boy-critics" who can't
        understand it.

71   SUTCLIFF, DENHAM. "Edwin Arlington Robinson: A Product of
        Seventeenth Century Puritanism." Bates College (Lewiston,
        Maine) Garnet, May, pp. 29-32.
            Gardiner's unsympathetic attitude toward poetry and poets
        is partially responsible for Robinson's ironical outlook on
        life, but even after he left Maine permanently he "retained
        not only the New England conscience but the shyness his
        treatment there had fostered."

72   TOWNSEND, ANNE B. "Edwin Arlington Robinson's Poem, 'King
        Jasper.'" Philadelphia Inquirer, December 14, p. 7.
            This is one of Robinson's finest poems; it has "greater
        vitality, clarity, and narrative power" than Tristram.

73   UNTERMEYER, LOUIS. Review of Amaranth. The American Mercury,
        34 (April), 507-508.
            "Amaranth is the apotheosis--or the reductio ad absurdum--
        of his preoccupation with the social and artistic misfits."
        The poem lacks direction and is somewhat confusing, but "if
        it is dubious allegory, it is compelling nightmare."

74   VAN DOREN, CARL. What Is American Literature? New York: Wil-
        liam Morrow, pp. 106-10.
            [Brief, appreciative overview with emphasis on the Arthur-
        ian poems as vehicles for psychological insights and rep-
        resentative of a myth vital for Americans.]

75   [VAN DOREN, MARK.] "Edwin Arlington Robinson." The Nation,
        140 (April 17), 434.
            Robinson's is "the oldest and solidest name in American
        poetry," although it is impossible to assess his future
        standing at the time of his death. The long narratives
        may have "too much steel...and too little gold." The Ar-
        thurian poems, The Man Who Died Twice, Amaranth, and some
        three dozen shorter poems will probably endure.

102

76 VINSON, ESTHER. "Tilbury Town." The Saturday Review of Lit-
    erature, 11 (April 20), 632.
    [Personal reminiscence of trip to Gardiner to find the
    Robinson house.]

77 WALTON, EDA LOU. "E. A. Robinson's Last Poem." New York
    Herald Tribune Books, November 24, p. 4.
    [Review of King Jasper.] Although Robinson has been pre-
    occupied with death in most of his late poems, his last one
    is concerned with life in that it is a study of social
    problems. He attacked materialism and industrialism be-
    cause they were "for him the powers of darkness."

78 _____. "Robinson's Last Poem." The Nation, 141 (December 25),
    749-50.
    [Review of King Jasper.] This poem can be compared to
    Merlin in that both deal with the disintegration of soci-
    ety. It is one of his best poems because Robinson felt so
    strongly about the issues raised.

79 WEBER, CARL J. "E. A. Robinson and Hardy." The Nation, 140
    (May 1), 508.
    [Letter to the editor asking if anyone can shed light on
    "For a Book by Thomas Hardy," which is quoted here.]

80 _____. "Two Sonnets." The Saturday Review of Literature, 11
    (April 27), 648.
    [Letter to the editor asking about Hardy's influence on
    Robinson and quoting "For a Book by Thomas Hardy" and "A
    Christmas Sonnet: For One in Doubt."]

81 Z[ABEL], M[ORTON] D. "Robinson in America." Poetry, 46
    (June), 157-62.
    Robinson's work is marked by the influence of New England
    empiricism, which he deplored, and his inability to hold
    illusions. His art "derives from his sense of the plainest
    use of speech." [Reprinted in 1937.B18 and 1970.A3.]

1936 A BOOKS

1 [COLLAMORE, BACON and LAWRANCE THOMPSON, eds.]. Edwin Arlington Robinson: A Collection of His Works from the Library
   of Bacon Collamore. Hartford: Privately Printed, 66 pp.
   ["To the Reader" by editors explains origin of the collection. Informal discussions of the publishing history of
   individual volumes.]

1936

*2   GROHS, ELISABETH. "Edwin Arlington Robinsons Längere Verser-
      zählungen." Ph.D. thesis, University of Vienna.
      [Cited in White, p. 12.]

 3   [HAGEDORN, HERMANN]. The Edwin Arlington Robinson Memorial.
      Gardiner, Maine: Privately printed, pp. [11-26].
      [Memorial address on the occasion of the unveiling of a
      tablet honoring Robinson, emphasizing his solitary nature
      and firm philosophy.] "He shared the dismay of the wisest
      of his generation, but not the despair."

 4   HOGAN, CHARLES BEECHER. A Bibliography of Edwin Arlington
      Robinson. New Haven: Yale University Press, 221 pp.
      [The standard bibliography, enumerating works separately
      published, books, pamphlets, periodicals and newspapers
      originally publishing works by Robinson, biographical and
      critical material dealing with Robinson, uncollected works
      by Robinson, translations, and spurious first editions.
      Chronological checklist includes exact dates of publica-
      tions by Robinson. Updated by 1941.B2 and 1971.A2.]

 5   RICHARDS, LAURA E. E. A. R. Cambridge, Mass.: Harvard Uni-
      versity Press, 61 pp.
      [Personal reminiscence of Robinson's boyhood in Gardiner
      and his association with the Richards family. Includes
      anecdotes concerning his name, high school pranks, and
      juvenilia, and reports on the three visits he made to Gar-
      diner after he left in 1897. Expansion of 1935.B64; par-
      tially reprinted in 1936.B21 and 1936.B22. Reprinted in
      1967.A4.]

 6   SCOTT, WINFIELD TOWNLEY. Elegy for Robinson. New York: Bach-
      rach Press, 16 pp.
      [Privately printed commemorative poem in five parts.]

1936 B SHORTER WRITINGS

 1   ANON. "Edwin Arlington Robinson." The Library Journal, 61
      (February 15), 158.
      [Announcement of Gardiner Memorial.]

 2   ANON. "Prince of Heartachers." Times Literary Supplement,
      No. 1774 (February 1), p. 91.
      [Review of King Jasper, noting Robinson's mastery of style
      and his treatment of the poem "with clarity and...charac-
      teristic humour."]

3   ANON. "Robinson Memorial." Publisher's Weekly, 129 (Febru-
    ary 22), 895.
    [Announcement of memorial tablet to be placed in Robin-
    son's home in Gardiner and purchase of Robinson's birth-
    place in Head Tide by some of his family.]

4   ARVIN, NEWTON. "King Jasper." The New Republic, 85 (January
    8), 262.
    Although the poem is disappointing and not entirely clear,
    Jasper apparently represents corrupt capitalism, Hebron so-
    cial change, and Zoë individualism. The introduction by
    Frost is also disappointing.

5   AUSLANDER, JOSEPH. "King Jasper: A Posthumous Poem." The
    North American Review, 241 (June), 375-76.
    "We do not feel that King Jasper adds a cubit to Robin-
    son's stature as a philosopher or a poet," although it does
    not detract. The Frost introduction is excellent.

6   BEACH, JOSEPH WARREN. The Concept of Nature in Nineteenth-
    Century English Poetry. New York: Macmillan, pp. 538-39.
    The bulk of Robinson's poetry suggests that he felt that
    ethical values give significance to life.

7   BOIE, MILDRED. "King Jasper: A Poem." The New England Quar-
    terly, 9 (March), 154-56.
    Although the symbolic content is somewhat timeworn, the
    dramatic story of King Jasper is skilfull. Robinson would
    have appreciated Frost's introduction.

8   BOYNTON, PERCY H. Literature and American Life. Boston:
    Ginn, pp. 800-805.
    Robinson's latter day fame is answer to "Jeremiahs who
    insist that America is hostile to creative art." "Captain
    Craig" is central to Robinson's philosophy: his disparage-
    ment of material success is one of his most notable char-
    acteristics.

9   BROOKS, PHILIP. "Notes on Rare Books." The New York Times
    Book Review, March 29, p. 27.
    [Report on Collamore-Thompson collection of Robinsoniana
    exhibited at Wesleyan University, noting that the catalog
    is valuable for editorial comments and excerpts from Rob-
    inson's letters to Collamore.]

10 BROWN, DAVID. "Some Rejected Poems of Edwin Arlington Robin-
    son." American Literature, 7 (January), 395-414.
    Robinson excised fourteen poems from his first two vol-
    umes when he published Collected Poems. Some are

stylistically poor, some are blatantly didactic, and some subjects are famous men about whom Robinson apparently changed his opinion. To make these deletions is "evidence of Robinson's unusual gift for understanding the defects of his own work."

11   CLARK, HARRY HAYDEN. "Edwin Arlington Robinson," in Major American Poets. New York: American Book Company, pp. 938-47.
      [Background material on Robinson in this anthology includes chronology, annotated bibliography of fifty books, brief notes on twelve individual poems, a general overview and a discussion of Robinson's poetic theory.]

12   HENDERSON, L. J. "Edwin Arlington Robinson." Proceedings of the American Academy of Arts and Sciences, 70 (March), 570-73.
      [Obituary, quoting copiously from "The First Seven Years," noting that Robinson's literary origin is to be found in Gardiner, Maine.]

13   HUBBELL, JAY B. and JOHN O. BEATY. An Introduction to Poetry. New York: Macmillan, passim.
      [References to Robinson scattered throughout this text as an exemplar of good technique. Twenty references and fifteen poems quoted.]

14   LUHAN, MABEL DODGE. Movers and Shakers. New York: Harcourt, Brace, passim.
      [Personal reminiscence of friendship with Robinson around 1914. Six letters reprinted, with some references to Gertrude Stein and one of Robinson's poems.]

*15   McKENNA, GERTRUDE. "Lovers of Rare Books Worship at Wesleyan Literary Shrine: H. B. Collamore, Noted Hartford Collector, Exhibits Treasures." Hartford Courant, February 23, Section V, p. 1.
      [Listed in Hogan, p. 135.]

16   MASON, DANIEL GREGORY. "Edwin Arlington Robinson: A Group of Letters." The Yale Review, 25 (June), 860-64.
      [Five early letters to Mason discussing Thoreau, Emerson, Emily Brontë, Moody, and Theodore Roosevelt. Comments by the recipient.]

17   MATTHIESSEN, F. O. "Society and Solitude in Poetry." The Yale Review, 25 (March), 603-604.

[Review of King Jasper, observing that Robinson is ill-
equipped to handle social problems and that the allegory
is "at once bare and obscure."]

18 P[ARSONS], E. O. "Last Work of E. A. Robinson." Worcester
    (Mass.) Sunday Telegram, January 5, Section IV, p. 8.
    [Review of King Jasper, noting the social commentary and
    the importance of the variety of characterizations.]

19 PHELPS, WILLIAM LYON. "Tribute to Robinson." New York Herald
    Tribune, November 13, pp. 14, 15.
    [Account of Phelps' association with Robinson, including
    two letters from Robinson and admission by Phelps of errors
    in judgment he made about Robinson's work. Reprinted in
    1939.B5 and 1939.B6.]

20 RANSOM, JOHN CROWE. "Autumn of Poetry." The Southern Review,
    1 (Winter), 612-14.
    [Review of King Jasper, noting that because of the
    "autumn-grey" tone and vagueness of the poem, only "an
    esoteric Robinsonian" can appreciate it. Suggests that a
    young poet couldn't get away with it, and that the intro-
    duction by Frost is superior to the poem.]

21 RICHARDS, LAURA E. "A Book and its Author." Yankee, 2 (June),
    26-29.
    [Reminiscence adapted from 1936.A5.]

22 ____. "Edwin Arlington Robinson." The Horn Book Magazine,
    12 (January-February), 52-53.
    [Biography for children adapted from 1936.A5.]

23 ROBBINS, HOWARD CHANDLER. "The Classicism of Edwin Arlington
    Robinson." The Congregational Quarterly, 14 (April), 166-
    71.
    Robinson's poetry is classic in four ways: the timeless-
    ness of its content, the symmetry of its form, the author's
    spiritual detachment, and his stoic acceptance of mortality.

*24 ROTH, GEORGES. "Edwin Arlington Robinson." Larousse Mensuel
    Illustré, 10 (February), 339-40.
    [Listed in White, p. 61.]

25 RYAN, KATHRYN WHITE. "The King is Dead." Voices, No. 85
    (Spring), pp. 54-57.
    [Review of King Jasper, suggesting that the poem is
    really about the burden of Robinson's success as a poet
    and his lack of success with women.]

1936

26 [SABEN, MOWRY.] "Robinson's Posthumous Poem." The Argonaut,
    114 (January 10), 4.
        [Review of King Jasper.] This poem is not the best Rob-
    inson, but it is respectable. It was probably influenced
    by John Strachey's The Coming Struggle for Power, an Eng-
    lish communist's book that Robinson reported he had read.

27 TATE, ALLEN. "Edwin Arlington Robinson," in Reactionary Es-
    says on Poetry and Ideas. New York: Charles Scribner's
    Sons, pp. 193-201.

28 TAYLOR, WALTER FULLER. A History of American Letters. New
    York: American Book Company, pp. 339-47.
        [Regarding Robinson as the principal modern American
    poet, Taylor divides the poems into three groups; the char-
    acter studies, the Arthurian material, and the psychologi-
    cal tales. Robinson's intellectuality and suggestiveness
    are emphasized, but the idea that he is a "futilitarian"
    is discounted.]

29 TODRIN, BORIS. "Edwin Arlington Robinson." The Book Collec-
    tor's Journal, 1 (July), 1, 14.
        [Obituary, noting especially Robinson's unusual depth
    and scope and singling out "Ben Jonson" as especially
    worthwhile.]

30 TURNER, C. J. M. "The Sonnets of Edwin Arlington Robinson."
    The Poetry Review, 27 (March-April), 121-27.
        [Review of Sonnets 1889-1927.] Although Robinson's son-
    nets do not compare with those of Rosetti and Browning be-
    cause the sound is not sufficiently musical; they are nev-
    ertheless the best sonnets written in America during that
    period.

31 UNTERMEYER, LOUIS. Modern American Poetry: A Critical An-
    thology. New York: Harcourt, Brace, pp. 139-43.
        [Sketch of career and assessment, emphasizing Robinson's
    ability at delineating characters and his precision; also
    mention of his declining powers since 1928.]

32 VAN DOREN, CARL. "Post-War: The Literary Twenties." Harper's
    Magazine, 173 (July), 154-56.
        [Reprinted in 1936.B33]

33 _____. Three Worlds. New York: Harper and Brothers,
    pp. 159-66, 198, 202-207.
        [Personal reminiscence about Robinson's association of
    Van Doren as editor of The Nation and as the member of the

Literary Guild advisory board who suggested Tristram should
be a club selection.]

34   WEBER, CARL J. "The Cottage Lights of Wessex." The Colby
      Mercury, 6 (February), 64-67.
         Robinson may have excluded "For a Book by Thomas Hardy"
      from Collected Poems because it was too personal. He re-
      portedly said that Hardy was the greatest poet of his gen-
      eration. The copy of The Torrent and the Night Before that
      Robinson sent Hardy was never acknowledged, but marginal
      comments were made by Hardy.

1937 A BOOKS

1   LIPPINCOTT, LILLIAN. A Bibliography of the Writings and Crit-
     icisms of Edwin Arlington Robinson. Boston: F. W. Faxon,
     86 pp.
        [Bibliography of books by Robinson, places of publication
     of individual poems, books and parts of books about Robin-
     son, periodical criticism, biographical articles, places of
     photograph publication, and bibliographical sources.]

1937 B SHORTER WRITINGS

1   ABERCROMBIE, LASCELLES. "King Jasper." Modern Language
     Notes, 52 (March), 218-20.
        King Jasper is a bold but unsuccessful experiment. Too
     much is left out of the story for it to be comprehensible,
     but Robinson's poetic ability is evident.

2   BENÉT, WILLIAM ROSE. "The Phoenix Nest." The Saturday Review
     of Literature, 16 (May 22), 19.
        [Letter from Howard G. Schmitt regarding a textual change
     in Amaranth.]

3   BOYNTON, PERCY H. "The Complete Robinson." The New Republic,
     91 (July 21), 314-15.
        [Review of Collected Poems, noting that Robinson has been
     important since the 1915 re-issue of Captain Craig and that
     Tristram and Talifer, though most admired, are least typi-
     cal.] He possessed "dexterity of thought and dexterity of
     of phrase."

4   BROWN, DAVID. "E. A. Robinson's Later Poems." The New Eng-
     land Quarterly, 10 (September), 487-502.
        The poems after Tristram deserve more attention, since
     "they achieve in varying degree the final aim of Robinson's

maturest purposes in thought and art." Cavender's House
is the first poem which fuses the presentation of vital
action and Robinson's own voice. Amaranth is the worst of
the late poems. [Reprinted in 1969.A4.]

5 _____. "A Note on 'Avon's Harvest.'" American Literature, 11
(November), 343-49.
This poem was revised when it was included in Collected
Poems because the reviewers had misinterpreted it. He re-
moved most of the references to the dagger, thus legitimiz-
ing the reviewers' interpretation of the poem.

6 BUCHAN, ALEXANDER M. "The First Citizen of Tilbury Town."
St. Louis Post-Dispatch, April 25, Section H, p. 4.
[Review of Collected Poems.] Robinson's poems are as
sorrowful and strange as the man, but, like Hawthorne, he
made gloomy places less terrible.

7 FLETCHER, JOHN GOULD. "Portrait of Edwin Arlington Robinson."
The North American Review, 244 (Autumn), 24-26.
[Sixty-five line commemorative poem.]

8 F[OSTER], I[SABEL]. "Robinson, Poet of America." Christian
Science Monitor Weekly Magazine, May 26, p. 10.
[Review of Collected Poems, noting that Robinson was not
a regionalist like Frost and Lowell but a reflector of
ideas whose influences are most notably William and Henry
James, Josiah Royce, Tennyson, and Browning.]

9 GREGORY, HORACE. "Poetry in 1937." New Masses Literary Supplement, 25 (December 7), 12.
Robinson was the most important poet of the first decade
of the century. He "foresaw disaster where others read
perpetual American success," and made vibrant his conven-
tional verse technique.

10 LOGGINS, VERNON. I Hear America.... New York: Thomas Y.
Crowell, pp. 51-60.
Robinson's subject is "rich for the critic but meagre for
the biographer" since he considered insignificant anything
not directly related to poetry. Obviously influenced by
Browning, he nevertheless writes with a philosophy of de-
spair. However, the bulk of his writing is portraiture,
"forming a verse comedie humaine wider in range than...any
other poet except Shakespeare."

11 MASON, DANIEL GREGORY. "Early Letters of Edwin Arlington Robinson: First Series." The Virginia Quarterly Review, 13
(Winter), 52-69.

[Report of friendship between the two men and letters from Robinson from July, 1899 to September, 1900. Partially reprinted in 1938.B20.]

12   _____. "Edwin Arlington Robinson to Daniel Gregory Mason: Second Series." The Virginia Quarterly Review, 13 (Spring), 223-40.
        [Letters from Robinson to Mason from September, 1900 to May 14, 1934. Early letters contain several critical statements about poetry. Partially reprinted in 1938.B20.]

13   MERTON, JOHN KENNETH. "A World His Own." The Commonweal, 26 (May 14), 79-80.
        [Review of Collected Poems.] "In the whole huge volume, there is not a single poem that is not distinguished. It stands as the most impressive poetic achievement in America."

14   PELTIER, FLORENCE. "Edwin Arlington Robinson, Himself." The Mark Twain Quarterly, 1 (Summer), 6, 11-14.
        [Personal reminiscence of author's acquaintance with Robinson from 1902 until his death.]

15   SCOTT, WINFIELD TOWNLEY. "The Unaccredited Profession." Poetry, 50 (June), 150-54.
        Despite the biographies now appearing, Robinson can best be found in his 45,000 lines of poetry. While there may be repetition and verbosity there, one also finds "a depth of understanding and an altitude of passion unmatched either in their quality or their frequency by any other American poet."

16   SMITH, RUSSELL. "E. A. Robinson." The Washington Post, May 2, Section III, p. 7.
        [Review of Collected Poems.] Robinson's work is not obscure but his spirit is elusive. His two chief qualities are symmetry and sophistication.

17   WOODALL, ALLEN E. "Edwin Arlington Robinson." Poet Lore, 43, No. 4, 363.
        [Elegaic sonnet to Robinson with allusions to his poetry.]

18   ZABEL, MORTON DAUWEN. "Robinson," in Literary Opinion in America. New York: Harper & Brothers, pp. 397-406.
        [Reprint of 1935.B81; reprinted in 1970.A3.]

19   _____. "Robinson: the Ironic Discipline." The Nation, 145 (August 28), 222-23.

1938

[Essay-review of <u>Collected Poems</u>.] Robinson made no con-
cession to current taste although he wrote about contemporary problems. His significance stylistically was "to cor-
rect the excesses of symbolism and romantic allegory."

1938 A BOOKS

1   HAGEDORN, HERMANN. <u>Edwin Arlington Robinson</u>. New York: Mac-
     millan, 402 pp.
     [The authorized and sympathetic biography, based on in-
     terviews with associates, letters, and personal recollec-
     tions of a twenty-five year friendship. Particular atten-
     tion to his early life in Gardiner, the years at Harvard,
     the circumstances surrounding the publication and reception
     of <u>Captain Craig</u>, and the first summer at Peterborough.
     Three-quarters of the book devoted to the years before 1916.
     Detailed index and appendix noting sources, but no formal
     documentation.]

1938 B SHORTER WRITINGS

1   BENÉT, WILLIAM ROSE. "Perfect Artistic Integrity." <u>The Mark</u>
     <u>Twain Quarterly</u>, 2 (Spring), 10.
        Robinson "was one of the sanest people who ever walked
     among us."

2   BROSNAN, THOMAS J. "Edwin Arlington Robinson." <u>Connecticut</u>
     <u>Teacher</u>, 5 (June), 3-4, 6.
        Robinson's skill with traditional forms, his gift of
     portraiture, and his psychological insights will assure
     him permanence. His one flaw is his lack of exuberance.

3   BROWN, ROLLO WALTER. "A Letter from Rollo Walter Brown."
     <u>The Mark Twain Quarterly</u>, 2 (Spring), 14, 24.
        [Personal reminiscence, noting Robinson's love of the
     romantic and spectacular and his sympathetic personality.]

4   BURTON, RICHARD. "Robinson As I Saw Him." <u>The Mark Twain</u>
     <u>Quarterly</u>, 2 (Spring), 9.
        [Personal reminiscence, noting Robinson's taciturnity.]

5   CARPENTER, FREDERIC IVES. "Tristram the Transcendent." <u>The</u>
     <u>New England Quarterly</u>, 11 (September), 501-23.
        [An examination of the place of <u>Tristram</u> in relation to
     Robinson's other work and to Emersonian idealism, conclud-
     ing that in this poem he realized the positive aspects of
     transcendentalism. Reprinted in 1969.A4.]

112

6   CESTRE, CHARLES. "Edwin Arlington Robinson...Maker of Myths." The Mark Twain Quarterly, 2 (Spring), 3-8, 24.
    Robinson was preoccupied with moral questions, investing his late poems with contemporary characters large enough to be regarded as mythological. [Readings of Cavender's House, The Man Who Died Twice, and King Jasper.]

7   CLEMENS, CYRIL. "E. A. Robinson: 1869-1935." The Mark Twain Quarterly, 2 (Spring), 1-2.
    [Biographical sketch about man to whom the entire issue is devoted, noting that Robinson was poetry chairman of the Mark Twain Society and posthumous recipient of the Mark Twain Medal.]

8   ____. "Robinson Collection at Gardiner, Maine." The Mark Twain Quarterly, 2 (Spring), 18.
    Robinson began the collection in the Gardiner library when he sent seven autographed copies there in 1930.

9   COFFIN, ROBERT PETER TRISTRAM. New Poetry of New England. Baltimore: Johns Hopkins Press, passim.
    [Comparison of Robinson and Frost in attitudes, techniques, and subject matter, suggesting that Robinson writes about "Big-House New Englanders"--those who once had wealth and power but became materially and spiritually bankrupt. Analysis of Amaranth. Reprinted in 1964.B2.]

10 COPELAND, C[HARLES] T. [An Appreciation]. The Mark Twain Quarterly, 2 (Spring), 16.
    Robinson had planned to visit Copeland on the night he went to the hospital for the last time.

11 DANIELS, MABEL. "Robinson's Interest in Music." The Mark Twain Quarterly, 2 (Spring), 15, 24.
    [Reprint of 1935.B37 and 1935.A1.]

12 DUBOIS, ARTHUR E. "The Cosmic Humorist." The Mark Twain Quarterly, 2 (Spring), 11-13, 24.
    Robinson was "a kind of cosmic coroner inquesting life." He shared similarities with Amy Lowell, Browning, and especially Hawthorne.

13 GUITERMAN, ARTHUR. "Epitaph on a Poet." The Mark Twain Quarterly, 2 (Spring), 12.
    [Quatrain to Robinson.]

14 HAGEDORN, HERMANN. "From the Official Biographer." The Mark Twain Quarterly, 2 (Spring), 16.

1938

[Author notes that he knows him better after working on the biography than he did when Robinson was alive.]

15 HOGAN, CHARLES BEECHER. "A Poet at the Phonic Shrine." The Colophon, N.S. 3 (Summer), 359-63.
[Discussion of "Isaac Pitman," Robinson's second poem, published in 1890 in The Phonographic World.]

16 LATHAM, G. W. "Robinson at Harvard." The Mark Twain Quarterly, 2 (Spring), 19-20.
At Harvard Robinson did not like Old English but did well in French and German. He admired Shakespeare most, but had also discovered Crabbe, Arnold, Thackery, and Hardy. His customary wedding gift was a leatherbound set of Austen.

17 LEDOUX, LOUIS V. "In Memoriam: Written in 1935." The Mark Twain Quarterly, 2 (Spring), 10.
[Reprint of 1935.B51.]

18 MacDOWELL, MRS. EDWARD. "Robinson at the MacDowell Colony." The Mark Twain Quarterly, 2 (Spring), 16.
Robinson was so reluctant to visit Peterborough the first year that he brought a false telegram with him in case he wanted to leave quickly, but liked it so much he stayed twenty-four years.

19 MARKHAM, EDWIN. "Dean of American Poets Pays Tribute." The Mark Twain Quarterly, 2 (Spring), 17.
Robinson is irreplaceable. [Quotes humorous quatrain Robinson wrote for Markham's birthday.]

20 MASON, DANIEL GREGORY. Music in My Time. New York: Macmillan, pp. 82-89, 116-18, 121-40.
[Personal reminiscence of friendship with Robinson between 1899 and 1907, including several letters and comments about Robinson's poems, especially Captain Craig and "Aunt Imogen." Reprint of 1937.B11 and 1937.B12.]

21 MAYNARD, THEODORE. The World I Saw. Milwaukee: Bruce Publishing Company, 232-38.
[Personal reminiscence, noting that Robinson was "a saint to literature" because he gave up marriage and money for his vocation and asserting that Robinson was basically religious if not entirely orthodox.]

22 MORLEY, CHRISTOPHER. [An Appreciation.] The Mark Twain Quarterly, 2 (Spring), 20.

[Morley declined opportunity to meet Robinson because he
had such respect for him as an artist that he did not want
to "add to his general human overhead."]

23 NEIHARDT, JOHN G. [An Appreciation.] The Mark Twain Quarter-
    ly, 2 (Spring), 10.
    [Report of Neihardt's meeting Robinson through Ledoux in
    1907.]

24 POWER, SISTER MARY JAMES. "Edwin Arlington Robinson: The
    First of the Seekers," in Poets at Prayer. New York:
    Sheed & Ward, pp. 71-82.
    Robinson was not a church member, but he had his own re-
    ligion; he was neither agnostic nor fatalistic, but searched
    for truth. [Special attention to Matthias at the Door, The
    Glory of the Nightingales, and Cavender's House.]

25 POWYS, JOHN COWPER. "The Big Bed." The Mark Twain Quarterly,
    2 (Spring), 2.
    [Reminiscence of meeting of the men, noting that Robin-
    son's bed filled the space in his rented room.]

26 STOVALL, FLOYD. "The Optimism Behind Robinson's Tragedies."
    American Literature, 10 (March), 1-23.
    Robinson's poetry is basically optimistic, as his more
    thoughtful critics have insisted. His dominant theme is
    "the growth of the human mind in its pursuit of truth
    through time and change." This theme can be seen in his
    poems about individuals, group relationships, and civili-
    zations. Matthias at the Door is the tragedy that is most
    persuasively optimistic. [Reprinted in 1969.A4.]

27 TORRENCE, OLIVIA H. D. "The Poet at the Dinner Table." The
    Colophon, N.S. 3 (Winter), 93-99.
    [Robinson's previously unpublished essay, "For Harriet
    Moody's Cookbook," included in an article about his eating
    habits.]

28 ULRICH, DOROTHY. "Edwin Arlington Robinson." Avocations, 2
    (June), 248-53.
    [Biographical sketch and overview of career. Reprinted
    in 1940.A4.]

29 VAN DOREN, MARK. "The Last Look." The Mark Twain Quarterly,
    2 (Spring), 21.
    [Twenty-eight line poem concerning Robinson's dying.]

1938

30   [WEBER, CARL J.] "Library Notes for E. A. R.'s Birthday."
     The Colby Mercury, 6 (November), 205-13.
         [Discussion and reprinting of letters from Robinson to
     Weber and Paul Lamperly regarding information about Robin-
     son editions.]

31   WEBER, CARL J. "The Sound of Cornish Waves Cold Upon Cornish
     Rocks." The Colby Mercury, 6 (November), 215-16.
         [Conjecture that Tristram was influenced by Robinson's
     visit to Hardy in 1923, a few months before Hardy's The
     Famous Tragedy of the Queen of Cornwell was published.]

32   WHEELOCK, JOHN HALL. "A Friend of Young Poets." The Mark
     Twain Quarterly, 2 (Spring), 20.
         [Personal reminiscence, indicating that Robinson was kind
     to young poets.]

1939 A BOOKS

 1   BARSTOW, JAMES S. My Tilbury Town. New York: Privately
     printed, 11 pp.
         [Reminiscence about growing up with Robinson in Gardiner.]

 2   HALL, JAMES NORMAN. The Friends. Muscatine, Iowa: Prairie
     Press, 34 pp.
         [Appreciation and assessment of Robinson's poetry in
     blank verse form.]

1939 B SHORTER WRITINGS

 1   CARLSON, C. LENNART. "Robinsoniana." The Colby Mercury, 6
     (December), 281-84.
         [Description and publication of seven early letters to
     men important to Robinson.]

 2   HERRON, IMA HONAKER. "E. A. Robinson," in The Small Town in
     American Literature. Durham, North Carolina: Duke Uni-
     versity Press, pp. 130-36.
         Robinson's critical attitude toward small towns is ap-
     parent in his realistic portrayal of character that anti-
     cipated Masters by seventeen years.

 3   MALONE, TED. A Listener's Aid to Pilgrimages of Poetry: Ted
     Malone's Album of Poetic Shrines. New York: Columbia
     University Press, n.p.
         [One-page discussion of Robinson's connection with house
     in Gardiner, with photograph.]

4   PAYNE, LEONIDAS WARREN, JR. "The First Edition of E. A. Rob-
     inson's The Peterborough Idea." The University of Texas
     Studies in English (July 8), pp. 219-31.
        [Collation of pamphlet and article in North American Re-
     view.]

5   PHELPS, WILLIAM LYON. Autobiography with Letters. New York:
     Oxford University Press.
        [Reprint of 1936.B19 and 1939.B6.]

6   _____. "Edwin Arlington Robinson," in Commemorative Tributes,
     The American Academy of Arts and Letters. New York: Acad-
     emy Publication No. 95, pp. 9-19.
        [Reprint of 1936.B19 and 1939.B5.]

7   SWIFT, BRUCE. "A Biographer of Souls." The Christian Leader,
     121 (December 16), 1194-95.
        Robinson's world view kept an even tenor. "There is a
     certain religious quality about his skepticism that reveals
     his mysticism."

8   UNCLE DUDLEY [pseud]. "The Poet in a Small Town." Boston Sun-
     day Globe, June 11, p. 4.
        Robinson's early life was difficult. "We charge our
     creators too dearly for the privilege of ennobling our ex-
     istence."

9   UNTERMEYER, LOUIS. From Another World. New York: Harcourt,
     Brace, pp. 222-27.
        [Personal reminiscence, noting that Frost admired Robin-
     son and including several anecdotes dealing with Robinson's
     wit.]

10   VAN DOREN, CARL and MARK VAN DOREN. American and British Lit-
     erature Since 1890. Revised edition. New York: Century,
     pp. 13-19.
        [Revision of 1925.B32.] Tristram received the greatest
     reception. The six poems which followed did not add mate-
     rially to his reputation, but Robinson "had done too much
     in his best poems for his next best to count against him."

1940 A BOOKS

1   KAPLAN, ESTELLE. Philosophy in the Poetry of Edwin Arlington
     Robinson. New York: Columbia University Press, 162 pp.
        Emersonian idealism, modified by Royce's interpretation
     of Schopenhauer, provides the basis for Robinson's thought.

1940

His four major themes, self-knowledge, love, marriage, and
social issues, reflect the stages of his intellectual growth.
[Analysis of "Captain Craig," "The Man Against the Sky,"
The Man Who Died Twice, Amaranth, Merlin, Cavender's House,
The Glory of the Nightingales, Matthias at the Door, "Diony-
sus in Doubt," and King Jasper.]

2   TORRENCE, RIDGELY. "Introduction" and "Notes," in Selected
     Letters of Edwin Arlington Robinson. New York: Macmillan,
     pp. vii-x, 181-91.
         This selection, chosen in collaboration with Hagedorn,
     Isaacs, and Ledoux, is intended to present Robinson the man;
     emphasis has been on his early letters since they are the
     less reserved. [Brief explanatory notes only documentary
     aid.]

3   TRYON, JAMES L. Harvard Days with Edwin Arlington Robinson.
     Waterville, Maine: Privately printed, 16 pp.
         [Address at Colby describing Robinson's professors and
     friends at Harvard and comments on his important courses
     and books.]

4   ULRICH, DOROTHY LIVINGSTON. Edwin Arlington Robinson. Hart-
     ford: Privately printed, 7 pp.
         [Reprint of 1938.B28.]

1940 B SHORTER WRITINGS

1   ANON. "Faith of E. A. Robinson." Times Literary Supplement,
     No. 2012 (August 24), p. 412.
         Selected Letters shows man of great reserve, but it is
     self-revealing in Robinson's firm faith in his vocation.

2   BROOKS, VAN WYCK. New England: Indian Summer 1865-1915.
     New York: E. P. Dutton, pp. 491-500.
         Robinson writes from the Yankee tradition inherited from
     Emerson, Dickinson, and Hawthorne and was the precurser of
     the American renaissance in poetry. He was "a wintry man."
     [Reprinted in 1949.B3.]

3   BUCKALEW, ANNE. "E. A. Robinson." Dallas Daily Times Herald,
     March 3, Section III, p. 16.
         [Review of Selected Letters.] "The entire group of let-
     ters indicates a life-long determination to succeed in the
     one thing that mattered to him."

*4   CAREW, HAROLD D. "A Poet to His Friends." Pasadena (Cal.)
     Star-News, March 16, Section II, p. 24.
       [Cited in White, p. 96, as a review of Selected Letters.]

5   CATHERINE, SISTER MARY. "The Psychology of Robinson." The
     Catholic Educational Review, 38 (June), 354-60.
       Since Robinson deals with character development his work
     is worth study in religion or English classes. "One never
     finds in his work revolting passages or language better
     left unsaid."

6   COUSINS, NATALIE A. "Gardiner's Poet." The Colby Mercury, 6
     (February), 285-88.
       [Biographical sketch.] "Robinson alive was hardly noticed
     but when he died he was eulogized on practically every edi-
     torial page in the country."

7   DUPEE, F[REDERICK] W. "The 'Long Animal.'" The Nation, 150
     (March 30), 427-28.
       [Review of Selected Letters, noting that it is as modest
     as the man himself.]

8   FICKE, ARTHUR DAVISON. "Cool Intelligent Astringence." New
     York Herald Tribune Books, February 25, p. 6.
       [Review of Selected Letters, observing that while Robin-
     son was modest about his own achievements, he had no hesi-
     tations about the importance of poetry.]

9   FINCH, JOHN. "Selected Letters of Edwin Arlington Robinson."
     The New England Quarterly, 13 (December), 733-35.
       Selected Letters is valuable not for Robinson's poetic
     theory but because of the portrait of the man.

10   GRISCOM, ISOBEL. "Moon's Other Side." Chattanooga Daily
     Times Magazine Section, April 7, p. 5.
       [Review of Selected Letters, noting that it reveals lit-
     tle about Robinson but is important in comments about con-
     temporary writers.]

11   HILL, ARCHIBALD A. "New Light on Some Literary Lives." The
     Virginia Quarterly Review, 16 (Summer), 450-55.
       [Review of Selected Letters, "a slight book of quiet and
     mildly acid charm."]

12   HUTCHISON, PERCY. "Edwin Arlington Robinson as Seen in His
     Letters." The New York Times Book Review, February 25,
     p. 5.
       [Review of Selected Letters, commenting particularly on
     the portrait of Robinson it provides.]

1940

13 JENCKES, EDWARD N. "A Poet's Letters." Springfield (Mass.)
    Daily Republican, February 24, p. 6.
        [Review of Selected Letters.] This book is important be-
    cause it reveals Robinson's personality and his literary
    tastes.

14 KUNITZ, STANLEY J. and HOWARD HAYCRAFT, eds. Twentieth Cen-
    tury Authors: A Biographical Dictionary of Modern Litera-
    ture. New York: H. W. Wilson, p. 1185.
        [Sketch emphasizing critical attitude toward Robinson
    during the last ten years of his life and citing brief
    critical assessments of his work.]

15 LORD, ALICE FROST. "Barstow House in Gardiner Was Frequented
    by Robinson." Lewiston (Me.) Journal Illustrated Magazine
    Section, March 16, p. A-8.
        [Article about the four Barstow brothers who were friends
    of Robinson.]

16 _____. "Colby College Acquires New Literary Distinction
    Through H. Bacon Collamore's Gift of Robinsoniana." Lewis-
    ton (Me.) Journal Illustrated Magazine Section, November
    16, p. A-8.
        [Description of Collamore collection, with explanation of
    why Colby is the recipient.]

17 _____. "Gardiner Associations of Poet Recalled by Present
    Resident." Lewiston (Me.) Journal Illustrated Magazine
    Section, March 30, p. 8.
        Robinson gave L. M. Barnard, a childhood friend, an in-
    scribed copy of The Torrent and the Night Before: "a book
    of untried stuff, more or less poetical.... I'm sick of
    the sight of [it]."

18 _____. "Gardiner Woman Cherishes Letters From Poet, Robin-
    son." Lewiston (Me.) Journal Illustrated Magazine Section,
    April 13, p. 8.
        [Thirteen letters written between 1927 and 1935 to Augus-
    tus and Alice Jordan, childhood friends, are printed.]

19 _____. "Glimpse of Robinson House Interior at Gardiner."
    Lewiston (Me.) Journal Illustrated Magazine Section, April
    20, p. A-8.
        [Photographs and description of Lincoln Street House in
    Gardiner.]

20 M[AYNARD], T[HEODORE]. "Selected Letters." The Catholic
    World, 151 (May), 248-49.
        Selected Letters gives important comments on other writers.

21   MILLETT, FRED B. _Contemporary American Authors_. New York:
      Harcourt, Brace, pp. 131-32, 548-54.
      [Brief biographical sketch and extensive bibliography.]

22   ORIANS, G. HARRISON. "The World War Decade," in _A Short His-
      tory of American Literature Analyzed by Decades_. New York:
      F. S. Crofts, pp. 292-93.
      [Brief overview emphasizing Robinson's traditional tech-
      niques and noting that he anticipated the dominant theme
      of the twenties in his character analysis of failures.]

23   PULSIFER, HAROLD R. "Books and Book Folks." _Portland_ (Me.)
      Press-Herald, March 23, p. 5.
      [Review of _Selected Letters_, noting that it is a good
      supplement to the Hagedorn biography.]

24   RITCHEY, JOHN. "'Dear Friends, Reproach Me Not....'" _Chris-
      tian Science Monitor Weekly Magazine Section_, March 30,
      p. 11.
      [Review of _Selected Letters_.] "He was not a great letter
      writer, and this book serves merely as a confirmation of
      his poems."

25   ROOT, E. MERRILL. "Foiled Circuitous Wanderer." _The Chris-
      tian Century_, 57 (March 6), 316.
      Selected Letters "underlines the fact that Robinson was
      a talented mediocrity."

26   SABEN, MOWRY. "Edwin Arlington Robinson." _The Argonaut_, 119
      (March 29), 21-22.
      [Review of _Selected Letters_ by friend of forty years,
      who notes that the letters reveal Robinson's characteristic
      humor.]

27   S[COTT], W[INFIELD] T. "Robinson." _Providence_ (R.I.) _Sunday
      Journal_, February 25, Section VI, p. 6.
      [Review of _Selected Letters_, suggesting that even com-
      plete letters will be of secondary importance.]

28   UNTERMEYER, LOUIS. "Fitful Glimpses." _The Saturday Review of
      Literature_, 21 (March 2), 7.
      [Review of _Selected Letters_.] "Most of Robinson's let-
      ters, like most of his conversations, were dull," but the
      book is valuable for the record of his friendship and his
      literary opinions.

29   WAGGONER, HYATT HOWE. "E. A. Robinson and the Cosmic Chill."
      The New England Quarterly, 13 (March), 65-84.

1940

> Robinson's most persistent theme is the problem of man's place in the universe. He rejected determinism, naturalism, and pessimism, finally returning to transcendentalism. "He lost his religion but he kept his faith." [Reprinted, revised in 1950.B8 and 1969.A4.]

30 W[EAVER], J[OHN] D. "Robinson's Letters to His Friends." _Kansas City_ (Mo.) _Star_, February 24, p. 5.
   Selected Letters does not illuminate "the darker mysteries of Robinson's character."

31 WEBER, CARL J. "A Maine Poet in a Maine College." _The Colby Alumnus_, 30 (November), 10-12.
   Bacon Collamore has given a large gift of Robinson materials to Colby College, which will "make Colby the headquarters of all future Robinson studies."

32 WELLS, HENRY W. _New Poets From Old_. New York: Columbia University Press, pp. 90-97, 316-20, and passim.
   Robinson is a follower of Browning in the tradition of the analytic style. He is most indebted to nineteenth century romanticism, but he managed to avoid its excesses through his rationalistic approach.

33 WILDER, AMOS N. _The Spiritual Aspects of the New Poetry_. New York: Harpers, pp. 174-75, 198-200.
   [Brief commentary on _Amaranth_.]

1941 A BOOKS - NONE

1941 B SHORTER WRITINGS

1 ANON. "Poetry Album: Edwin Arlington Robinson." _Scholastic_, 39 (October 13), 22.
   [Overview of career, emphasizing his skill at writing character sketches.]

2 HOGAN, CHARLES BEECHER. "Edwin Arlington Robinson: New Bibliographical Notes." _Papers on the Bibliographical Society of America_, 35 (Second Quarter), 115-44.
   [Updating of Hogan's _Bibliography_ (1936.A4), included in White's _Bibliography_ (1971.A2).]

3 KNICKERBOCKER, FRANCES WENTWORTH. "Faith in the Pieces." _The Sewanee Review_, 49 (January-March), 125-26.
   [Review of _Selected Letters_, noting that the volume reveals Robinson's integrity and devotion to his art.]

4   LORD, ALICE FROST. "Winthrop Once Harbored Gardiner's Poet, Robinson." Lewiston (Me.) Journal Illustrated Magazine Section, January 4, p. A-8.
       [Article about Robinson's 1898 visit with Arthur Blair in Winthrop, where he completed "Captain Craig."]

5   RITTENHOUSE, JESSIE B. "Edwin Arlington Robinson." Rollins College Bulletin, 36 (June), 5-10.
       [Reminiscence, including comments about Robinson's deafness, his inability to portray women, and his refusal to join the Poetry Society of America.]

6   RUSH, N. ORWIN. "Our Latest Robinson Accession." The Colby Mercury, 7 (January), 14-15.
       [Notice of acquisition of journal which first printed "For a Book by Thomas Hardy."]

7   SABEN, MOWRY. "Memories of Edwin Arlington Robinson." The Colby Mercury, 7 (January), 13-14.
       [Reminiscence by Harvard classmate, commenting on his lack of philosophic ability, his vacillating opinions about writers, and his capacity for self-deception.]

8   VAN NORMAN, C. ELTA. "Captain Craig." College English, 2 (February), 462-75.
       [Analysis of "Captain Craig" through a review of criticism, brief examination of structure, and lengthy interpretation of theme in light of Robinson's philosophic stance.]

9   WEBER, CARL J. "Three Newly Found Articles by Edwin Arlington Robinson." The Colby Mercury, 7 (December), 69-72.
       [Reprinting of three prose pieces attributed to Robinson. (Attribution refuted in 1942.B14).]

10 WILSON, JAMES SOUTHALL. "Selected Letters of Edwin Arlington Robinson." American Literature, 12 (January), 512-14.
       Selected Letters is of literary interest in that it reveals a personality, but it is not a scholarly piece of editing.

1942 A BOOKS - NONE

1942 B SHORTER WRITINGS

1   BATES, JAMES M. L. "Robinson's Letters to George Burnham." The Colby Mercury, 7 (May), 93-94.

1942

[Bates, in making a typescript of a group of Robinson
letters, learned a few things about the man but little
about his work.]

2   BATES, R. C. "The Robinson Gift." The Yale University Ga-
    zette, 17 (October), 33-35.
        [Description of large collection of Robinsoniana recently
    donated to Yale by Lucius Beebe.]

3   BLANCK, JACOB. "News from the Rare Book Sellers." Publish-
    er's Weekly, 141 (January 31), 525.
        Robinson may have written juvenilia because his name is
    included in "The Golden Days Puzzlers Directory" for 1886.

4   _____. "News from the Rare Book Sellers." Publisher's Week-
    ly, 141 (May 23), 1924.
        Robinson may have contributed to Golden Days for Boys and
    Girls under the pseudonym "1812." [See 1942.B13.]

5   BURNS, WINIFRED. "Edwin Arlington Robinson in the Hands of
    the Reviewers." Poet-Lore, 48 (Summer), 164-75.
        [Brief overview of critics' reaction to Robinson's po-
    etry, noting that it was more negative than positive. Bib-
    liography included.]

6   DAUNER, LOUISE. "Avon and Cavender: Two Children of the
    Night." American Literature, 14 (March), 55-65.
        Just as Robinson's light imagery represents knowledge,
    his night imagery represents ignorance of moral nature or
    moral action. Avon and Cavender are Robinson's extreme
    examples of spiritual failures. Significantly, both poems
    take place at night.

7   _____. "Vox Clamantis: Edwin Arlington Robinson as a Critic
    of American Democracy." The New England Quarterly, 15
    (September), 401-26.
        [Study of Robinson's social poems as they reflect an
    anti-materialistic stance. Special attention given to the
    Demos and Dionysius poems and King Jasper.]

8   DOYLE, JOHN R. "The Shorter Poems of E. A. Robinson." Bul-
    letin of the Citadel, 6, 3-18.
        Robinson's short poems resemble those of the seventeenth
    century more closely than those of his immediate predeces-
    sors: they deal with "unpoetic" subjects treated individ-
    ually and with density of language. [Reprinted in 1969.A4.]

9   PHELPS, WILLIAM LYONS. "Edwin Arlington Robinson," in Ameri-
    can Academy of Arts and Letters: Commemorative Tributes,
    1905-41. New York: The Academy, pp. 323-28.
        [Reprint of 1939.B6.]

10 WALSH, WILLIAM THOMAS. "Some Recollections of E. A. Robin-
    son." The Catholic World, 155 (August-September), 522-31,
    703-712.
        [Record of Walsh's acquaintance with Robinson at Peter-
    borough, and his unsuccessful attempt to convert Robinson
    to Catholicism. Walsh claims to have been influential in
    the writing of "Nicodemus" and "Ponce de Leon."]

11 WEARING, THOMAS. "Edwin Arlington Robinson--New England Poet-
    Philosopher." Colgate-Rochester Divinity School Bulletin,
    14 (February), 152-74.
        Critical commentary places Robinson in both a poetic and
    philosophical perspective. "Calvary" and "Captain Craig"
    refute Wilder's assertion that Robinson "could not go be-
    yond an heroic stoicism." [See 1940.B33.]

12 WEBER, CARL J. "Additions to Our Robinson Collection." The
    Colby Mercury, 7 (May), 94-96.
        [Notice of four books added to the Robinson collection
    at Colby.]

13 _____. "A Robinson Wild-Goose Chase." The Colby Mercury, 7
    (May), 96.
        Blanck's conjecture about Robinson contributing to Golden
    Days for Boys and Girls cannot be corroborated. [See
    1942.B3 and 1942.B4.]

14 WILLIAMS, ALICE MEACHAM. "Edwin Arlington Robinson, Journal-
    ist." The New England Quarterly, 15 (December), 715-24.
        [Article about Robinson's attempts to write for news-
    papers, including reprint of correspondence with Clarence
    Stedman and his single editorial, "A Balm of Custom."]

1943 A BOOKS

1   BETSKY, SEYMOUR. "Some Aspects of the Philosophy of Edwin
    Arlington Robinson: Self-Knowledge, Self-Acceptance, and
    Conscience." Ph.D. thesis, Harvard University.
        [An examination of the "Christianized Platonism" that is
    the basis of Robinson's thought, with additional discus-
    sions of his relationship to Emersonian transcendentalism
    and his individualistic sympathetic attitude. (Harvard
    University Summary of Theses: 1943-1945, pp. 457-60.)]

1943

2   WEBER, CARL J., ed. <u>Letters of Edwin Arlington Robinson to</u>
     <u>Howard George Schmitt.</u> Waterville, Me.: Colby College
     Library, 31 pp.
          [Introductory explanation of relationship between Schmitt
     and Robinson, with extensive notes on the letters.]

<u>1943 B SHORTER WRITINGS</u>

1   BEERS, SAMUEL G. "A Poet for Pastors." <u>Religion in Life</u>, 12
     (Summer), 421-30.
          [Discussion of Robinson's integrity, artistry, insight,
     religious philosophy and prophetic qualities. Poems from
     <u>The Children of the Night</u> and the Arthurian narratives dis-
     cussed.]

2   BENÉT, WILLIAM ROSE. "The Phoenix Nest." <u>The Saturday Review</u>
     <u>of Literature</u>, 26 (February 20), 18.
          Ben Ray Redmon reports that Robinson told him "The Whip"
     is a poem about the stock market, with the whip symbolizing
     the margin and the lover representing Anthony Comstock.

3   _____. "The Phoenix Nest." <u>The Saturday Review of Litera-</u>
     <u>ture</u>, 26 (April 17), 54.
          Robinson sent letter to Carl Weber saying that "The Whip"
     is meant to be taken literally.

4   COLLAMORE, H. B. "Robinson and the War." <u>Colby Library Quar-</u>
     <u>terly</u>, 1 (March), 30-31.
          [Letter to Edith Brower in 1918 regretting that his age
     prevents him from active service.]

5   DAUNER, LOUISE. "The Pernicious Rib: E. A. Robinson's Con-
     cept of Feminine Character." <u>American Literature</u>, 15
     (May), 139-58.
          Robinson's women are more individualized than his men,
     but his composite woman is intelligent, sensitive, cynical
     and amoral. "She is the tragic instrument for man's fall."
     [Analysis of women in <u>Matthias at the Door</u>, <u>Talifer</u>, <u>Mer-</u>
     <u>lin</u>, and <u>Tristram</u>. Reprinted in 1969.A4.]

6   HUDSON, HOYT H. "Robinson and Praed." <u>Poetry</u>, 61 (February),
     612-20.
          Robinson shows affinity to Praed in syntax, style, and
     subject matter. Both poets combined the comic and the
     serious. While there is no record of Robinson's having
     read Praed, he was quite popular during the 1880's.

7   LORD, ALICE FROST. "Friendly Contacts with Maine Poet Reveal
    Personality of the Man." Lewiston (Me.) Journal Magazine
    Section, October 23, p. A-8.
        [Interview with Esther Willard Bates, Robinson's typist
    at Peterborough.]

8   PETTIT, HENRY. "Robinson's 'The Whip.'" The Explicator, 1
    (April), Item 50.
        This poem is similar in theme to Keats' "La Belle Dame
    Sans Merci" in the speculation of a surviving lover in a
    triangle after the death of the other one.

9   SCHMITT, HOWARD GEORGE. "Some Robinson Letters in My Collec-
    tion." Colby Library Quarterly, 1 (January), 8-12.
        [Publication of and commentary on four letters by Robin-
    son.]

10 SIMON, CHARLIE MAY. Lays of the New Land: Stories of Some
    American Poets and their Work. New York: E. P. Dutton,
    pp. 131-43.
        [Biographical sketch and introduction to Robinson's
    poems for juvenile readers.]

11 STOVALL, FLOYD. "Robinson and Frost," in American Idealism.
    Norman: University of Oklahoma Press, pp. 169-77.
        Robinson believed with Whitman that all men can intuit
    truth, but he felt that the power of illusion, being
    stronger, can frequently overwhelm it. [Analysis of
    Amaranth, Matthias at the Door, and King Jasper.]

12 SUTCLIFFE, W. DENHAM. "The Original of Robinson's 'Captain
    Craig.'" The New England Quarterly, 16 (September), 407-
    431.
        [Biographical sketch of Alfred H. Louis, the eccentric
    Jewish lawyer who was acquainted with literary circles in
    England and America and who became the model for Captain
    Craig.]

13 WEBER, CARL J. "Poet and President." The New England Quar-
    terly, 16 (December), 615-26.
        [Publication of and commentary on the dozen letters
    Theodore Roosevelt wrote Robinson.]

14 _____. "Robinson's Prose: A Retraction." Colby Library
    Quarterly, 1 (March), 31-32.
        Robinson probably did not write articles previously at-
    tributed to him. [See 1941.B9 and 1942.B13.]

1943

15   WELLS, HENRY W. "The New England Conscience," in The American
     Way of Poetry. New York: Columbia University Press,
     pp. 89-105.
        [Analysis of all the non-Arthurian narratives from Roman
     Bartholow to King Jasper, with the thesis that Robinson's
     awareness of inner spiritual states infuses his poetry.

1944 A BOOKS

1   ANON. Edwin Arlington Robinson at Colby College. Waterville,
     Me.: Colby College Library, 4 pp.
        Pamphlet containing a list of the lectures delivered at
     Colby on Robinson as well as a bibliography of books and
     articles on Robinson published by the faculty there.

2   BATES, ESTHER WILLARD. Edwin Arlington Robinson and His
     Manuscripts. Colby College Monograph No. 11. Waterville,
     Me.: Colby College Library, 32 pp.
        [Personal reminiscences of Robinson's typist, with vi-
     gnettes concerning Robinson's attitudes about his own po-
     ems, the writing of poetry, and the business of publish-
     ing.]

3   CROWDER, RICHARD H. "Three Studies of Edwin Arlington Robin-
     son: His Male Characters, His Emergence, and His Contem-
     poraneous Reputation." Unpublished Ph.D. thesis, State
     University of Iowa, 245 pp.
        [The three studies are reprinted in 1945.B2, 1946.B2,
     and 1946.B3.]

4   DAUNER, MARGARET L[OUISE]. "Studies in Edwin Arlington Rob-
     inson." Unpublished Ph.D. thesis, State University of
     Iowa.
        [Three of the five chapters are reproductions of 1942.B6,
     1942.B7, and 1943.B5. The other two are on Robinson's
     views of art and a technical analysis of several short
     lyrics.]

1944 B SHORTER WRITINGS

1   BEATTY, FREDERICKA. "Edwin Arlington Robinson as I Knew Him."
     The South Atlantic Quarterly, 43 (October), 375-81.
        [Reminiscence of acquaintance with Robinson for two sum-
     mers at Peterborough, emphasizing his dry humor, reserve,
     and kindness.]

1944

2   GIERASCH, WALTER. "Robinson's 'Luke Havergal.'" The Explica-
     tor, 3 (October), Item 8.
         The "western gate" may be either a symbol for Luke's
     lover's fidelity or a gate in a walled city. The "crimson
     leaves" are perhaps Luke's vain insistence upon perfection.

3   GREGORY, HORACE and MARYA ZATURENSKA. "The Vein of Comedy in
     E. A. Robinson's Poetry." The American Bookman, 1 (Fall),
     43-64.
         Robinson uses wit "with greater poise" than any poet in
     English since the eighteenth century. "Captain Craig" is
     the most important of his major poems and is reminiscent of
     James. The Man Who Died Twice is the last poem to show the
     wit "that had been the true rewards of the author's maturi-
     ty." [Analysis of "Captain Craig" and "Ben Jonson." Re-
     printed in 1946.B8.]

4   HALL, JAMES NORMAN. "Reading and Meditating: Edwin Arlington
     Robinson's Poems." Atlantic Monthly, 174 (September), 57-
     58.
         [Forty-seven line poem to Robinson, principally in coup-
     lets].

5   LEDOUX, LOUIS V. "Robinson, Edwin Arlington," in Dictionary
     of American Biography, Vol. 21 (Supplement One). Edited by
     Harris E. Starr. New York: Charles Scribner's Sons, 632-
     34.
         [Biographical sketch and critical assessment, emphasizing
     the importance of his New England heritage on his work.]

6   NOTOPOULOS, JAMES A. "Sophocles and 'Captain Craig.'" The
     New England Quarterly, 17 (March), 109.
         Two passages in "Captain Craig," pp. 117-18 and 140, are
     translations of lines 332-3 and 337-47 in Antigone. [See
     1944.B8.]

7   RAVEN, A. A. "Robinson's 'Luke Havergal.'" The Explicator,
     3 (December), Item 24.
         The gloomy imagery is typical of Robinson, but the "in-
     tellectual meaning" of the poem is that the bereaved lover
     should look to the future with faith.

8   WEBER, CARL J. "E. A. Robinson's Translation of Sophocles."
     The New England Quarterly, 17 (December), 604-605.
         Notopolous (1944.B6) suggested that Robinson stole the
     translations from Antigone, but Robinson's own translation
     is at Colby.

1945

1945 A BOOKS

1   McCULLOCH, WARREN STURGIS. One Word After Another. Chicago:
     Chicago Literary Club, 27 pp.
        [Address presented to the Chicago Literary Club. Assess-
     ment of Robinson's contributions to poetry, emphasizing his
     diction, light imagery, emotional inflexibility, syntacti-
     cal complexity, and understatement.]

1945 B SHORTER WRITINGS

·1   ANON. "He Saw the Gleam of Lancelot: Edwin Arlington Robin-
     son, 1869-1935." Senior Scholastic, 46 (April 2), 17
        [Sketch of Robinson's personality and career. "Miniver
     Cheevy" is quoted but Lancelot is not mentioned.]

2   CROWDER, RICHARD. "'Here Are the Men...': E. A. Robinson's
     Male Character Types." The New England Quarterly, 18 (Sep-
     tember), 346-67.
        Although most of Robinson's characters are failures, they
     can be classified according to the seven personality types
     of Edward Spranger and Gordon W. Allport: the theoretic,
     the economic, the aesthetic, the social, the political, the
     religious, and the sensual. [Reprinted in 1969.A4.]

3   _____. "Robinson's 'An Old Story.'" The Explicator, 4 (De-
     cember), Item 22.
        The obscurity of the second stanza is clarified by re-
     versing the order of the lines. The persona realizes that
     his original anger is envy.

·4   PARLETT, MATHILDE M. "Robinson's 'Luke Havergal.'" The Ex-
     plicator, 3 (June), Item 57.
        This poem may be about religious experience rather than
     love. If the woman personifies truth she may be calling
     Luke from study of eastern religions back to the Christian
     fold.

5   SUPER, R. H. "Robinson's 'For a Dead Lady.'" The Explicator,
     3 (June), Item 60.
        "The breast where roses could not live" perhaps is an al-
     lusion to Joyce's Ulysses.

6   WINTERS, YVOR. "Religious and Social Ideas in the Didactic
     Work of E. A. Robinson." The Arizona Quarterly, 1 (Spring),
     70-85.
        [Essay emphasizing Robinson's fuzzy thinking, a result of
     his Calvinist/Unitarian background. Revised and reprinted
     in 1946.A1 and 1969.A4.]

130

1946 A BOOKS

1   WINTERS, YVOR. Edwin Arlington Robinson. The Makers of Mod-
     ern Literature Series. Norfolk, Connecticut: New Direc-
     tions Books, 162 pp.
        [Brief assessment containing chapters on Robinson's life,
     background, and influences, as well as analyses of his po-
     ems grouped according to length.] His short poems about
     individuals are his best; some eleven are in the first rank
     and twenty-two are in the second. Lancelot is far superior
     to Tristram, but his long poems generally are mediocre.
     [Partially reprinted in 1970.A3.]

1946 B SHORTER WRITINGS

1   ANON. "Your Town: Your People." Scholastic, 48 (May 13), 23.
        [Brief sketch of career. "Mr. Flood's Party" is quoted.]

2   CROWDER, RICHARD. "E. A. Robinson's Craftsmanship: Opinions
     of Contemporary Poets." Modern Language Notes, 61 (Janu-
     ary), 1-14.
        Contemporary poet-critics objected to Robinson's lack of
     concrete imagery, circumlocution, and obscurity, but from
     1916 until his death they applauded the quality of his
     blank verse, his austerity, dignity, and honesty.

3   _____. "The Emergence of E. A. Robinson." The South Atlantic
     Quarterly, 45 (January), 89-98.
        Although critics were surprisingly kind to Robinson when
     he published his first volumes, they praised him for the
     wrong things. No one noticed his attention to making
     verses out of colloquial speech, which was his chief inno-
     vation.

4   _____. "Robinson's 'For a Dead Lady.'" The Explicator, 5
     (December), Item 19.
        The lady is Robinson's mother. Perhaps the line "the
     laugh that love could not forgive" refers to Robinson's
     feeling unwanted. [See 1945.B5.]

5   _____. "Robinson's 'The Sheaves.'" The Explicator, 4 (March),
     Item 38.
        The final sestet is ironic because "convention forbids
     our associating material gain with poetic 'girls with
     golden hair.'"

6   FIGUEIRA, GASTON. "Poetas y Prosistas Americanos: I. Edwin
     Arlington Robinson. II. Thomas Wolfe." Revista Ibero-
     americano, 11 (October), 329-32.

1946

> Although Robinson and Whitman wrote different kinds of poetry, the two are linked because no other American poet of their stature appeared in the interim between them.

7   FREEMAN, JESSIE WHEELER. "The Poet of Tilbury Town." The Winged Word, 5 (Autumn), 79-81.
    [Appreciation, emphasizing Robinson's love for the river.]

8   GREGORY, HORACE and MARYA ZATURENSKA. "La Comedie Humaine of E. A. Robinson," in A History of American Poets: 1900-1940. New York: Harcourt, Brace, pp. 107-32.
    [Reprint of 1944.B3 along with biographical sketch, assessment of career, and review of criticism.]

9   HOERNECKE, ALMA ELLIS. "Remembering a Maine Poet." The Winged Word, 5 (Autumn), 82.
    [Two sonnets about Robinson after reading Robinson's Sonnets 1889-1927.]

10 MORGAN, A. E. The Beginnings of Modern American Poetry. London: Longmans, Green, pp. 10-11.
    Robinson presented realistic portrait of society "with economy of phrase and accuracy of form." He resembles Hardy in his insistence on honesty.

11 NEWMAN, ISRAEL. "Of the Immortals." The Winged Word, 5 (Autumn), 81.
    [Sonnet about Robinson.]

12 ROOSEVELT, THEODORE. Letters to Kermit from Theodore Roosevelt: 1902-1908. Edited by Will Irwin. New York: Scribners, passim.
    [Scattered references to Roosevelt's reading Robinson's poetry and securing a job for him.]

1947 A BOOKS

1   SUTCLIFFE, DENHAM. "Introduction," in Untriangulated Stars: Letters of Edwin Arlington Robinson to Harry de Forest Smith 1890-1905. Edited by Denham Sutcliffe. Cambridge: Harvard University Press, pp. xiii-xxvii.
    These letters, which were written when Robinson was at Harvard and after he returned to Gardiner, cover the most important of his developing years. "Almost anything else would have been better for Robinson than his return from Harvard to Gardiner--but America might have lost a poet."

1947 B SHORTER WRITINGS

1   ANON. "Additions to the Census of the TORRENT." Colby Library Quarterly, 2 (August), 52.
     Three more copies of The Torrent and the Night Before are located.

2   ANON. "Robinson, Edwin Arlington," in National Cyclopedia of American Biography, Vol. 33. New York: J. T. White, pp. 145-46.
     [Biographical sketch with attention to geneological data.]

3   BENÉT, WILLIAM ROSE. "The Phoenix Nest." The Saturday Review of Literature, 30 (January 18), 32.
     [Disagreement with Winters' explication of "The Whip," (1946.A1) and query about the meaning of "En Passant."]

4   _____. "The Phoenix Nest." The Saturday Review of Literature, 30 (March 8), 48.
     [Winters' reply to complaint about his interpretation of "The Whip" (1946.A1) and two other letters concerning that poem and "En Passant."]

5   BLANCK, JACOB. "News for the Rare Book Sellers." Publisher's Weekly, 152 (November 22), B354.
     [Announcement of the Isaacs collection of Robinsoniana at the New York Public Library. (See 1948.B11.)]

6   CROWDER, RICHARD. "E. A. Robinson's Camelot." College English, 9 (November), 72-79.
     [A review of contemporaneous criticism of the three Arthurian poems, organized by character, qualities of verse, plots and themes, and the poets' contemporaniety. Critical comments of some sixteen writers are given, but no conclusions are drawn.]

7   DUNBAR, OLIVIA HOWARD. A House in Chicago. Chicago: University of Chicago Press, passim.
     [Scattered references throughout of Robinson's association and correspondence with Harriet Converse Moody. Letter from Robinson about Cavender's House, p. 250.]

8   NEFF, EMERY. "The Intimate Robinson." The Nation, 145 (November 8), 506-507.
     [Review of Untriangulated Stars.] "The clash of his ambition with his environment is the dramatic core" of this collection of letters.

1947

9   O., M. N. "Robinson's 'Sonnet: Oh for a Poet.'" The Expli-
    cator, 5 (May), Query 21.
        Perhaps this poem is one of unconscious irony since Rob-
    inson appears to be doing the thing for which he is up-
    braiding the "little sonnet-men."

10 PERRINE, LAURENCE. "Robinson's 'Veteran Sirens.'" The Expli-
    cator, 6 (November), Item 13.
        Contrary to what Winters (1946.A1) suggests, this poem is
    about spinsters who refuse to grow old gracefully.

11 RANSOM, JOHN CROWE. "On a New England Lyre." The New York
    Times Book Review, January 19, pp. 7, 28.
        [Review of Edwin Arlington Robinson, by Yvor Winters.]
    While Robinson and Hardy are both traditionalists, Robin-
    son's idiom is far different from Hardy's in that "Robin-
    son appears to cultivate the poetry of the indefinite
    phrase." While another poet works hard at rendering posi-
    tive qualities, Robinson intimates that his object is too
    mysterious to be rendered. "This is a strange kind of
    poetry, and takes some studying."

12 SUPER, R. H. "Robinson's 'For a Dead Lady.'" The Explicator,
    5 (June), Item 60.
        [Denial of the validity of Crowder's comments (1946.B4)
    about Super's earlier explication (1945.B5).]

13 WEBER, CARL J. "The Jubilee of Robinson's Torrent." Colby
    Library Quarterly, 2 (February), 1-12.
        Of the 112 copies Robinson mailed of The Torrent and the
    Night Before, 56 have been located.

14 _____. "A New Poem by Edwin Arlington Robinson." Colby Li-
    brary Quarterly, 2 (February), 12-13.
        [Printing of an octave Robinson sent to Edith Brower in
    1897.]

15 WHITE, WILLIAM. "E. A. Robinson and A. E. Housman." Colby
    Library Quarterly, 2 (August), 42-43.
        [Publication of a letter from Robinson to Edmund R. Brown
    refusing to write an introduction to a new edition of A
    Shropshire Lad.]

1948 A BOOKS

1   ISAACS, EDITH J. R. Edwin Arlington Robinson: A Descriptive
    List of the Lewis M. Isaacs Collection of Robinsoniana.
    New York: New York Public Library, 15 pp.
        [Reprint of 1948.B11.]

2   NEFF, EMERY. Edwin Arlington Robinson. The American Man of
    Letters Series. New York: William Sloane Associates,
    286 pp.
        [Critical biography which closely follows Hagedorn's bio-
    graphy but with relatively more attention to individual po-
    ems, notably "Captain Craig" and "The Man Against the Sky."
    No footnotes; detailed indices. Reprinted in 1968.A6.]

*3 PERRINE, LAURENCE D. "Edwin Arlington Robinson and the Ar-
    thurian Legend." Ph.D. thesis, Yale University, 118 pp.
        [Cited in White, pp. 113.]

1948 B SHORTER WRITINGS

1   ANON. "Poet in America." Time, 51 (March 8), 110, 112.
        [Review of Untriangulated Stars.] "Readers of this book
    may realize some of...the terrible consumption of human
    resources that go to make a poet in America."

2   ANON. "Untriangulated Stars." Times Literary Supplement,
    February 21, p. 111.
        [Announcement in "Books Received" section.]

3   ANON. "Untriangulated Stars." The United States Quarterly
    Booklist, 4 (March), 39.
        This book "provides the most important sort of clues to
    the poet's youthful and maturing character."

4   BATES, ESTHER WILLARD. "The Letters of Edwin Arlington Rob-
    inson." Christian Science Monitor, January 3, p. 8.
        Untriangulated Stars is a model job of editing.

5   BISHOP, JOHN PEALE. "The Intelligence of Poets," in Collected
    Essays of John Peale Bishop. Edited by Edmund Wilson.
    New York: Scribner's, pp. 264-66.
        [Review of Collected Poems from article in Vanity Fair,
    1922.] If Robinson "has not always written well, he has
    at least written wisely." The Arthurian poems are impres-
    sive, but his dramatic monologues are not successful.

6   COWLEY, MALCOLM. "Edwin Arlington Robinson: Defeat and Tri-
    umph." The New Republic, 119 (December 6), 26-30.
        [Review of Edwin Arlington Robinson, by Emery Neff.]
    Robinson's difficulty in getting his work published at the
    turn of the century was similar to that of other writers

1948

such as Dreiser. The starkness of his apartment, even after
he could afford better quarters, suggests that he was ob-
livious to his surroundings, accounting for his lack of
visual imagery in his poetry. [Reprinted in 1964.B3.]

7   CROWDER, RICHARD. "Robinson's 'Luke Havergal.'" The Expli-
     cator, 7 (November), Item 15.
          Contrary to Parlett's view (1945.B4), this poem is an ex-
     ercise in the symbolist mode.

8   DAUNER, LOUISE. "Untriangulated Stars." American Literature,
     20 (March), 78-80.
          This book is essential for Robinson scholars or "anyone
     who wishes an inner guide to the poetry."

9   _____. "Untriangulated Stars." The New England Quarterly,
     21 (March), 111-114.
          This book is more important psychically than factually,
     but it is the most important documentation so far of the
     real Robinson.

10   GREGORY, HORACE. "A Poet's Honest Self-Appraisal." The New
     York Times Book Review, February 8, pp. 1, 24.
          Robinson's prose is rather awkward, but the letters in
     Untriangulated Stars are fascinating because of their
     bluntness; they reveal more about him than the biographers
     have.

11   ISAACS, EDITH J. R. "Edwin Arlington Robinson: A Descriptive
     List of the Lewis M. Isaacs Collection of Robinsoniana."
     Bulletin of the New York Public Library, 52 (May), 211-33.
          [A description of the collection which includes all of
     Robinson's published books, over seventy manuscripts, and
     numerous letters to, by, and about Robinson. Reprinted in
     1948.A1.]

*12 LE BRETON, MAURICE. "E. A. Robinson," in Anthologie de la
     Poésie Américaine Contemporaine. Paris: Editions Denoël,
     pp. 40-41.
          [Cited in White, p. 41.]

13   MAYNARD, THEODORE. "Untriangulated Stars." The Catholic
     World, 168 (October), 87.
          Although this book is not so important as the earlier
     collection of letters or the Hagedorn biography, it is a
     valuable addition to Robinson scholarship.

1948

14   MIMS, EDWIN. The Christ of the Poets. Nashville, Tennessee:
      Abington-Cokesbury, pp. 222-24 and passim.
         One explanation of Robinson's melancholy is that he found
      little faith in his generation. "Nicodemus" and "Calvary"
      are examples of Christian influence.

15   PERRINE, LAURENCE. "Robinson's 'Tristram' ix-x." The Expli-
      cator, 6 (May), Item 44.
         Yvor Winters (1946.A1) was incorrect about the ship,
      which has no function in the plot but symbolizes transcen-
      dent love.

16   QUINN, M. B., SISTER. "E. A. Robinson: Vision and Voice."
      America, 79 (May 15), 141-43.
         Although Robinson's reputation is growing, misconceptions
      about him exist. He is both optimistic and sympathetic
      toward Christianity, as such poems as "Calvary," "The Three
      Taverns," and "Ponce de Leon" indicate.

17   TATE, ALLEN. "Edwin Arlington Robinson," in On The Limits of
      Poetry: Selected Essays, 1928-1942. New York: William
      Morrow, pp. 358-65.
         [Reprint of 1933.B26 and 1936.B27; reprinted in 1959.B5
      and 1968.B16.]

18   T[HOMAS], E[LSIE]. "Untriangulated Stars." Wisconsin Library
      Bulletin, 44 (April), 82.
         These letters "reveal Robinson's mental and spiritual ex-
      periences as he tried to remain true to his ideal of a
      literary career."

19   WEBER, CARL J. "Two More 'Torrents.'" Colby Library Quar-
      terly, 2 (August), 122-23.
         [Report of location of two copies of The Torrent and the
      Night Before.]

20   _____. "With Admiration and Love." Colby Library Quarterly,
      2 (May), 85-108.
         [Description of Colby's collection of association books:
      those given or received by Robinson.]

21   WHICHER, GEORGE F. "A Poet to His Friend." New York Herald
      Tribune Books, January 11, p. 4.
         [Review of Untriangulated Stars.] This book is "a quiet
      chronicle of heroism not exceeded in the literary records
      of our time. There has been nothing like it since Keats."

1948

22 WILLIAMS, STANLEY T. "Edwin Arlington Robinson," in Literary
    History of the United States. Edited by Robert E. Spiller,
    et al. New York: Macmillan, pp. 1157-70.
        [Overview of career, emphasizing Robinson's romanticism,
    melancholy, and position as a transition figure between the
    old and the new poetry.]

23 WILLIAMS, WILLIAM CARLOS. "Eat Rocks." The Nation, 167 (Oc-
    tober 30), 498-99.
        [Review of Edwin Arlington Robinson, by Emery Neff.]
    Robinson more properly belongs to the new poetry than the
    old. One has to get through the "flinty shell of art" of
    his traditional verse forms. "Take his shell and call it
    the end of the period, but his meat...begins the new tree."

1949 A BOOKS

*1 FUSSELL, EDWIN S. "The Early Poetry of Edwin Arlington Robin-
    son." Ph.D. thesis, Harvard University, 169 pp.
        [Cited in White, p. 113. Published 1954.A1.]

1949 B SHORTER WRITINGS

1   ADAMS, LEONIE. "The Ledoux Collection of Edwin Arlington Rob-
    inson." The Library of Congress Quarterly Journal of Cur-
    rent Acquisitions, 7 (November), 9-13.
        [Analyses of variant passages in manuscript versions of
    Tristram and "Many Are Called," part of the Ledoux collec-
    tion of Robinsoniana at the Library of Congress. Sugges-
    tion that while the Ledoux collection is smaller than the
    Isaacs collection at the New York Public Library, it is
    more interesting.]

2   ANON. "News Notes." Poetry, 74 (May), 122.
        [Announcement of the acquisition of the Ledoux collection
    by the Library of Congress.]

3   BROOKS, VAN WYCK. "Edwin Arlington Robinson," in Chilmark
    Miscellany. New York: E. P. Dutton, pp. 254-62.
        [Reprint of 1940.B2.]

4   BROWN, R. W. "Mrs. MacDowell and Her Colony." Atlantic
    Monthly, 180 (July), 42-46.
        [Occasional reference to Robinson in sketch of how and
    why Mrs. MacDowell established the colony at Peterborough.]

5   COMMAGER, HENRY STEELE. "Traditionalism in American Poetry."
    The Nineteenth Century and After, 146 (November), 322-26.
        Robinson, "the most distinguished of American men of let-
    ters of his generation," used traditionalism to advantage.
    He is "a Calvinist who flirted with transcendentalism oc-
    casionally." He can be compared to Browning but wrote more
    than Emerson or Whitman. [Reprinted in 1950.B1.]

6   CONNER, FREDERICK WILLIAM. "Robinson," in Cosmic Optimism.
    Gainesville: University of Florida Press, pp. 365-74.
        "Robinson was a transcendentalist...to the extent of
    denying the mechanistic determinism of the naturalists...
    and he was an optimist to the extent of believing that
    somehow and some time the injustice of men's lives would
    be corrected." Evolutionary theories were of little com-
    fort to him.

7   CROWDER, RICHARD. "E. A Robinson's Symphony: 'The Man Who
    Died Twice.'" College English, 11 (December), 141-44.
        The Man Who Died Twice would be good for class-room study
    because it is a relatively short book-length poem, it is
    well organized, and the imagery is impressive.

8   DYKES, MATTIE M. "Trying to Spell God: A Study of Edwin Arl-
    ington Robinson." Northwest Missouri State Teachers Col-
    lege Studies, 13 (June), 85-124.
        [Overview of life and work with copious quotations.] The
    aim of the paper is to show "how the poet struggled to
    spell God for himself,...how he tried to help individuals
    spell God for themselves, and finally how he tried to help
    nations."

9   ISAACS, LEWIS M. "E. A. Robinson Speaks of Music." The New
    England Quarterly, 22 (December), 499-510.
        The Man Who Died Twice is notable for Robinson's ability
    to use musical imagery well and is possibly autobiographi-
    cal, since Robinson wrote a musical composition which was
    published years later. [Letter by Robinson quoted on the
    relationship of poetry and music.]

10 PERRINE, LAURENCE. "Robinson's 'Eros Turannos.'" The Expli-
    cator, 8 (December), Item 20.
        This carefully structured poem can be divided evenly into
    two parts, dealing with the before and the after of a bad
    marriage. Part I represents madness; part II, tragedy.

11 ____. "Robinson's 'Tristram.'" The Explicator, 7 (March),
    Item 33.

1949

> Isolt dies of love in all the sources; Robinson makes her
> death more realistic by adding shock.

12   T., W. P. "A Composer in Words." The Christian Science Moni-
     tor, July 23, [p. 8].
>   [Reminiscence by a college friend who points out that
>   Robinson is essentially a musical poet and that his poems
>   are deceptively simple; Robinson claimed to have spent two-
>   hundred hours writing "The House on the Hill."]

13   WEBER, CARL J. "Two Friends of Robinson." Colby Library
     Quarterly, 2 (February), 147-52.
>   [Report of acquisition of libraries of Thomas S. Perry
>   and Harold Pulsifer by Colby College Library.]

14   _____. "Two More 'Torrents' Turn Up." Colby Library Quar-
     terly, 2 (May), 161-62.
>   Sixty-four copies of Robinson's first volume are now lo-
>   cated.

1950 A BOOKS

1   HUMPHRY, JAMES, III. The Library of Edwin Arlington Robinson:
     A Descriptive Catalogue. Colby College Monograph, No. 19.
     Waterville, Me.: Colby College Press, 52 pp.
>   [Introduction about Robinson's reading and a list of some
>   300 books in Robinson's library.]

1950 B SHORTER WRITINGS

1   COMMAGER, HENRY STEELE. "The Traditionalists," in The Ameri-
     can Mind. New Haven: Yale University Press, pp. 155-61.
>   [Reprint of 1949.B5.]

2   CROWDER, RICHARD. "Robinson's 'The Field of Glory.'" The
     Explicator, 8 (February), Item 31.
>   Levi, "a misfit in a materialistic world," would be more
>   heroic if he thought of more important things than earthly
>   glory.

3   JACOBS, WILLIS D. "E. A. Robinson's 'Mr. Flood's Party.'"
     College English, 12 (November), 110.
>   Critics are wrong when they call Mr. Flood a drunkard,
>   since he is too physically and mentally fit to be an alco-
>   holic.

4   JANE, MARY C. "Journey to Head Tide." The Christian Science
     Monitor, Magazine Section, 42 (February 25), 10.
          [Feature story about visit to Robinson's birthplace.]

5   MILLETT, FRED B. Reading Poetry. New York: Harper & Broth-
     ers, pp. 80-81, 165-66.
          [Six poems anthologized; "Flammonde" discussed.]

6   OWNBEY, E. SYDNOR. "Robinson's 'Mr. Flood's Party.'" The
     Explicator, 8 (April), Item 47.
          Mr. Flood resembles Roland in physical appearance and
     action, but he is a comic Roland.

7   SOUTHWORTH, JAMES GRANVILLE. "Edwin Arlington Robinson," in
     Some Modern American Poets. New York: Macmillan, pp. 28-
     41.
          Robinson has more historic than intrinsic importance
     since he tried to do for poetry what Meredith and James
     had done for the novel. He does not deserve his high repu-
     tation because he lacks empathy and control.

8   WAGGONER, H. H. "E. A. Robinson: The Cosmic Chill," in The
     Heel of Elohim: Science and Values in Modern American Po-
     etry. Norman: University of Oklahoma Press, pp. 18-40.
          [Revision of 1940.B29 and reprinted in 1970.A3.]

9   WEBER, CARL J. "Humphry's Catalogue of Robinson's Library."
     Colby Library Quarterly, 2 (November), 271-72.
          [Announcement of gift of Robinson's library to Colby
     College Library.]

1951 A BOOKS - NONE

1951 B SHORTER WRITINGS

1   BARTLETT, PHYLISS. Poems in Process. New York: Oxford Uni-
     versity Press, p. 104-106.
          No other American poet can be studied as easily as Robin-
     son because of the large collections of manuscripts in li-
     braries and his methodical revisions.

2   BOGAN, LOUISE. Achievement in American Poetry 1900-1950.
     Chicago: Henry Regnery, pp. 19-22.
          Robinson's early poetry marks an important shift from
     sentimentality to realism. His tone and diction are his
     most original qualities. His late poems eventually became
     obsessions rather than creations. He is a poet of the town,
     not the country.

1951

3   DAVIS, CHARLES T. "The Poetic Drama of Moody, Robinson, Tor-
    rence, and MacKaye, 1894-1909." Ph.D. thesis, New York
    University, 184 pp.
        [Comparative chapters on the four playwrights' friend-
    ship, dramatic poetry, and philosophy. Robinson's "Captain
    Craig," Van Zorn, and The Porcupine analyzed.]

4   FITZELL, LINCOLN. "The Sword and the Dragon." The South At-
    lantic Quarterly, 50 (April), 214-32.
        [In an article dealing with poetic integrity, Robinson is
    one of some twenty poets included. "Luke Havergal" is men-
    tioned as a good example of "the scrutiny of individual
    disaster."]

5   FUSSELL, EDWIN S. "An Unpublished Poem by E. A. Robinson."
    American Literature, 22 (January), 487-88.
        ["Broadway," found in a fair copy at Harvard, is pub-
    lished.] Perhaps Robinson never published it because the
    art was too brittle.

6   ____. "A Note on E. A. Robinson's 'Credo.'" Modern Lan-
    guage Notes, 66 (June), 398-400.
        [An explanation and resolution of syntactic difficulties
    of the word "for" in line 12 of "Credo."]

7   ____. "Robinson to Moody: Ten Unpublished Letters." Ameri-
    can Literature, 23 (May), 173-87.
        Robinson's letters to Moody (from 1899 to 1908) reveal
    the depth of their friendship and the mutual awareness that
    each might change the direction of poetry. [Ten letters
    published from the Harvard collection.]

8   ____. "Robinson's 'For a Dead Lady.'" The Explicator, 9
    (March), Item 33.
        "The laugh that love could not forgive" probably refers
    to possessiveness and the desire to be taken seriously.

9   POLICARDI, SILVIO. Breve Storia della Letteratura Americana.
    Milano, Varese: Instituto Edioriale Cisalpino, pp. 218-19.
        [Overview of literary career, emphasizing Robinson's ori-
    ginal use of traditional style and his basic dramatic qual-
    ity.]

10 WESTBROOK, PERRY D. Acres of Flint: Writers of Rural New
    England, 1870-1900. Washington, D.C.: The Scarecrow
    Press, pp. 111-13.
        Robinson shared with Mary E. Wilkins Freeman a tendency

to probe "the psychological wreckage of Calvinism" in New England, but his Tilbury Town is too bleak to be a representative picture.

11 WHICHER, GEORGE F. "The Twentieth Century," in The Literature of the American People: An Historical and Critical Survey. Edited by Arthur Hobson Quinn. New York: Appleton-Century-Crofts, pp. 819-22.
    Robinson's poetry is marked by his psychological studies, his attacks on complacency in his countryman, and his concentration on the life of the artist. The Man Who Died Twice is one of his most significant poems. He is similar to Keats in his devotion to poetry.

1952 A BOOKS

1 BARNARD, ELLSWORTH. Edwin Arlington Robinson: A Critical Study. New York: Macmillan, 318 pp.
    [This full-scale critical study is organized by analyses of Robinson's obscurities, diction, poetic forms, characterization, and philosophical stance. While all Robinson's books are mentioned, emphasis is on the early work. No sustained reading of individual poems. Extensive notes and an index. Re-issued 1969.A1.]

*2 BAUMGARTNER, ALFRED. "Das Lyrische Werk Edwin Arlington Robinson." Ph.D. thesis, Mainz University.
    [Cited in White, p. 114.]

1952 B SHORTER WRITINGS

1 DEUTSCH, BABETTE. Poetry in Our Time. New York: Henry Holt, pp. 55-60.
    Robinson, who resembles Browning, Praed, and James, is best at New England portraiture, but his "pedestrian reasonableness generally prevented him from transmitting his ideas into the stuff of poetry." [Reprinted in 1963.B7.]

2 FUSSELL, EDWIN. "The Americanism of E. A. R." Claremont Quarterly, 1:9-12.
    Robinson is being accused of being "un-American," as Jeffers was, but it is silly to condemn a poet who died in 1935 for not taking part in the cold war.

3 HART, SYLVIA and ESTELLE PAIGE. "Robinson's 'For a Dead Lady.'" The Explicator, 10 (May), Item 51.
    Possibly "the laugh that love could not forgive" refers to her love, not his.

1952

4 SCHERMAN, DAVID E. and ROSEMARIE REDLICH. Literary America.
   New York: Dodd, Mead, pp. 114-51.
   [Sketch of career with illustration of Gardiner, Maine,
   Robinson's Tilbury Town. Quotations from "Mr. Flood's
   Party" and Amaranth.]

5 STAGEBERG, NORMAN C. and WALLACE ANDERSON. Poetry as Experience. New York: American Book Company, pp. 189-92 and
   passim.
   [Introduction to poetry, using 6 poems by Robinson to
   illustrate various poetic devices.]

6 WAGGONER, H. H. "Robinson's 'New England.'" The Explicator,
   10 (March), Item 33.
   "We're told," in line 10 suggests that outsiders are at-
   tacking New England. Perhaps Robinson was referring to
   Ludwig Lewisohn.

7 WILSON, EDMUND. "Mr. E. A. Robinson's Moonlight," in The
   Shores of Light: A Literary Chronicle of the Twenties and
   Thirties. New York: Farrar, Straus and Young, pp. 36-38.
   [Reprint of 1923.B34.]

1953 A BOOKS

1 BURTON, DAVID H. "Christian Conservatism in the Poetry of
   Edwin Arlington Robinson." Ph.D. thesis, Georgetown Uni-
   versity, 345 pp.
   [A study of Robinson's intellectual background and the
   Christian theology in his poems, concluding that while
   Christian ethical views pervade his poetry, his own theo-
   logical stance is that found in "Nicodemus."]

2 THOMPSON, LAWRANCE, ed. Tilbury Town: Selected Poems of Edwin Arlington Robinson. New York: Macmillan, pp. ix-xvii;
   133-43.
   [Introduction emphasizing Robinson's wit and profundity
   and notes on each of the sixty-five poems.]

1953 B SHORTER WRITINGS

1 CROWDER, RICHARD. "'Man Against the Sky.'" College English,
   14 (February), 269-76.
   [Close reading of the poem.] The poem suffers from dis-
   cursiveness and lack of conclusion, but "the general in-
   conclusiveness is, however, the meaning of the poem, which...
   gives the reader the dilemma of the twentieth century man."

2   WRIGHT, CELESTE TURNER. "Robinson's 'Lost Anchors.'" The Ex-
    plicator, 11 (June), Item 57.
        Robinson used the wrong verb tense in line 8; it should
    be "had" instead of "have." The last line refers to the
    old sailor.

1954 A BOOKS

1   FUSSELL, EDWIN S. Edwin Arlington Robinson: The Literary
    Background of a Traditional Poet. Berkeley and Los Angeles:
    University of California Press, 211 pp.
        [An examination of Robinson's influences, established by
    his subject matter, stylistic parallels, and his comments
    about other writers in letters and conversations. Two
    principal chapters focus on American and British influen-
    ces, with briefer studies on European naturalism, Classical
    influences, and the English Bible. A concluding chapter
    compares Robinson's use of tradition with that of T. S.
    Eliot. Publication of 1949.A1; partially reprinted in
    1970.A3.]

2   STEPHENS, ALAN ARCHER, JR. "The Shorter Narrative Poems of
    Edwin Arlington Robinson." Ph.D. thesis, University of
    Missouri, 235 pp.
        In spite of his reputation as a traditionalist, an exam-
    ination of Robinson's short narratives reveals that he fre-
    quently used experimental techniques.

1954 B SHORTER WRITINGS

1   BROWN, JOHN. Panorama de la Littérature Contemporaine aux
    États-Unis. Nrf. Paris: Librarie Gallimard, pp. 260-61.
        Robinson is a liaison between the Puritan tradition and
    the anguish of The Waste Land. The simplicity of his rhyme
    and conversational tone are commendable.

2   COXE, LOUIS O. "E. A. Robinson: The Lost Tradition." The
    Sewannee Review, 62 (Spring), 247-66.
        [Close readings of "Eros Turannos," "The Clerks," and
    "The Gift of God" to support the thesis that Robinson did
    not receive the attention he deserves because readers have
    neither seen the subtleties of verse nor appreciated the
    excellence of his prosody. Reprinted in 1969.A4 and
    1970.A3.] Robinson has written more poems of high merit
    than any other American, which makes him "the major Ameri-
    can poet of our era, with only T. S. Eliot as a peer."

1954

3   ECKMAN, FREDERICK WILLIS. "The Language of American Poetry:
     1900-1910." Ph.D. thesis, Ohio State University, 338 pp.
         Of the poets writing in the first decade of the century,
     only Robinson and Pound have more than historic interest.
     Robinson avoided the excesses of romanticism by using the
     vocabulary and syntax of realistic fiction. [DA 20:2798-
     2800.]

4   KNIGHT, GRANT C. The Strenuous Age in American Literature.
     Chapel Hill: The University of North Carolina Press,
     pp. 74-75, 209-210.
         Robinson's poetry is comparable to that of Housman, but
     "Robinson's humanity was warmer." "Captain Craig" was "the
     most concentrated, the most tender, and the wisest an Amer-
     ican had yet published."

5   LEARY, LEWIS. Articles on American Literature, 1900-1950.
     Durham, North Carolina: Duke University Press, pp. 258-63.
         [A bibliographical listing of 221 articles on Robinson
     in serial publications.]

6   LOWE, ROBERT LIDDELL. "Two Letters of Edwin Arlington Robin-
     son: A Note on his Early Critical Reception." The New
     England Quarterly, 27 (June), 257-61.
         That Robinson wrote two letters to William Allen Neilson
     regretting that they had not met suggests that he was ap-
     preciative of early supporters. [Two letters by Robinson
     and a review of Captain Craig printed.]

7   STARR, NATHAN C. King Arthur Today. Gainesville: University
     of Florida Press, pp. 21-39, 72-83.
         [A detailed comparison of Robinson's treatment of Arthur-
     ian materials with other modern writers, emphasizing his
     aim "to illuminate the commonplace" and his exclusive in-
     terest in character revelation. Tristram considered the
     least successful of the Arthurian trilogy.]

8   TATE, ALLEN. Sixty American Poets 1896-1944, Selected, with
     Preface and Critical Notes. Revised. Washington, D.C.:
     The Library of Congress, pp. 107-113.
         [A check list of works by Robinson and bibliographical
     and critical materials about him in the Library of Congress
     Catalog and the Union Catalog.] "Robinson's achievement is
     in all respects comparable to that of the chief English
     poets of the nineteenth century. He is the only American
     poet in our entire history of whom that may be said."

9   WEBER, CARL J. "Another 'Torrent' Turns Up." Colby Library
    Quarterly, 3 (February), 220.
    [Sixty-five copies of Robinson's first book now located.]

1955 A BOOKS

1   DECHERT, PETER. "Edwin Arlington Robinson and Alanson Tucker
    Schumann: A Study in Influences." Ph.D. thesis, Univer-
    sity of Pennsylvania, 225 pp.
    Schumann was a facile but mediocre poet who influenced
    Robinson's reading, his early experiments in poetic forms,
    his attitude toward the role of the poet, and certain phil-
    osophic stances. [DA 15:822-23.]

2   FRYXELL, LUCY DICKINSON. "Edwin Arlington Robinson as a Dra-
    matist and Dramatic Poet." Ph.D. thesis, University of
    Kentucky, 161 pp.
    Robinson's interest in theatre and the time he spent
    writing plays have a demonstrable effect on his late poetry
    in that a dramatic structure is imposed on them and other
    dramatic devices are evident. [DA 20:4110-11.]

1955 B SHORTER WRITINGS

1   AIKEN, CONRAD. "Edwin Arlington Robinson." Times Literary
    Supplement, October 14, p. 605.
    [Letter to the editor insisting that Robinson was well
    received by his contemporaries, contrary to comment in re-
    cent review of Fussell's book. Reprinted in 1956.B1.]

2   CHILDERS, WILLIAM C. "Edwin Arlington Robinson's Proper
    Names," Names: Journal of the American Name Society, 3
    (December), 223-29.
    [Conjecture on the sources for some of the names of the
    Tilbury Town characters, such as John Evereldown, Miniver
    Cheevy, Eben Flood, Aaron Stark, and Cliff Klingenhagen.]

3   SPILLER, ROBERT E. "Problems in Dynamism: Adams, Norris,
    Robinson," in The Cycle of American Literature: An Essay
    in Historical Criticism. New York: Macmillan, pp. 208-
    210.
    "With Henry Adams, Robinson rescued from the collapse of
    of nineteenth-century idealism his undying faith in human-
    ity and, thus fortified, rode out to meet the dragon of
    modern scientific determinism."

1955

4   UNTERMEYER, LOUIS. "Edwin Arlington Robinson," in <u>Makers of
     the Modern World</u>. New York: Simon and Schuster, pp. 399-
     404.
          [Biographical sketch emphasizing the painfully slow start
     of his career and noting that he is not an innovator but a
     revitalizer of old forms.]

1956 A BOOKS

1   MOON, ELMER SAMUEL. "Organic Form in the Shorter Poems of
     Edwin Arlington Robinson." Ph.D. thesis, University of
     Michigan, 283 pp.
          [A study of the influence of Robinson's transcendental
     attitudes on stylistic matters of history, syntax, symbol,
     and design in his shorter poems. <u>DA</u> 17:145.]

2   MORRILL, PAUL HAMPTON. "Psychological Aspects of the Poetry
     of Edwin Arlington Robinson." Ph.D. thesis, Northwestern
     University, 189 pp.
          [A study of fifty-three short poems and eleven long ones
     using current psychological theories of inter-personal re-
     lationships, concluding that Robinson's use of the psycho-
     logical was indicative of his reaction to the genteel
     romanticism of the nineteenth century. <u>DA</u> 17:363-64.]

3   STEVICK, ROBERT DAVID. "E. A. Robinson's Principles and Prac-
     tice of Poetry: The Effects of his Principles of Poetry on
     the Technique and Structure of the Poems." Ph.D. thesis,
     University of Wisconsin, 305 pp.
          Robinson's use of diction and his allusions provide a
     structural element to his poetry. He is not successful
     when he is only abstract and didactic, but his most com-
     plex structural method is the combination of character and
     abstract statement. [<u>DA</u> 16:2463.]

1956 B SHORTER WRITINGS

1   AIKEN, CONRAD. "On Edwin Arlington Robinson." <u>Colby Library
     Quarterly</u>, 4 (February), 95-97.
          [Reprint of 1955.B1.]

2   CHILDERS, WILLIAM C. "Robinson's 'Amaryllis.'" <u>The Explica-
     tor</u>, 14 (February), Item 34.
          Amaryllis may stand for a symbol of poetry as well as a
     lament for old age.

1957

3 HILL, ROBERT W. "More Light on a Shadowy Figure: A. H. Louis, the Original of E. A. Robinson's 'Captain Craig.'" Bulletin of the New York Public Library, 60 (August), 373-77.
   [One sonnet and three letters by Louis.]

4 KINDILIEN, CARLIN T. "Edwin Arlington Robinson," in American Poetry in the Eighteen-Nineties. Providence, R.I.: Brown University Press, pp. 96-105.
   Robinson achieved poetic individuality in the Nineties through his unique combination of mood, form, and subject matter. In diction he tried to maintain the normal word order and at the same time to be artistic. He is not so much a pessimist as he is a qualified optimist.

5 SCOTT, WINFIELD TOWNLEY. "To See Robinson." The New Mexico Quarterly, 26 (Summer), 161-78.
   [Personal reminiscence of Scott's visiting Robinson at Peterborough in 1927 and a record of their friendship until Robinson's death. Reprinted in 1961.B5.]

6 WEBER, CARL J. "What's in a Name?--or in a Signature?" MSS, 8:185-88.
   Robinson's handwriting grew "increasingly microscopic" until it was almost illegible by the 1920's.

7 WHITE, WILLIAM. "What is a Collector's Item: Emily Dickinson, E. A. Robinson, and D. H. Lawrence? (An Essay in the Form of a Bibliography)." The American Book Collector, 6 (Summer), 6-8.
   [Disquisition on whether or not Tilbury Town is a collector's item, noting that there are three previously unpublished poems in the notes.]

8 ZARDOYA, CONCHA. "Edwin Arlington Robinson," in Historia de la Literatura Norteamericana. Barcelona: Editorial Labor, S.A., pp. 320-33.
   [Brief biographical and critical sketch emphasizing Robinson's lyricism, traditionalism, and optimism.]

1957 A BOOKS - NONE

1957 B SHORTER WRITINGS

1 ANGOFF, ALLAN, ed. American Writing Today: Its Independence and Vigor. The Times (London) Literary Supplement. New York: New York University Press, pp. 354-56.
   [Reprint of 1922.B5.]

1957

2   SLOTE, BERNICE. "Robinson's 'En Passant.'" The Explicator,
     15 (February), Item 27.
        This poem, a microcosm of Robinson's work, depends upon
     a move in chess for clarification. One man has killed
     another because the victim refused to stop and talk with
     the murderer.

1958 A BOOKS - NONE

1958 B SHORTER WRITINGS

1   ADLER, JACOB H. "Robinson's 'Gawaine.'" English Studies, 39
     (February), 1-20.
        Robinson has made Gawaine a well-rounded, sympathetic
     figure who is important to the plot and serves as a unify-
     ing figure for all three Arthurian poems.

2   AIKEN, CONRAD. Collected Criticism of Conrad Aiken from 1916
     to the Present: A Reviewer's ABC. New York: Meridian
     Books, pp. 333-46.
        [Reprint of 1921.B1, 1922.B1, and 1927.B1. Reprinted in
     1970.A3.]

3   GARVIN, HARRY R. "Poems Pickled in Anthological Brine." CEA
     Critic, 20 (October), 1, 4.
        Robinson is more sympathetic to Cory than are the towns-
     people, who are bitterly aware that Cory is indifferent to
     others and feel "a retributive satisfaction" at his suicide.
     [Reprinted in 1962.B9.]

4   MILLER, PERRY. "The New England Conscience." American Schol-
     ar, 28 (Winter), 49-58.
        [Brief mention of "New England" as comic treatment of
     conscience.]

5   WAGENKNECHT, EDWARD. The Seven Worlds of Theodore Roosevelt.
     New York: Longmans-Green, pp. 60-61, 153.
        [Report of Roosevelt's patronage of Robinson and the
     critics response to the Outlook article. Two unpublished
     letters cited.]

1959 A BOOKS - NONE

1959 B SHORTER WRITINGS

1   CIARDI, JOHN. How Does A Poem Mean. Boston: Houghton
     Mifflin, p. 712.

[Brief comment on symbolic significance of the name Eben
Flood in "Mr. Flood's Party."]

2 OLIVER, EGBERT S. "Robinson's Dark-Hill-to-Climb Image."
   Literary Criterion, 3 (Summer), 36-52.
      Robinson is one of three or four most significant Ameri-
   can poets since Whitman. His central image of climbing a
   hill to look for light is first seen in Captain Craig and
   continues through several poems in The Man Against the Sky,
   Cavender's House, The Glory of the Nightingales, Matthias
   at the Door, and Nicodemus. It is perhaps most notable in
   "Mr. Flood's Party." [Reprinted in 1965.B12.]

3 ROSENFIELD, LEONORA COHEN. "The Philosopher and the Poet."
   Palinurus, 1 (April), 24-40.
      [Commentary on an edition of notes on Robinson by Morris
   Cohen, the philosopher who shared a sitting room at Peter-
   borough for years. Cohen reports conversations concerning
   Robinson's literary tastes and opinions of his own poetry.
   He assesses Robinson's poetry as high "B" work rather than
   "A" because Robinson so isolated himself.]

4 STEVICK, ROBERT D. "Robinson and William James." The University of Kansas City Review, 25 (June), 293-301.
      Comparing "The Man Against the Sky" with William James'
   "Is Life Worth Living?" is valid since Robinson called his
   poem "a protest against the material explanation of the
   universe." This comparison increases our understanding of
   this religious rather than philosophical poem.

5 TATE, ALLEN. "Edwin Arlington Robinson," in Collected Essays.
   Denver: Alan Swallow, pp. 358-64.
      [Reprint of 1933.B26, 1936.B27, 1948.B17, and reprinted
   in 1968.B16.]

6 UNTERMEYER, LOUIS. "Edwin Arlington Robinson," in Lives of
   the Poets: The Story of One Thousand Years of English and
   American Poetry. New York: Simon and Schuster, pp. 623-
   29.
      [Biographical sketch and brief assessment.] Robinson
   will be remembered for short lyrics of social commentary.

1960 A BOOKS

1 DAVIS, CHARLES T. "Introduction" and "Notes," in E. A. Robinson: Selected Early Poems and Letters. Edited by Charles
   T. Davis. New York: Holt, Rinehart and Winston, pp. ix-
   xxx; 223-38.

1960

Robinson is a modern poet because of his diction, irony,
and narrative technique. In his attempt to become "a gen-
uine Emersonian idealist" he was a unique writer of the
1890's. [Notes give publishing data for each poem included
in Robinson's first three volumes, many of which were
omitted from Collected Poems. Explanatory notes for most
of the thirty-three letters included.]

1960 B SHORTER WRITINGS

1   BROOKS, CLEANTH and ROBERT PENN WARREN. Understanding Poetry.
     Third edition. New York: Holt, Rinehart and Winston,
     pp. 214-17.
        [Detailed explication of "Mr. Flood's Party."] Pathos
     and humor, but not mawkishness, prevail in this poem about
     "a drunken derelict."

2   BROWN, MAURICE F. "Moody and Robinson." Colby Library Quar-
     terly, 5 (December), 185-94.
        Robinson and William Vaughan Moody were friends and each
     admired the other's work, although Robinson was less gener-
     ous in his praise than Moody, possibly because Robinson was
     jealous of Moody's success.

3   BURKHART, CHARLES. "Robinson's 'Richard Cory.'" The Explica-
     tor, 19 (November), Item 9.
        This poem is impressively balanced with a series of con-
     trasts: active and passive, light and dark, royal and com-
     mon. "The exemplum becomes deeply ambiguous: that knowl-
     edge may be an illusory good."

4   CARY, RICHARD. "In Memoriam: Edwin Arlington Robinson."
     Colby Library Quarterly, 5 (December), 169.
        On the twenty-fifth anniversary of Robinson's death this
     issue of the journal is dedicated to "Maine's most dis-
     tinguished native poet and his perdurable accomplishment."

_____. "Robinson's Notes to His Nieces." Colby Library Quar-
     terly, 5 (December), 195-202.
        The sixty-five letters to Robinson's nieces, Ruth, Marie,
     and Barbara, in the Colby library reveal that Robinson was
     generous, modest, soberly witty, moderately pessimistic,
     and dedicated to the writing of poetry.

6   CROWDER, RICHARD. "Robinson's Talifer: The Figurative Tex-
     ture." Boston University Studies in English, 4 (Winter),
     241-47.

1961

[Reassessment of Talifer with review of criticism, suggesting that it deserves more attention and emphasizing its
allegorical significance.]

7 EBY, CECIL D., JR. "Edwin Arlington Robinson on Higher Educa-
tion." Colby Library Quarterly, 5 (September), 163-64.
[Letter to Waitman Barbe about why colleges don't produce
more writers. Robinson doesn't know.]

8 HILLYER, ROBERT. In Pursuit of Poetry. New York: McGraw-
Hill, pp. 82-87 and passim.
[References to Robinson scattered throughout this discussion of poetry. Examples of his work frequently used to
illustrate a verse form. Elaborate praise for Amaranth.]

9 NIVISON, DAVID S. "Does it Matter how Annandale Went Out?"
Colby Library Quarterly, 5 (December), 170-85.
[Cautious but supported speculation by Robinson's grand-
nephew that "Miniver Cheevy," "Cortege," and the Annandale
poems are especially autobiographical. Reprinted in
1969.A4.]

10 ROSENTHAL, M. L. "Rival Idioms: The Great Generation: Robinson and Frost," in The Modern Poets: A Critical Introduction. New York: Oxford University Press, pp. 104-112.
Robinson, whose principal themes are mutability and failure, is better at narrative poetry that avoids self-pity
than at philosophical enquiry. [Commentary on "Clavering,"
"The Man Against the Sky," "The Tree in Pamela's Garden,"
and "Cassandra."]

11 THORP, WILLARD. "E. A. Robinson," in American Writing in the
Twentieth Century. Cambridge: Harvard University Press,
pp. 38-42.
Robinson is one of the most significant American poets.
His interest in failures is often pointed out, but not the
fortitude that the failures possess.

1961 A BOOKS

1 FOY, JOHN VAIL. "Character and Structure in Edwin Arlington
Robinson's Major Narratives." Ph.D. thesis, Cornell University, 268 pp.
After Robinson's attempts at prose and drama failed he
worked out a realistic and dramatic treatment for his characters in his narratives. The Arthurian poems show the re-
sults of this attempt, but his narratives on contemporary

1961

    themes have characters that are so subtly delineated that
they seem too much alike. His later narratives have a
clearer plot structure and characterization. [DA 22:1996.]

1961 B SHORTER WRITINGS

1   ADAMS, RICHARD P. "The Failure of Edwin Arlington Robinson."
    Tulane Studies in English, 11:97-151.
      Robinson's poetry is too negative to be truly romantic.
He spent so much time rejecting materialism that he had no
energy for stating a positive position. [Close readings of
"Luke Havergal," "The Man Against the Sky," "To a Dead
Lady," and "Eros Turannos."]

2   CROWDER, RICHARD. "E. A. Robinson and the Meaning of Life."
    The Chicago Review, 15 (Summer), 5-17.
      [A discussion of Robinson as an existentialist through an
examination of some twenty poems, concluding that his existentialism is closer to that of Tillich and Kierkegaard
than that of Sartre.]

3   DAVIS, CHARLES T.   "Image Patterns in the Poetry of Edwin
    Arlington Robinson." College English, 22 (March), 380-86.
      While light and dark images dominate Robinson's verse,
other image patterns are evident. Those most frequently
seen are houses, gardens, ashes and flame, and the sea.
[Reprinted in 1969.A4.]

4   PEARCE, ROY HARVEY. The Continuity of American Poetry.
    Princeton: Princeton University Press, pp. 256-68.
      Robinson's contribution to American poetry is his mastery
of the objective, intense, dramatic poem. He saw the limitation of the form and tried unsuccessfully to go beyond
it in philosophical poems, such as "The Man Against the
Sky" and the late narratives. [Explication of "Eros Tur-
ranos."]

5   SCOTT, WINFIELD TOWNLEY. "To See Robinson," in Exiles and
    Fabrications. Garden City, New York: Doubleday, pp. 154-
    70.
      [Reprint of 1956.B5.]

*6   SMITH, RAY. "Robinson, Edwin Arlington," in Lexikon der Welt-
    literatur im 20. Jahrhundert, Vol. 2. Freiburg, Sasel,
    Wein: Herder, col. 758-59.
      [Cited in White, p. 46.]

7   SULLIVAN, LUCY D. "Edwin Arlington Robinson, Disinherited
     Puritan." The Gordon Review, 6 (First Issue), 11-20.
          Robinson, unable to approve of the current practice of
     Christianity, sought all his life for a substitution. His
     poetry, however, reveals attitudes about God, sin, and re-
     generation that are grounded in Puritan theology.

8   WHICHER, STEPHEN and LARS AHNEBRINK, eds. "Edwin Arlington
     Robinson," in Twelve American Poets. New York: Oxford
     University Press, pp. 68-71.
          One must appreciate Robinson's angle of vision to enjoy
     his work. "He combatted the naturalistic disillusion of
     his day, not by arguing that human life is happy, since it
     plainly is not, but by dramatizing the significance of the
     individual destiny."

1962 A BOOKS

1   COXE, LOUIS. Edwin Arlington Robinson. University of Minne-
     sota Pamphlets on American Writers No. 17. Minneapolis:
     University of Minnesota Press, 48 pp.
          [General introduction, incorporating much of 1954.B2 and
     adding the assessment that Robinson shared with the nine-
     teenth century British poets both their excellence and ex-
     cesses: his reputation has suffered because of the number
     of mediocre poems he published in the second half of his
     career. Brief bibliography.]

*2   MALOF, JOSEPH FELTER. "The Engaging Mask: Isolation in the
     Early Poems of Edwin Arlington Robinson." Ph.D. thesis,
     University of California, Los Angeles.
          [Cited in White, p. 76.]

3   ROBINSON, WILLIAM RONALD. "Edwin Arlington Robinson: The
     Poetry of the Act." Ph.D. thesis, Ohio State University,
     239 pp.
          [An examination of Robinson's aesthetic, which posits
     that metaphysical answers are not possible through philo-
     sophy but through the creation of poetry itself. While the
     Robinsonian attitude bears resemblances to William James's
     radical empiricism, romanticism, and existentialism, it is
     essentially an individual world view centering on the
     search for truth and the reconciliation between man and
     society. "Flammonde" singled out as the most significant
     poem in demonstrating this stance. DA 24:303-304; pub-
     lished 1967.A5.]

1962

1962 B SHORTER WRITINGS

1   ALLEN, JAMES L., JR. "Symbol and Theme in 'Mr. Flood's Par-
     ty.'" Mississippi Quarterly, 15 (Fall), 139-43.
         [Explication of "Mr. Flood's Party," emphasizing the use
     of metaphorical language and lamenting that Robinson did
     not write more poetry in this vein.]

*2   BOMPARD, PAOLA. "Un Gran Precursore di Spoon River: Edwin
     Arlington Robinson Doganiere del Pessimismo." La Fiera
     Letteraria, 36 (September 7), 4.
         [Cited in White, p. 77.]

3   CARY, RICHARD. "Robinson on Moody." Colby Library Quarterly,
     6 (December), 176-83.
         At Harvard Robinson was awed by the editor of the Harvard
     Monthly, William Vaughan Moody. His letters about him are
     complimentary but they reveal a rivalry between the two.
     Moody was "a providential obstruction, the irritant rock
     Robinson needed to thrust his blade against--and so sharpen
     it."

4   CROWDER, RICHARD. "Redemption for the Man of Iron." The Per-
     sonalist, 43 (January), 46-56.
         Talifer may be regarded as a symbolic representation of
     the pattern of Christian redemption. Talifer's rejection
     of Althea for Karen and subsequent divorce and remarriage
     are roughly parallel to the Christian experience of sin,
     confession, and reconciliation. The meanings of the names
     of the characters support this view.

5   _____. "Robinson, Edwin Arlington," in The Reader's Encyclo-
     pedia of American Literature. Edited by Max J. Herzberg.
     New York: Thomas Y. Crowell, pp. 965-66.
         [Biographical sketch with cross references to twelve
     poems. Assessment of Robinson as writer with many faults
     but finally the chief perpetrator of the poetic renaissance.]

6   DANIELS, MABEL. "Edwin Arlington Robinson: A Muscial Memoir."
     Radcliffe Quarterly, 46 (November), 5-11.
         [Reminiscence of composer who established a friendship
     with Robinson at Peterborough and put some of his poems to
     music.] Both "Captain Craig" and The Man Who Died Twice
     demonstrate Robinson's knowledge of music, which he loved
     next to poetry.

7   DERLETH, AUGUST. "Old Voices and New." Voices: A Journal of
     Poetry, No. 177 (January-April), p. 62.

1962

[Brief recommendation for Selected Early Poems and Letters.]

8   FAIRCHILD, HOXIE NEALE. "Realists," in Religious Trends in
    English Poetry; Volume 5: 1880-1920, Gods of a Changing
    Poetry. New York and London: Columbia University Press,
    pp. 238-43.
        Robinson's idealism is diluted transcendentalism, which
    is diluted Puritanism, which makes him sound like a high
    school valedictorian. "As with his master, Browning, his
    simplicities undermine his complexities."

9   GARVIN, HARRY R. "Comprehensive Criticism: A Humanistic Dis-
    cipline." Bucknell Review, 10 (May), 305-327.
        [Expansion of 1958.B3, using the explication of "Richard
    Cory" as a paradigm for analytic criticism that is "com-
    prehensive."]

10 HERTZ, ROBERT N. "Two Voices of the American Village: Robin-
    son and Masters." Minnesota Review, 2 (April), 345-58.
        [Analysis of the characteristic Tilbury Town and Spoon
    River as keys to the poet's perception of life. The Til-
    bury characters are divided into five groups: failures,
    non-entities, paradoxes, victims and stoics.]

11 KLOTZ, MARVIN. "Robinson's 'The Tree in Pamela's Garden.'"
    The Explicator, 20 (January), Item 42.
        Since Apollo is mentioned in the poem, Pamela may be
    analogous to Daphne. In that case she herself is the tree
    in the title and is not to be construed as a pitiable
    creature but a "destructively frigid" one.

12 KUNTZ, JOSEPH M. Poetry Explication: A Checklist of Inter-
    pretation since 1925 of British and American Poems Past and
    Present. Revised edition. Denver: Alan Swallow, pp. 212-
    15.
        [A bibliography of forty explications, listed by poem
    title.]

13 LOWE, ROBERT LIDDELL. "Edwin Arlington Robinson to Harriet
    Monroe: Some Unpublished Letters." Modern Philology, 60
    (August), 31-40.
        [As well as printing thirteen letters by Robinson, this
    article traces the literary relationship between him and
    Monroe, stressing her guarded admiration for the poet and
    her unrelenting dislike of the Arthurian poems.]

1962

14   PERRINE, LAURENCE. "Contemporary Reference to Robinson's Arthurian Poems." Twentieth Century Literature, 8 (July),
74-82.
    While Merlin and Lancelot are not political allegories,
there are contemporary attitudes expressed: war is not to
be glorified, the death of the common soldier is as tragic
as that of an aristocrat, kings are corrupt, and women
should be given more of a place in the affairs of men.

15   _____. "A Reading of 'Miniver Cheevy.'" Colby Library Quarterly, 6 (June), 65-74.
    "Miniver Cheevy" is a remarkable poem because of the
diction, technical excellence, tone, and autobiographical
elements: his attitudes about materialism and classical
antiquity and his brush with alcoholism.

1963 A BOOKS

1   UNTERMEYER, LOUIS. Edwin Arlington Robinson: A Reappraisal,
with a Bibliography and a List of Materials in the Edwin
Arlington Robinson Exhibit on Display at the Library of
Congress, April 15 to July 15, 1963. Washington, D.C.:
Library of Congress, 39 pp.
    [Biographical sketch and assessment.] Robinson is over-
shadowed by Frost, but deserves more attention. His emo-
tions are shaped and controlled by traditional poetic
forms. [Reprinted in 1973.B9.]

1963 B SHORTER WRITINGS

1   BARRY, JAMES D. "Robinson's 'Firelight.'" The Explicator, 22
(November), Item 21.
    This technically superior sonnet deals with the wisdom of
using only the illusory firelight rather than submitting to
the harsh reality of full light.

2   CAMBON, GLAUCO. "Edwin Arlington Robinson: Knight of the
Grail," in The Inclusive Flame: Studies in American Poetry.
Bloomington: Indiana University Press, pp. 53-78.
    Robinson's Camelot is an inversion of his Tilbury Town.
Both his contemporary and Arthurian characters search for
the fulfillment of their dreams. His characters do not
succumb to defeat but "have reconquered innocence through
experience." Robinson may be considered a precursor to
Yeats, Eliot, Stevens, and Robert Lowell, among others.

1963

3 CARY, RICHARD. "E. A. Robinson as Soothsayer." Colby Library
    Quarterly, 6 (June), 233-45.
       Robinson made several predictions about the success of
    his own poems and the work of other writers, but not all of
    them proved to be correct. Possibly his friendship with
    such correspondents as Edith Brower adversely colored his
    view. [Reprinted in 1969.A4.]

4 _____. "Robinson Bonanza." Colby Library Quarterly, 6 (June),
    261.
       [Announcement of acquisition of fifty-four holographic
    letters to Arthur Davis Variell, a school friend of Robin-
    son. [See 1974.B8.)]

5 _____. "Robinson on Browning." Victorian Newsletter, 23
    (Spring), 19-21.
       Robinson was not pleased by the frequent comparison by
    reviewers of his work and Browning's. His letters show
    that while he once admired Browning's poems, he grew less
    and less enthusiastic about them, possibly because of what
    he considered an invidious comparison.

6 _____. "Robinson on Dickens." American Notes & Queries, 2
    (November), 35-36.
       [Three letters from Robinson to Edith Brower extolling
    Dickens' virtues.] Robinson felt that Dickens was "the
    greatest thing since Shakespeare."

7 DEUTSCH, BABETTE. Poetry in Our Time: A Critical Survey of
    Poetry in the English-Speaking World 1900-1960. Second
    edition, revised and enlarged. Garden City, New York:
    Doubleday, pp. 59-64.
       [Reprint of 1952.B1.]

8 JOE, WANNE J. "A Brief Discussion of Edwin Arlington Robinson
    Based on His Life and Poetry." The English Language and
    Literature, No. 14, pp. 18-39.
       [Examination of Robinson's career with emphasis on his
    cultural milieu of Puritan moralism and Roycian idealism
    and centering primarily on his anti-materialistic stance
    that led eventually to a "prophecy for the downfall of
    American democracy" in King Jasper.]

9 LOWELL, AMY. "A Bird's Eye View of E. A. Robinson," in A Dial
    Miscellany. Edited by William Wasserstrom. Syracuse:
    Syracuse University Press, pp. 75-87.
       [Reprint of 1922.B22 and 1930.B20.]

1963

10   MORAN, RONALD. "Avon's Harvest Re-examined." Colby Library
     Quarterly, 6 (June), 247-54.
        [A plot summary, a review of contemporary criticism, a
     notice of the textual changes, and a survey of later criti-
     cal commentary, indicating that when Robinson took out the
     dagger he intended that the poem should be read as a ghost
     story instead of a tale about a man who has hallucinations.]

11   M[OTTRAM], E. N. W. "Robinson, Edwin Arlington," in The Con-
     cise Encyclopedia of English and American Poets and Poetry.
     Edited by Stephen Spender and Donald Hall. New York: Haw-
     thorne, pp. 275-76.
        [Biographical sketch with assessment.] Robinson's "genu-
     ine personal and fin-de-siècle gloom never reached tragic
     power." His best poem is "Isaac and Archibald."

12   REIN, DAVID N. "The Appeal of 'Richard Cory.'" CEA Critic,
     26 (November), 6.
        Students laugh at the end of "Richard Cory" because they
     are more envious than sympathetic with Cory. They identify
     with the narrator.

13   SAMPLEY, ARTHUR M. "Quiet Voices, Unquiet Times." Midwest
     Quarterly, 3 (Spring), 247-56.
        Using as a criterion the poet who has a tragic sense and
     addresses spiritual problems, Robinson is one of four great
     twentieth century poets, in company with Eliot, Yeats, and
     Frost. Robinson sees spiritual failure as central to modern
     life and the "light" as salvation.

14   SOMKIN, FRED. "Tocqueville as a Source for Robinson's 'Man
     Against the Sky.'" Colby Library Quarterly, 6 (June),
     245-47.
        Although there is no direct evidence that Robinson read
     Alexis de Tocqueville, Democracy in America is a possible
     source for the first scene in "The Man Against the Sky."

15   SPILLER, ROBERT et al., eds. "Edwin Arlington Robinson," in
     Literary History of the United States: Bibliography and
     Supplement, Vol. 2. Third edition; revised. New York:
     Macmillan; London: Collier-Macmillan, pp. 705-708; 184-85.
        [Reprinting of 1948 bibliography and 1959 supplement of
     primary and secondary sources on Robinson in one volume of
     LHUS.]

16   WELLMAN, MANLY WADE. "The Richard Cory Murder Case," Ellery
     Queen's Mystery Magazine, February, pp. 80-87.

1964

[Short story in which Miniver Cheevy discovers that someone other than Richard put a bullet through his head.]

17 WRIGHT, ELIZABETH. "Robinson's 'The Tree in Pamela's Gar-
    den.'" The Explicator, 21 (February), Item 47.
        Klotz (1962.B11) is wrong in suggesting that Pamela is
    "a warped personality." She is pathetic in that she prob-
    ably has been unable to convince herself as she has the
    town that she doesn't need a man.

1964 A BOOKS - NONE

1964 B SHORTER WRITINGS

1   ALLEN, JAMES L., JR. "Edwin Arlington Robinson: Poet or
    Versifier?" English Record, 14 (February), 9-15.
        Many critics agree that figurative language is essential
    to poetry, but Robinson apparently had a low regard for it;
    he often used a minimum of concrete images in his poetry.
    See, for example, "Richard Cory."

2   COFFIN, ROBERT P. TRISTRAM. New Poetry of New England. New
    York: Russell & Russell, passim.
        [Reprint of 1938.B9.]

3   COWLEY, MALCOLM. "Edwin Arlington Robinson," in After the
    Genteel Tradition: American Writers, 1910-1930. Edited by
    Malcolm Cowley. Carbondale: Southern Illinois University
    Press, pp. 28-36.
        [Reprint of 1948.B6.]

4   FROST, ROBERT. Selected Letters of Robert Frost. Edited by
    Lawrance Thompson. New York: Holt, Rinehart and Winston,
    passim.
        [Eight letters, to, by, or about Robinson.]

5   GROSS, HARVEY. Sound and Form in Modern Poetry: A Study of
    Prosody from Thomas Hardy to Robert Lowell. Ann Arbor:
    University of Michigan Press, pp. 63-74.
        [A study of the metrical qualities of Robinson's blank
    verse through an examination of "Isaac and Archibald."]

6   LEOFF, EVE. Review Notes and Study Guide to Twentieth Century
    British and American Poets. New York: Monarch Press,
    pp. 39-41.
        [Comments on "Richard Cory," "Miniver Cheevy," "Bewick
    Finzer," "The Unforgiven," and "The Mill."]

161

1964

7   LOWE, ROBERT LIDDELL. "A Letter of Edwin Arlington Robinson
     to James Barstow." The New England Quarterly, 37 (Septem-
     ber), 390-92.
         [Letter regarding poems Barstow had reprinted in the
     Kansas City Star in 1899.]

8   PISANTI, TOMMASO. "La Poesia de Edwin A. Robinson tra Otto-
     cento e Novencento." Ausonia, 19:32-35.
         [Brief introduction to four translated poems.]

9   TANSELLE, G. THOMAS. "Robinson's 'Dark Hills.'" CEA Critic,
     26 (February), 8-10.
         This poem is useful for composition of poetry classes be-
     cause of its simplicity, grammatical structure, and diction.

10   WIDDEMER, MARGARET. Summers at the Colony. Syracuse: Syra-
     cuse University Library Associates, 36 pp.
         [Memoir regarding triangular courtship at Peterborough,
     hampered by Mrs. MacDowell, observed by Robinson, with the
     suggestion that "Job the Rejected" is written about the
     triangle.]

1965 A BOOKS

1   DICKEY, JAMES. "Introduction: Edwin Arlington Robinson, the
     Many Truths," in Selected Poems of Edwin Arlington Robinson.
     Edited by Morton Dauwen Zabel. New York: Macmillan,
     pp. xi-xxviii.
         [Reassessment emphasizing Robinson's speculative quality,
     his craftsmanship, and his sensitivity. Particular atten-
     tion paid to "Calverly's," "Isaac and Archibald," and "Lef-
     fingwell." Reprinted in 1968.B7, 1970.A3, and 1972.B3.]

*2   GIULIANI, ALFREDO, trans. Uomini e Ombre, by Edwin Arlington
     Robinson. Milano: Mondadori, 168 pp.
         [Cited in White, p. 48.]

3   MOTT, SARA LOUISE. "The Happy Ending as a Controlling Comic
     Element in the Poetic Philosophy of Edwin Arlington Robin-
     son." Ph.D. thesis, University of South Carolina, 183 pp.
         Throughout his career, in every type of poem, and in ap-
     proximately one-half of the corpus of his work, Robinson
     employes an actual or implied happy ending beyond the
     gloominess of the current situation. [DA 26:6047.]

4   SMITH, CHARD POWERS. Where the Light Falls: A Portrait of
     Edwin Arlington Robinson. New York: Macmillan; London:
     Collier-Macmillan, 420 pp.

162

[Combination memoir and critical biography, advancing the
hitherto unconsidered view that the majority of Robinson's
poems are autobiographical; specifically, Robinson's great
tragedy, the loss of his only love, Emma, to his brother
Herman, is the impetus and theme (a love triangle) for the
majority of his poems. Further, Lancelot is considered the
most truly autobiographical poem. Principal among the
sources are Hagedorn's biography, the undocumented "Legend
of Emma" and the slightly dissenting family legend, and the
Collected Poetry, of which "899 pages of the 1488" deal
"with the triangle or two or one of its members."]

5   ZIETLOW, PAUL NATHAN. "The Shorter Poems of Thomas Hardy and
     Edwin Arlington Robinson: A Study in Contrasts." Ph.D.
     thesis, University of Michigan, 224 pp.
        [A study of the conservatism, colloquialism, pessimism,
     and regionalism of Hardy and Robinson, demonstrating that
     while they approach poetry from different directions they
     arrive at remarkably similar effects. DA 26:2765.]

1965 B SHORTER WRITINGS

1   ANON. "Robinson, Edwin Arlington," in The Reader's Encyclope-
     dia. Second edition, Edited by William Rose Benét. New
     York: Thomas Y. Crowell, p. 865.
        [Brief biographical sketch with cross references to six
     poems. Emphasis on Robinson as a bridge between centuries.]

2   ANON. "Selected Poems." The Booklist, 62 (December), 392.
        [One paragraph summarizing the introduction and describ-
     ing the contents of Selected Poems.]

3   BERTHOFF, WARNER. "The 'New' Poetry: Robinson and Frost,"
     in The Ferment of Realism: American Literature, 1884-1919.
     New York: The Free Press, pp. 263-77.
        Although Robinson's poetry is narrow and monotonous, he
     has "the most flexible working vocabulary in modern American
     poetry...entirely within the framework of the plain style."
     Two versions of "The House on the Hill" show his growth si-
     multaneously toward specificity and obliquity. "Captain
     Craig" is probably "his greatest achievement" and surely
     influenced Stevens' "The Comedian of the Letter C." [Re-
     printed in 1970.A3.]

4   BROOKS, VAN WYCK. An Autobiography. New York: E. P. Dutton,
     pp. 496-98.
        [Brief comparison of Robinson and Hawthorne.]

1965

5   DONOGHUE, DENIS. "Edwin Arlington Robinson, J. V. Cunningham,
    Robert Lowell," in <u>Connoisseurs of Chaos: Ideas of Order
    in Modern American Poetry</u>. New York: Macmillan pp. 129-
    59.
        Both J. V. Cunningham and Robert Lowell use variations of
    Robinson's principal theme: the juxtaposition of reason
    and passion. ["Demos and Dionysus," "Maya," and "New Eng-
    land" are analyzed. A list of the thirty-one "successful"
    poems is given. <u>Amaranth</u> is called the only "mere failure"
    of the long poems.]

6   HART, JAMES D. "Edwin Arlington Robinson," in <u>Oxford Companion
    to American Literature</u>. Fourth edition. New York: Oxford
    University Press, pp. 718-19.
        [Biographical sketch, with short description of each vol-
    ume of verse, and a brief overview. Cross-references to
    twenty-two Robinson poems.]

7   HEPBURN, JAMES G. "E. A. Robinson's System of Opposites."
    <u>Publications of the Modern Language Association of America</u>,
    80 (June), 266-74.
        "Robinson associates his poetry of opposites with objec-
    tivity and realism; he sees such poetry to be divorced from
    his own voice and vision; and he seems generally to regard
    it as lesser work." [Discussions of many early poems, no-
    tably "The Night Before," "Captain Craig," "The House on
    the Hill," and "Luke Havergal." Reprinted in 1969.A4.]

8   JENKINS, RALPH E. "Robinson's 'Lost Anchors.'" <u>The Explica-
    tor</u>, 23 (April), Item 64.
        Critics have missed the most obvious interpretation of
    this poem: just as the men who sought buried treasure
    found only rusted anchors, so the sailor who sought adven-
    ture on the sea found nothing.

9   LATHAM, HAROLD S. <u>My Life in Publishing</u>. New York: E. P.
    Dutton, pp. 42-47.
        [Reminiscence of Robinson's association with the editor-
    in-chief of Macmillan, including account of Robinson's
    preparation of <u>King Jasper</u> during his last illness.]

*10 MIRAZZI, PIERO. "Tilbury Town (Lettura dell apesia di Edwin
    Arlington Robinson)." <u>Annali della Facoltà di Lettre e
    Filosofia dell'Università di Bari</u>, 10:217-79.
        [Cited in White, p. 79.]

11 MORRIS, CHARLES R. "Robinson's 'Richard Cory.'" <u>The Expli-
    cator</u>, 23 (March), Item 52.

The diction in this poem is particularly British, perhaps
because Gardiner had an English atmosphere or because Robinson enjoyed Hardy's "Life's Little Ironies." Richard
Cory may resemble Miniver Cheevy in that he was too British
to fit into an American town.

12 OLIVER, EGBERT S. "Robinson's Dark-Hill-to-Climb Image," in
     Studies in American Literature: Whitman, Emerson, Mel-
     ville, and Others. New Delhi: Eurasia Publishing House,
     pp. 139-54.
       [Reprint of 1959.B2.]

13 SØRENSEN, POUL. "Edwin Arlington Robinson," in Modern Ameri-
     kansk Lyrik Fra Whitman til Sandburg. [Købehhavn]: Borgen
     Bellegloger 28, pp. 200-204.
       [Introductory material for seventeen anthologized and
     translated lyrics.]

14 STRAUCH, CARL F. "Edwin Arlington Robinson," in American
     Literary Masters, Vol. 2. Edited by Charles Anderson. New
     York: Holt, Rinehart and Winston, pp. 505-563.
       [Introduction and head notes for each poem in an anthol-
     ogy, bibliography, and biographical sketch.] "Isaac and
     Archibald" and "Rembrandt to Rembrandt" "are Robinson's
     highest achievements."

15 UNTERMEYER, LOUIS. "E. A. R.: A Remembrance." The Saturday
     Review, 48 (April 10), 33-34.
       [Anecdotal reminiscence, emphasizing Robinson's shyness,
     wit, and generosity.]

16 WEEKS, LEWIS E., JR. "E. A. Robinson's Poetics." Twentieth
     Century Literature, 11 (October), 131-145.
       [Discussion of Robinson's aesthetic, divided into four
     sections: why and how a poet writes, what poetry is, and
     what it is for. Reprinted in 1969.A4.] Robinson's "ex-
     alted opinion of the poetic art ultimately leads him to
     consider the expression of truth through the blinding
     flashes of poetic insight to be the supreme function of
     poetry."

17 WHITE, WILLIAM. "A Bibliography of Edwin Arlington Robinson,
     1941-1963." Colby Library Quarterly, 7 (March), 1-26.
       [Additions to Hogan's bibliography. Reprinted in
     1971.A2.]

1966

1966 A BOOKS

1 AYO, NICHOLAS. "Robinson and the Bible." Ph.D. thesis, Duke
   University, 251 pp.
       The Bible is Robinson's most important literary source;
   it provided him the subject for numerous poems as well as
   material for his principal theme--the emergence of light
   from darkness. "The Three Taverns," "Lazarus," and "Nicodemus" are among the most profound religious poems in
   American letters. (DA 27:469A-470A.]

2 EWERS, PATRICIA O'DONNELL. "Merlin, Lancelot, and Tristram:
   E. A. Robinson's Poems of Man's Dilemma." Ph.D. thesis,
   Loyola University, 198 pp.
       [Close readings of the Arthurian poems, concluding that
   they were failures because the material was inappropriate
   to Robinson's abilities.]

3 JOYNER, NANCY CAROL. "Edwin Arlington Robinson's View of
   Poetry: A Study of His Theory and His Techniques in the
   Late Narratives." Ph.D. thesis, University of North Carolina at Chapel Hill, 258 pp.
       An examination of Robinson's ideas about poetry and his
   poetic career reveals that in spite of his greater success
   with short poems his preference was always for the book-
   length narrative. A study of the late long poems them-
   selves reveals a progressive incorporation of his discur-
   sive, symbolic mode into the narrative framework. [DA
   27:2531A-2532A.]

4 MORAN, RONALD WESSON, JR. "With Firm Address: A Critical
   Study of Twenty-six Shorter Poems of E. A. Robinson."
   Ph.D. thesis, Louisiana State University, 201 pp.
       [A review of criticism and a close reading of short poems
   from Robinson's early, middle, and late periods, concluding
   with a description of consistent subjects, themes, and
   techniques recognizable in these poems. DA 27:1378A.]

5 REICHERT, VICTOR EMANUEL. Spelling God With the Wrong Blocks:
   An Appreciation of Edwin Arlington Robinson. Covington,
   Kentucky: The Literary Club, 23 pp.
       [Overview of Robinson's life, touching on his obscurity,
   idealism, and pessimism. Particular attention is given the
   significance of Tilbury Town, with commentary on "Mr.
   Flood's Party."]

1966 B SHORTER WRITINGS

1   ANON. "Selected Poems." The Virginia Quarterly Review, 42
    (Winter), xviii.
    [Review of Selected Poems, noting that it would have been
    a better book if one long poem had been included.]

2   ANON. "Selected Poems." American Literature, 37 (January),
    521.
    [Review of Selected Poems, praising the selection but
    noting that the introduction is poor.]

3   BOOTH, PHILIP. "He Survives His Popularity." The Christian
    Science Monitor, 58 (February 24), 11.
    [Review of Selected Poems.] Robinson is no longer thought
    to be a great poet because of his repetition and "over-
    extended blank verse." His characters are more often pa-
    thetic than tragic, but at least he is still measured
    against Frost and Hardy.

4   BRUBAKER, BILL RAY. "The Political Appointment of American
    Writers." Ph.D. thesis, Ohio State University, 282 pp.
    [Robinson is one of several political appointees con-
    sidered in a study that shows that political appointment
    generally failed to stimulate writers. DA 27:3005A-3006A.]

5   COWAN, S. A. "Robinson's 'Lost Anchors.'" The Explicator,
    24 (April), Item 68.
    Jenkins (1965.B8) is careless in his interpretation and
    overlooks the possibility that Robinson uses "seized" in
    the nautical sense; i.e. the anchors were made ready for
    use. The futility of the sailor's life is thereby under-
    scored by the doubly ironic anchors.

6   DONALDSON, SCOTT. "The Alien Pity: A Study of Character in
    E. A. Robinson's Poetry." American Literature, 38 (May),
    219-29.
    Robinson's poetry, more narrative than dramatic, focuses
    on characters who are failures who appear successful or
    vice versa. They don't want pity but understanding. Al-
    though these characters move through a grim world, some are
    saved from despair through "a capacity for illusion."

7   FISHER, JOHN HURT. "Edwin Arlington Robinson and Arthurian
    Tradition," in Studies in Language and Literature in Honour
    of Margaret Schlauch. Edited by Mieczyslaw Brahmer, Stan-
    islow Helsztynski, and Julian Krzyzanowski. Warsaw:
    Panstwowe Wydawnictwo Naukowe, pp. 117-31.

1966

> Robinson's Arthurian trilogy may represent three aspects
> of the chilvaric dilemma: between <u>Merlin</u> there is a con-
> flict between love and duty, in <u>Lancelot</u>, earthly and di-
> vine love, and in <u>Tristram</u> the conflicting nature of love
> itself.

8   FREE, WILLIAM J. "E. A. Robinson's Use of Emerson." <u>American</u>
      <u>Literature</u>, 38 (March), 69-84.
      Robinson reported being impressed by Emerson's "Compen-
      sation," and the influence of that essay is apparent in
      many of his early poems.

9   GORLIER, CLAUDIO. "E. A. Robinson e Robert Frost." <u>Paragone</u>,
      N.S. 12 (February), 126-32.
      [Essay review of Giuliani's translation, <u>Uomini e Ombre</u>,
      in which Robinson is compared to many other American writ-
      ers, notably Frost, Eliot, and Robert Lowell.]

10   GRAFF, GERALD E. "Statement and Poetry." <u>Southern Review</u>,
      N.S 2 (Summer), 499-515.
      An analysis of "Hillcrest" refutes the contention that
      poetry should never be discursive rather than dramatic.

11   PARISH, JOHN E. "The Rehabilitation of Eben Flood." <u>The</u>
      <u>English Journal</u>, 55 (September), 696-99.
      Contrary to the interpretation offered by Brooks and
      Warren (1960.B1), Mr. Flood probably has doors shut where
      he was once welcome because he has outlived all of his
      friends in Tilbury Town.

12   PELL, EDWARD. "Character in Verse." <u>The New Leader</u>, 49 (Jan-
      uary), 29-30.
      [Review of <u>Selected Poems</u>.] Robinson is a good poet when
      he focuses on character and keeps it short, but "Isaac and
      Archibald" fails because it is too rambling and "For a Dead
      Lady" has fuzzy characterization.

13   SAUL, GEORGE BRANDON. "Selected Poems." <u>College English</u>, 27
      (March), 517.
      [Brief review complimenting selection, introduction, and
      bibliographical data.]

14   SKARD, SIGMUND. "E. A. Robinson: 'Eros Turannos,' A Critical
      Survey," in <u>Americana Norvegica: Norwegian Contributions to</u>
      <u>American Studies</u>, Vol. 1. Oslo: Glydendal Norsk Forlag;
      Philadelphia: University of Pennsylvania Press, pp. 286-
      330.

1966

[Textual variants, critical reception, classical background, interpretation, and bibliography of criticism of
"Eros Turannos."] "'Eros Turannos' is Robinson's best poem
and most typical. It reflects the impact of his classical
background on his work."

15 SPECTOR, ROBERT D. "Other Voices, Other Rhythms." The Satur-
    day Review, 49 (February 19), 42-44.
    [Review of Selected Poems.] This book will probably not
    revive interest in Robinson because "his absence of poetic
    imagery and superficial garrulousness" will keep readers
    away.

16 STAFFORD, WILLIAM. "There Yet Remains What Fashion Cannot
    Kill." Poetry, 108 (June), 187-88.
    [Review of Selected Poems, commenting on its usefulness.]

17 THOMPSON, LAWRANCE. Robert Frost: The Early Years, 1874-1915.
    New York: Holt, Rinehart and Winston, pp. 414, 589.
    [Mention of Frost's discussions with Ezra Pound and May
    Sinclair about Robinson.]

18 WALCUTT, CHARLES CHILD and J. EDWIN WHITESELL, eds. The Ex-
    plicator Cyclopedia, Vol. 1. Chicago: Quadrangle Books,
    pp. 245-62.
    [Reprint of the twenty-six articles about Robinson orig-
    inally published in The Explicator.]

19 WARREN, AUSTIN. "Edwin Arlington Robinson," in The New Eng-
    land Conscience. Ann Arbor: University of Michigan Press,
    pp. 182-93.
    Robinson's Puritan background accounted for his belief
    that being a success and being a poet were mutually exclu-
    sive--his sense of conscience is similar to that of Thoreau.
    [Brief discussions of "New England" and "The Man Against
    the Sky."]

20 WHITE, GERTRUDE M. "Robinson's 'Captain Craig': A Reinter-
    pretation." English Studies, 47 (December), 432-39.
    "Captain Craig" should not be considered a character
    sketch but a drama in which the narrator wrestles with the
    correct response to the Captain. It is central to Robin-
    son's poetry as well as his career in its speculation about
    the life and lot of the poet.

21 WHITE, WILLIAM. "E. A. R. in India." The American Book Col-
    lector, 16 (May), 32.
    [Brief notice of Robinson's growing international reputa-
    tion.]

1966

22 _____. "Where is E. A. Robinson?" The American Book Collector, 16 (March), 7.
The omission of Robinson from a recent collection of essays, The Twenties Poetry and Prose, is unfortunate.

23 ZIFF, LARZER. "In and Out of Laodicea: The Harvard Poets and
Edwin Arlington Robinson," in The American 1890's: Life
and Times of a Lost Generation. New York: Viking,
pp. 325-33.
[Biographical sketch and assessment, with discussion of
"The Clerks" and "Isaac and Archibald." Robinson is compared to Whitman and Pound.]

24 ZILLMAN, LAWRENCE JOHN. The Art and Craft of Poetry: An Introduction. New York: Macmillan, pp. 158-59.
[Commentary on "Mr. Flood's Party" as example of a character sketch.]

1967 A BOOKS

1 ANDERSON, WALLACE L. Edwin Arlington Robinson: A Critical
Introduction. Riverside Studies in Literature. Boston:
Houghton Mifflin, 165 pp.
[Overview containing chapters on the intellectual milieu,
Robinson's background, his aesthetics, commentary on some
twenty of his best known poems, and a concluding assessment
that puts Robinson in the first rank of poets and names depiction of character as his "most notable achievement." Bibliography.]

2 ISLEY, ELISE DORT. "The Sources of the Imagery in the Poetry
of E. A. Robinson." Ph.D. thesis, University of Arkansas,
189 pp.
Major sources of Robinson's imagery other than literary
ones are people, especially children, domestic surroundings,
music, and the outdoors. Most of his images come from
early events and surroundings; New York is rarely alluded
to, for instance. [DA 28:1436A.]

3 MOSELEY, RICHARD SAMUEL, III. "Narrative Form in the Long
Poems of Edwin Arlington Robinson." Ph.D. thesis, University of Cincinnati, 282 pp.
[Analysis of the narrative structure of Robinson's last
dozen long poems, concentrating on Lancelot, Matthias at
the Door, and Amaranth, concluding that his combination of
traditional and modern elements suggest a new direction for
poetry. DA 28:3193A.]

4   RICHARDS, LAURA E. E. A. R. New York: Russell & Russell.
     [Reprint of 1936.A5.]

5   ROBINSON, W. R. Edwin Arlington Robinson: A Poetry of the
     Act. Cleveland, Ohio: The Press of Western Reserve Uni-
     versity, 183 pp.
     [Publication of 1962.A3; partially reprinted in 1970.A3.]

1967 B SHORTER WRITINGS

1   ANDERSON, WALLACE L. "E. A. Robinson's 'Scattered Lives.'"
     American Literature, 38 (January), 498-507.
     Before Robinson published his frist book of poetry he had
     planned and presumably completed a collection of short sto-
     ries called "Scattered Lives." These prose character
     sketches possibly were the basis of his poetic character
     sketches.

2   CARY, RICHARD. "'Go Little Book': An Odyssesy of Robinson's
     The Torrent and the Night Before." Colby Library Quarterly,
     7 (December), 511-27.
     Robinson's first book was early a collector's item; he
     did not sell them, but one in good condition is now prob-
     ably worth $1000.

3   _____. "The Library of Edwin Arlington Robinson: Addenda."
     Colby Library Quarterly, 7 (March), 398-415.
     [A list of the 173 books from Robinson's library that
     have been added to the collection at Colby since the cata-
     log was published (1950.A1).]

4   _____. "Torrents Come in Driblets." Colby Library Quarterly,
     7 (December), 548.
     [A note on three more copies of The Torrent and the Night
     Before.]

5   CROWDER, RICHARD. "E. A. Robinson and the Garden of Eden."
     Colby Library Quarterly, 7 (December), 527-35.
     Robinson's frequent use of the Eden myth indicates his
     knowledge of Milton and Genesis. He believed, in spite of
     his romanticism, that "to try to gain re-entry into para-
     dise was impracticable and finally futile."

6   GENTHE, CHARLES. "E. A. Robinson's 'Annandale' Poems." Colby
     Library Quarterly, 7 (March), 392-98.
     The Annandale trilogy is based on Molière's Le Malade
     Imaginaire.

1967

7   GRIMM, CLYDE L. "Robinson's 'For a Dead Lady': An Exercise
     in Evaluation." Colby Library Quarterly, 7 (December),
     535-47.
         [Close reading of "For a Dead Lady," noting the ironic
     Christian allusions and emphasizing its technical excel-
     lence. Reprinted in 1969.A4.]

8   KOHRING, KLAUS HEINRICH. Die Formen des "long poem" in der
     Modernen Amerikanischen Literatur. Heidelberg: Carl Win-
     ter, pp. 192-200.
         [Comparison of Merlin and Jeffers' Tamar, noting that
     Merlin is the more abstract of the two. Robinson is placed
     in idealistic rather than naturalistic tradition.]

9   LEWIS, J. S. "A Note of Robinson's 'Forestalling.'" American
     Notes & Queries, 5 (March), 106.
         Robinson's use of "forestalling" in "For a Dead Lady" is
     probably a technical term from photo-engraving meaning "to
     dodge."

10   MARR, CARL W. "The Torrent and the Night Before." Colby Li-
     brary Quarterly, 7 (December), opp. p. 511.
         [Twenty-four line poem, written in iambic quatrains.]

11   MARTIN, JAY. "Edwin Arlington Robinson," in Harvests of
     Change: American Literature 1865-1914. Englewood Cliffs,
     New Jersey: Prentice-Hall, pp. 152-58.
         Robinson's cautious idealism led him to create characters
     like Captain Craig. "Dramatizing the reign of the anti-
     hero, he defined and made relevant a hero for the modern
     world." His outlook is similar to that of Sarah Orne Jew-
     ett and other regional prose writers.

12   MORAN, RONALD. "Meaning and Value in 'Luke Havergal.'" Colby
     Library Quarterly, 7 (March), 385-91.
         The "paraphrasable element" in this poem is that Luke is
     being urged by a dead wife or lover to join her by commit-
     ting suicide.

13   ST. ARMAND, BURTON L. "The Power of Sympathy in the Poetry of
     Robinson and Frost: The 'Inside' vs. the 'Outside' Narra-
     tive." American Quarterly, 19 (Fall), 564-74.
         Robinson differs from Frost in that Robinson's reader can
     get inside his characters and look out, whereas the reader
     of Frost looks from the outside of his character. Frost is
     a naturalist in that his characters are against some

172

external force; Robinson is a somewhat existentialist "sympathist," a follower of James, who showed people's thoughts as well as their actions. [Captain Craig is discussed extensively.]

14   STOVALL, FLOYD. "Edwin Arlington Robinson in Perspective," in Essays on American Literature in Honor of Jay B. Hubbell. Edited by Clarence Gohdes. Durham, N.N.: Duke University Press, pp. 241-58.
[Review of career, changing critical reactions, amount of representation in anthologies, and the two principal critical attitudes about him since 1930. Table classifying length, metrical patterns, etc., of Robinson's poems.]

15   SUBBINA, C. "Robinson on Verlaine." American Studies Research Centre Newsletter, no. 11, pp. 52-54.
Robinson's sonnet on Verlaine is appropriate to the subject in his allusion to Verlaine's "autumn song" and his accurate description of the French poet's personality.

16   ZIETLOW, PAUL. "The Meaning of Tilbury Town: Robinson as a Regional Poet." The New England Quarterly, 40 (June), 188-211.
Robinson's regionalism differs from that of Frost and Hardy in that his "usable past" is myth rather than a fixed time or place. The materialism of Tilbury is a deterrent to "transcendental wholeness," and thus is a place to escape from, not return to, as Frost's and Hardy's regions are presented.

1968 A BOOKS

1   BROWER, EDITH. "Memories of Edwin Arlington Robinson," in Edwin Arlington Robinson's Letters to Edith Brower. Edited by Richard Cary. Cambridge: Harvard University Press, Belknap Press, pp. 203-15.
[Memoir recounting the circumstances of the friendship between Robinson and Brower, and her assessment of his personality, emphasizing his honesty and independence.]

2   CARY, RICHARD. "Introduction and Notes," in Edwin Arlington Robinson's Letters to Edith Brower. Edited by Richard Cary. Cambridge: Harvard University Press, Belknap Press, pp. 1-13 and passim.
[Biographical sketch of Edith Brower and explanation of her importance to Robinson as a sympathetic recipient of

1968

       his letters for most of his career. Copious and detailed
notes accompany most of the 189 letters. Index and appendices.]

3   FRANCHERE, HOYT C. <u>Edwin Arlington Robinson.</u> Twayne's United
States Author's Series No. 137. New York: Twayne, 148 pp.
    [Brief critical biography, emphasizing the importance of
Robinson's unhappy love affair on his poetry and dealing
principally with his themes.]

4   GOWEN, JAMES ANTHONY. "Some Puritan Characteristics in the
Poetry of Edwin Arlington Robinson." Ph.D. thesis, Stan-
ford University, 216 pp.
    Fundamental Puritan concepts, such as human depravity,
grace, and predestination pervade Robinson's poetry. What
his critics called pessimism is actually an expression of
this Calvinistic terminology and thought. [<u>DA</u> 29:1538A.]

5   MORRIS, CELIA B. "The MAKARIS of Camelot." Ph.D. thesis,
City University of New York, 360 pp.
    A study of the use of the Arthurian materials by Malory,
Tennyson, and Robinson reveal that the story moves "from
the primarily objective, through an uncertain, ambivalent
middle ground, to the primarily subjective." [<u>DA</u> 29:1516A-
1517A.]

6   NEFF, EMERY. <u>Edwin Arlington Robinson.</u> New York: Russell &
Russell, 286 pp.
    [Reprint of 1948.A2.]

1968 B SHORTER WRITINGS

1   ANON. "Edwin Arlington Robinson's Letters to Edith Brower."
<u>The Booklist,</u> 45 (November 15), 344.
    "The collection has both literary interest and psycholog-
ical import."

2   ANON. "Edwin Arlington Robinson's Letters to Edith Brower."
<u>Publisher's Weekly,</u> 194 (July 1), 48-49.
    These letters were for Robinson therapeutic and for the
reader interesting because of his literary opinions.

3   BRIEN, DOLORES E. "Edwin Arlington Robinson's 'Amaranth':
A Journey to 'The Wrong World.'" <u>Research Studies of Washington State University,</u> 36 (June), 143-50.
    [Close reading of <u>Amaranth</u>, with the thesis that here
Robinson adumbrates the absurd, has a pessimistic attitude
toward art as a vocation, and indicates an affinity to
atheistic existentialism.]

1968

4   BROOKE, RUPERT. The Letters of Rupert Brooke. Edited by
     Geoffrey Keynes. New York: Harcourt, Brace & World,
     pp. 473, 494.
         [Two letters praising Robinson as the only poet in Amer-
     ica worth reading. "For a Dead Lady" noted as especially
     well written.]

5   BURTON, DAVID H. "Theodore Roosevelt and Edwin Arlington Rob-
     inson: A Common Vision." The Personalist, 49 (Summer),
     331-50.
         Although Robinson and Roosevelt were of different phil-
     osophical persuasions, they share a strong reaction against
     materialism. This attitude is expressed in "Cassandra,"
     "The Master," "On the Way," "The Revealer," and the three
     Demos and Dionysus poems.

6   CUNNINGHAM, J. V. "Edwin Arlington Robinson: A Brief Bio-
     graphy." Denver Quarterly, 3 (Spring), 28-31.
         [Biography and assessment.] "Though he wrote too much,
     he wrote much that was distinctive and good."

7   DICKEY, JAMES. "Edwin Arlington Robinson," in Babel to Byzan-
     tium: Poets and Poetry Now. New York: Farrar, Straus
     and Giroux, pp. 209-30.
         [Reprint of 1965.A1; reprinted in 1970.A3 and 1972.B3.]

*8   K[ENNY], H[ERBERT] A. "Silent Approval," Boston Sunday Globe,
     September 8, p. 46-A.
         [Review of Edwin Arlington Robinson's Letters to Edith
     Brower. Cited in White, p. 105.]

9   KOHN, MARJORIE. "Edwin Arlington Robinson's Letters to Edith
     Brower." Library Journal, 93 (October 15), 3788.
         "The 189 letters owned by Colby College...provide addi-
     tional insight into Robinson's life of self-doubt."

10   KRAMER, AARON. The Prophetic Tradition in American Poetry:
     1835-1900. Rutherford, N.J.: Fairleigh Dickinson Univer-
     sity Press, pp. 323-24 and passim.
         [Scattered references to Robinson pertaining to his at-
     titude toward war, with particular attention to "Captain
     Craig."]

11   LANDINI, RICHARD G. "Metaphor and Imagery in E. A. Robinson's
     'Credo.'" Colby Library Quarterly, 8 (March), 20-22.
         "Credo," informed by a journey metaphor and Nativity im-
     ages, "implies an affirmation of the Christian faith, or as
     close to one as we are likely to find in the Robinson canon."

1968

12 LEVENSON, J. C. "Robinson's Modernity." Virginia Quarterly
    Review, 44 (Autumn), 590–610.
        [Discussion of Robinson's assimilation of the philoso-
    phical stances of both William James and Royce, resulting
    in a combination of pragmatic and idealistic attitudes that
    is distinctly modern. "Isaac and Archibald" explicated as
    an example of these influences in both matter and manner.
    Reprinted in 1969.A2 and 1970.A3.]

13 MATTFIELD, MARY S. "Edwin Arlington Robinson's 'The Sheaves.'"
    CEA Critic, 31 (November), 10.
        In one of Robinson's few nature poems the principal feel-
    ing conveyed is one of melancholy.

14 PHILIPS, DAVID E. "Edwin Arlington Robinson's Letters to
    Edith Brower." Down East, 15 (November), 66.
        These letters, which cover Robinson's entire career, "are
    as revealing of the soul of one our most reticent major
    writers as anything yet published."

15 READ, ARTHUR M., II. "Robinson's 'The Man Against the Sky.'"
    The Explicator, 26 (February), Item 49.
        Donne's pun on sun in "Good Friday, 1613, Riding West-
    ward" is alluded to in this poem, but Robinson's lack of
    capitalization of sun gives depth to the line.

16 TATE, ALLEN. "Edwin Arlington Robinson," in Essays of Four
    Decades. Chicago: Swallow Press, pp. 341–47.
        [Reprint of 1933.B26, 1936.B27, 1948.B17, and 1959.B5.]

17 WAGER, WILLIS. American Literature: A World View. New York:
    New York University Press; London: University of London
    Press, pp. 185–89.
        [Brief review of Robinson's career, suggesting that the
    late nineteenth-century interest in prose fiction is re-
    flected in his blank verse narratives.]

18 WAGGONER, HYATT H. "The Idealist in Extremis: Edwin Arling-
    ton Robinson," in American Poets: From the Puritans to the
    Present. Boston: Houghton Mifflin, pp. 262–92.
        Robinson's philosophy reflects that of Emerson, especially
    in his first three and last two volumes and most pervasively
    in Captain Craig. Stylistically, however, he is most like
    Hawthorne.

1969 A BOOKS

1   BARNARD, ELLSWORTH. Edwin Arlington Robinson: A Critical
    Study. New York: Octagon Books, 318 pp.
    [Reprint of 1952.A1.]

2   _____, ed. Edwin Arlington Robinson: Centenary Essays.
    Athens: University of Georgia Press, 192 pp.
    [Eleven original essays, cited below, and reprint of
    1968.B12. Chronology, bibliography, index.]

3   BIERK, JOHN CASHION. "Edwin Arlington Robinson as Social
    Critic and Moral Guide." Ph.D. thesis, Northwestern Uni-
    versity, 211 pp.
    [Discussion of Robinson as a proponent of idealism and an
    opponent of materialism, with particular attention to King
    Jasper, concluding that a continuity and development of
    these dual attitudes may be traced through his poetry. DA
    30:2997A-2998A.]

4   CARY, RICHARD, ed. Appreciation of Edwin Arlington Robinson:
    28 Interpretive Essays. Waterville, Me.: Colby College
    Press, 356 pp.
    [Foreword by Cary and reprints of 1930.B31, 1932.B43,
    1935.B58, 1937.B4, 1938.B5, B26, 1940.B29, 1942.B8,
    1943.B5, 1945.B2, B6, 1954.B2, 1960.B9, 1961.B3, 1963.B3,
    1965.B7, 1967.B7, B16, 1969.B6, B12, B24, B27, B35, B37-B38,
    B41, B46, and B48.]

5   COXE, LOUIS O. Edwin Arlington Robinson: The Life of Poetry.
    New York: Pegasus, 188 pp.
    [Critical biography presenting Robinson as "a hick from a
    hick town" who was also a man of genius. Explanation of
    the social climate that influenced his writing and the aca-
    demic attitudes that have prevented his poetry from receiv-
    ing the attention it merits. Emphasis on explication of
    selected individual poems. Assessment of him as an old-
    fashioned writer and a modernist. Brief bibliography and
    index, but no formal documentation.]

6   DARIEN, PETER. "A Centennial Occasion," in his edition of A
    Tilbury Score, by Edwin Arlington Robinson. Summit, N.J.:
    Masterwork Press, n.p.
    [One-page introduction to centennial celebration of
    "crucial" poet. Twenty sonnets reprinted.]

7   MORRIS, LLOYD. The Poetry of Edwin Arlington Robinson. New
    York: Haskell House, 116 pp.
    [Reprint of 1923.A1.]

1969

8   SATTERFIELD, LEON JAMES. "Major Categories of Irony in the
     Poetry of Edwin Arlington Robinson." Ph.D. thesis, Uni-
     versity of Nebraska, 195 pp.
         [Definition of irony and division of Robinson's use of it
     in the categories of verbal irony, irony of allusion, dra-
     matic irony, and double-image irony, concluding that Robin-
     son is a better ironist than he has been given credit for.
     DA 30:3022A.]

1969 B SHORTER WRITINGS

1   AIKEN, CONRAD. "Three Meetings with Robinson." Colby Library
     Quarterly, 8 (September), 345-46.
         [Aiken's report of Robinson's high reputation at Harvard
     in 1907 and their subsequent friendship which cooled after
     Lucius Beebe published a report of the two poets' "alco-
     holiday" in England.]

2   ANDERSON, HILTON. "Robinson's 'Flammonde.'" Southern Quar-
     terly, 7 (January), 179-83.
         Many parallels between Christ and Flammonde can be found.

3   ANDERSON, WALLACE L. "The Young Robinson as Critic and Self-
     Critic," in Edwin Arlington Robinson: Centenary Essays.
     Edited by Ellsworth Barnard. Athens: University of Geor-
     gia Press, pp. 68-87.
         Robinson's detailed criticism of poetry by Josephine
     Preston Peabody shows his concern for the combination of
     substance and form. Ironically, Miss Peabody was success-
     ful in publishing her work at the time Robinson was unable
     to get Captain Craig published. He was aware of critical
     fashions while he was determined not to compromise his art
     for them.

4   ANON. "Edwin Arlington Robinson's Letters to Edith Brower,"
     American Literature, 40 (January), 594.
         [Brief mention of "consequential addition" to Robinson
     material.]

5   ANON. "Edwin Arlington Robinson's Letters to Edith Brower,"
     The Virginia Quarterly Review, 45 (Winter), xxx.
         "Although characterized, like his poems, by impeccable
     restraint, the letters disclose Robinson's personal warmth
     as well as his 'almost intolerable situation.'"

6   AYO, NICHOLAS. "Robinson's Use of the Bible." Colby Library
     Quarterly, 8 (March), 250-65.
         [Summary of dissertation (1966.A1). Reprinted in
     1969.A4.]

7   BARBOUR, BRIAN M. "Robinson's 'Veteran Sirens.'" The Expli-
     cator, 28 (November), Item 20.
        Contrary to other opinions, this poem is about prosti-
     tutes. The title is an oxymoron because the mythological
     sirens are eternally young. Ninon, the seventeenth-century
     courtesan who was both old and attractive, is the unifying
     symbol.

8   BARNARD, ELLSWORTH. "Edwin Arlington Robinson," in Fifteen
     Modern American Authors: A Survey of Research and Criti-
     cism. Edited by Jackson Bryer. Durham, N.C.: Duke Uni-
     versity Press, pp. 345-67.
        [Overview of Robinson bibliography, editions, letters and
     manuscripts, biography, and criticism, concluding that in-
     terest in Robinson is increasing.]

9   _____. "'Of This or That Estate': Robinson's Literary Repu-
     tation." Edwin Arlington Robinson: Centenary Essays.
     Edited by Ellsworth Barnard. Athens: University of Geor-
     gia Press, pp. 1-14.
        Robinson's twenty years of neglect, twelve years of rec-
     ognition, and thirty years of obscurity may be attributed
     to the lack of approval of his late poems, his unpopular
     philosophy, his personality, his lack of appeal to the
     "new" critics, and the lack of sensuality in his poetry.
     Currently his reputation is increasing.

10   BROOKHOUSE, CHRISTOPHER. "Imagery and Theme in Lancelot," in
     Edwin Arlington Robinson: Centenary Essays. Edited by
     Ellsworth Barnard. Athens: University of Georgia Press,
     pp. 120-29.
        Both Robinson and Malory use the destruction of Camelot
     as a symbol of national disaster. Temporal and spatial
     setting is symbolic of the characters' relationship with
     each other, as is the light and dark imagery. The poem
     goes beyond the destruction of Arthur's world to the pri-
     vate, spiritual salvation of Lancelot and Guinivere.

11   BUDD, LOUIS. "Edwin Arlington Robinson's Letters to Edith
     Brower." The South Atlantic Quarterly, 68 (Summer), 430-31.
        Book shows that "both Robinson's humor and dedication to
     poetry were inveterate."

12   BURTON, DAVID H. "E. A. Robinson's Idea of God." Colby Li-
     brary Quarterly, 8 (June), 280-94.
        [Examination of Robinson's various attitudes about God
     based on statements in his poetry from "The Children of the
     Night" to The Glory of the Nightingales, concluding that

1969

his emotional need to believe in a Diety was overcome by
his intellectual inability to affirm such an existence.
Reprinted in 1969.A4.]

13 _____. "The Intellectualism of Edwin Arlington Robinson."
Thought, 44 (Winter), 565-80.
The conflict between idealism and scientific materialism
in Robinson's thought adumbrates current attitudes of American intellectuals.

14 _____. "Robinson, Roosevelt, and Romanism: An Historical Re-
flection of the Catholic Church and the American Ideal."
Records of the American Catholic Historical Society of
Philadelphia, 80 (March), 3-16.
Both Robinson and Roosevelt admired the faith of individual Catholics but distrusted the Church and its theology as
an institution.

15 CARY, RICHARD. "Robinson Books and Periodicals: I." Colby
Library Quarterly, 8 (March), 266-77.
[Bibliography of books by Robinson, his proof sheets, and
his work in periodicals in the Colby College Library.]

16 _____. "Robinson Books and Periodicals: II." Colby Library
Quarterly, 8 (June), 334-43.
[Bibliography of works by others inscribed by Robinson in
the Colby College Library.]

17 _____. "Robinson Books and Periodicals: III." Colby Library
Quarterly, 8 (September), 399-413.
[Bibliography of books and periodicals written by others,
inscribed by others, in the Robinson collection at the
Colby College Library.]

18 _____. "Robinson Manuscripts and Letters." Colby Library
Quarterly, 8 (December), 479-87.
[Bibliography of manuscripts and letters by and about
Robinson in the Colby College Library.]

19 CLARK, HARRY HAYDEN. "The Poet as Critic." CEA Critic, 3
(February), 3.
Edwin Arlington Robinson's Letters to Edith Brower is
useful to critics to discover Robinson's critical views,
although they were not consistent. "Robinson may have
shown humility about his personal life, but his aesthetic
standards were high."

1969

20 CLIFTON, LINDA J. "Two Corys: A Sample of Inductive Teaching." English Journal, 58 (March), 414-15.
A comparison between Robinson's "Richard Cory" and the
musical version by Simon and Garfunkel shows students important differences between the two.

21 CROWDER, RICHARD. "Robinson's Reputation: Six Observations."
Colby Library Quarterly, 8 (March), 220-38.
Since the peak of Robinson's popularity in 1927, critical
attention has been modest but steady, as a survey of dissertations, critical essays by poets, foreign articles,
books, and periodical articles indicates.

22 DAUNER, LOUISE. "Two Robinson Revisions: 'Mr. Flood's Party'
and 'The Dark Hills.'" Colby Library Quarterly, 8 (June),
309-16.
Close analysis of two versions of these poems reveals
that among Robinson's aesthetic principles are "emphasis
upon logical and metaphorical unity, phonematic symbolism,
and syntactical and rhythmic appropriateness."

23 DAVIS, CHARLES T. "Robinson's Road to Camelot," in Edwin Arlington Robinson: Centenary Essays. Edited by Ellsworth
Barnard. Athens: University of Georgia Press, pp. 88-105.
[Source study of the Arthurian poems, which are based
primarily on Malory and Tennyson, with Arnold's attitude
and Swinburne's sea imagery of secondary importance. Wagner's Tristan is recognized as an influence, but the three
poems are seen finally as being informed by Robinson's own
vision of Camelot.]

24 DECHERT, PETER. "He Shouts to See Them Scamper So: E. A.
Robinson and the French Forms." Colby Library Quarterly,
8 (September), 386-98.
Although Robinson practiced French forms under the tute-
lage of A. T. Schumann, he has kept relatively few examples
of the ballade, rondeau, and villanelle. Two versions of
"The House on the Hill" indicate the improvement he made in
this vallanelle from particularization to universality in
theme. [Reprinted in 1969.A4.]

25 DOMINA, LYLE. "Fate, Tragedy and Pessimism in Robinson's
'Merlin.'" Colby Library Quarterly, 8 (December), 471-78.
Merlin is not as pessimistic as is commonly thought because Merlin experiences a spiritual victory in spite of
the failure of his love for Vivian.

181

1969

26 DONALDSON, SCOTT. "The Book of Scattered Lives," in Edwin
   Arlington Robinson: Centenary Essays. Edited by Ellsworth
   Barnard. Athens: University of Georgia Press, pp. 43-44.
   The poems about New York characters in The Town Down the
   River show an empathy that is not apparent in the Tilbury
   poems. [Explication of the Calverly poems.]

27 FOY, J. VAIL. "Robinson's Impulse for Narrative." Colby Library Quarterly, 8 (March), 238-49.
   [Analysis of "The Night Before."] Although this poem was
   a failure it was Robinson's first attempt at the long narrative form. Reprinted in 1969.A4.]

28 FREE, WILLIAM J. "The Strategy of 'Flammonde,'" in Edwin Arlington Robinson: Centenary Essays. Edited by Ellsworth
   Barnard. Athens: University of Georgia Press, pp. 15-30.
   "Flammonde" succeeds where the early lyrics and "Captain
   Craig" fail because of the distance achieved through the
   perception of the persona. Robinson's poems about characters are better than his lyrics because he lacked fresh
   metaphors and was essentially abstract.

29 HINDEN, MICHAEL C. "Edwin Arlington Robinson and the Theatre
   of Destiny." Colby Library Quarterly, 8 (December), 463-
   71.
   [Comparison of Van Zorn and Eliot's The Cocktail Party
   with the thesis that Robinson's two dramas deserve study
   not only for their intrinsic worth but also because Robinson anticipated Eliot by more than thirty years.]

30 HIRSCH, DAVID H. "'The Man Against the Sky' and the Problem
   of Faith," in Edwin Arlington Robinson: Centenary Essays.
   Edited by Ellsworth Barnard. Athens: University of Georgia Press, pp. 31-42.
   [Analysis of Biblical allusions and comparison of Robinson's man with that in Paradise Lost, emphasizing Robinson's
   negative attitude toward faith.]

31 JARRELL, RANDALL. "Fifty Years of American Poetry," in The
   Third Book of Criticism. New York: Farrar, Straus & Gi-
   roux, pp. 296-97.
   "Robinson wrote a great deal of poetry but only a few
   good poems; and yet there is a somber distinction and honesty about him." "Mr. Flood's Party" is his best poem.

32 JOYNER, NANCY. "Robinson's Pamela and Sandburg's Agatha."
   American Literature, 40 (January), 548-49.

1969

Robinson changed the name of the protagonist in "The Tree
in Pamela's Garden" to Pamela from Agatha because Sandburg
used the name Agatha in a similar context in his poem
"Plaster."

33   _____. "An Unpublished Version of 'Mr. Flood's Party.'" English Language Notes, 7 (September), 55-57.
A variant conclusion of this poem differs from the published version in diction, dramatic action, and in a mock-
ing rather than sympathetic attitude toward Mr. Flood.

34   LUCAS, JOHN. "The Poetry of Edwin Arlington Robinson." Renaissance & Modern Studies, 13:132-47.
Robinson's greatest strength is his ability to write hon-
estly and sympathetically about insignificant people. His
"acceptance of the mysteriousness of people...is the mark
of an unfailing compassion, and it makes Robinson one of
the necessary poets."

35   MacLEISH, ARCHIBALD. "On Rereading Robinson." Colby Library
Quarterly, 8 (March), 217-19.
Robinson's contribution to American literature is his
uniquely ironic voice. [Reprinted in 1969.A4.]

36   MARTIN, JAY. "A Crisis of Achievement: Robinson's Late Narratives," in Edwin Arlington Robinson: Centenary Essays.
Edited by Ellsworth Barnard. Athens: University of Georgia Press, pp. 130-156.
[Overview of Robinson's career as it was affected by a
milieu inimical to his popular acceptance, suggesting that
the late narratives result from a "crisis of achievement"
similar to what Erik Erikson calls the "crisis of genera-
tivity," and are essentially a search for self-identity.
Brief comments on the nine late narratives, with particular
attention to Roman Bartholow.]

37   MORAN, RONALD. "The Octaves of E. A. Robinson." Colby Library Quarterly, 8 (September), 363-70.
Robinson's twenty-eight extant octaves are important because they are personal statements that deal with poetry,
belief, and attitude about the times. [Reprinted in
1969.A4.]

38   MORRILL, PAUL H. "'The World is...a Kind of Spiritual Kinder-
garten.'" Colby Library Quarterly, 8 (December), 435-48.
[Study of Robinson's psychological studies as they relate
to infantilism, classified into the categories of the
search for affection and understanding, the quest for power,

1969

man as creator, and aberrants. Table of sixty-four poems
illustrating these categories included. Reprinted in
1969.A4.]

39 PERRINE, LAURENCE. "Tennyson and Robinson: Legalistic Moral-
ism vs. Situation Ethics." Colby Library Quarterly, 8 (December), 416-33.
Tennyson's moral stance in Idylls of the King is conven-
tionally Victorian in that he insists upon the sanctity of
marriage. Robinson anticipates situation ethics in his
Arthurian poems in his exaltation of love over marriage.

40 RANDALL, DAVID A. Dukedom Large Enough. New York: Random
House, pp. 230-34.
[Reminiscence of a book dealer who once inveigled Robinson into writing answers to questions in several of his
first editions.]

41 ROBINSON, W. R. "E. A. Robinson's Yankee Conscience." Colby
Library Quarterly, 8 (September), 371-85.
[Close reading of "New England" and discussion of the
tension between conscience and the intellect created by
Robinson's New England background and his antipathy toward
the puritan ethic. Reprinted in 1969.A.]

42 SHERMAN, DEAN. "Robinson's 'Battle After War.'" The Explicator, 27 (April), Item 64.
"Robinson is here equating light with Reason and Intelligence and darkness with Chaos and Death" because of the
Platonic use of the term Erebus.

*43 SOLOMON, PETRE. "Un Destin Bizar: Edwin Arlington Robinson."
Romania Literara, June 19, p. 23.
[Cited in White, p. 83.]

44 SQUIRES, RADCLIFFE. "Tilbury Town Today," in Edwin Arlington
Robinson: Centenary Essays. Edited by Ellsworth Barnard.
Athens: University of Georgia Press, pp. 175-83.
[Comparison of Robinson's poetry with that of Stevens and
Eliot suggesting that Robinson's work is the more durable
because it proves rather than assumes its themes and be-
cause the style is less obtrusive.]

45 STARR, NATHAN COMFORT. "The Transformation of Merlin," in
Edwin Arlington Robinson: Centenary Essays. Edited by
Ellsworth Barnard. Athens: University of Georgia Press,
pp. 106-19.
Robinson's Merlin is different from other versions in

1969

that the hero is not a magician and is only metaphorically
enchanted by Vivian, who is both sensuous and intelligent.
Robinson's treatment of his materials here is that of a
realist, not a romantic.

46 STEVICK, ROBERT D. "Formulation of E. A. Robinson's Principles
    of Poetry." Colby Library Quarterly, 8 (June), 295-308.
       Because Robinson wrote in a well established tradition,
    he had no particular need to formulate a sympathetic theory.
    His poetics were intuitive and included an insistence upon
    metrical and syntactical regularity along with full ex-
    ploitation of semantic possibilities. [Analysis of "Many
    Are Called" and two Octaves. Reprinted in 1969.A4.]

47 _____. "The Metrical Style of E. A. Robinson," in Edwin Arl-
    ington Robinson: Centenary Essays. Edited by Ellsworth
    Barnard. Athens: University of Georgia Press, pp. 54-68.
       "Robinson's poetic worth can be reliably assessed through
    study of his style." "Eros Turannos" is superior to "The
    Unforgiven" because of the superior diction and metrical
    style. In the short poems Robinson pays scrupulous atten-
    tion to metrical style, but in the long poetry his blank
    verse becomes increasingly irregular with more syntactical
    peculiarities, an index of his lessening poetic powers.

48 SUSS, IRVING D. "The Plays of Edwin Arlington Robinson."
    Colby Library Quarterly, 8 (September), 347-63.
       Need rather than ability prompted Robinson to spend seven
    years writing plays. Van Zorn and The Porcupine, here ana-
    lyzed, were published but only the first was produced.
    Neither has ever been well received. [Reprinted in
    1969.A4.]

49 UNTERMEYER, LOUIS. "Simon Simple." Colby Library Quarterly,
    8 (December), 415.
       [Reprint of 1916.B20.]

50 VAN DOREN, MARK. "Edwin Arlington Robinson." Colby Library
    Quarterly, 8 (June), 279.
       [Brief appreciation emphasizing Robinson's lack of vanity
    and mastery of form.]

51 WEEKS, LEWIS E., JR. "Maine in the Poetry of Edwin Arlington
    Robinson." Colby Library Quarterly, 8 (June), 317-34.
       Maine is reflected in Robinson's poetry in his images,
    especially those of the sea, his character types, and
    themes relating to the Protestant ethic and destruction and
    decay.

1969

52 WHITE, WILLIAM. "A Bibliography of Edwin Arlington Robinson,
    1964-1969." Colby Library Quarterly, 8 (December), 448-62.
    [Supplement to Hogan's bibliography, incorporated in
    1971.A2.]

53 _____. "Three Literary Giants." The American Book Collector,
    19 (April-May), 4.
    [Review of Edwin Arlington Robinson's Letters to Edith
    Brower.] With Cary's notes and Miss Brower's memoir, "the
    volume is almost a biography in itself."

1970 A BOOKS

1   FISH, ROBERT STEVENS. "A Dramatic and Rhetorical Analysis of
    'The Man Against the Sky' and Other Selected Poems of E. A.
    Robinson." Ph.D. thesis, University of Oklahoma, 184 pp.
    [Certain poems generally considered only from a philo-
    sophical point of view are analyzed as dramatic and rhetor-
    ical works, notably "The Man Against the Sky," "Credo,"
    "The Children of the Night," "Hillcrest," "L'Envoi," and
    "Demos." DAI 30:6196A.]

2   MILLER, JOHN HERMAN. "E. A. Robinson's Changing Beliefs About
    Living in the World." Ph.D. thesis, Indiana University,
    219 pp.
    [An examination of Robinson's progressive pessimism about
    his society by tracing four major themes established in his
    first volume and continuing through the last: art, death,
    light, and living in this world. His early tentative ide-
    alism is finally replaced by a conviction that capitalism
    has corrupted the world beyond repair. DAI 31:4783A.]

3   MURPHY, FRANCIS, ed. Edwin Arlington Robinson: A Collection
    of Critical Essays. Twentieth Century Views. Englewood
    Cliffs, New Jersey: Prentice-Hall, 186 pp.
    [Introduction (pp. 1-7) by editor noting defensive tone
    of Robinson criticism; a new essay by Josephine Miles,
    cited below; and reprints or partial reprints of 1922.B35;
    1935.A2, B81; 1946.A1; 1950.B8; 1954.A1, B2; 1958.B2;
    1965.A1, B3; 1967.A5; 1968.B12.]

4   [PYE, JOHN WILLIAM.] Edwin Arlington Robinson: A Bio-
    Bibliography. Hartford, Connecticut: Watkinson Library,
    Trinity College, 44 pp.
    [Short title catalog with biographical and bibliographi-
    cal notes of the H. Bacon Collamore Collection of Robinson-
    iana at Trinity College. Includes excerpts from letters
    and two deleted stanzas of "Twilight Song."]

1970 B SHORTER WRITINGS

1 BURTON, D. H. "Edwin Arlington Robinson and Christianity."
   Spirit: A Magazine of Poetry, 37 (Spring), 30-35.
       Much of Robinson's poetry expresses affinity to the
   Christian ethic although Robinson disavowed Christianity.
   "The fact is that neither orthodox theology nor established
   ecclesiastical institutions meant very much for a man for
   whom philosophical idealism and scientific doubt had become
   integral."

2 CRAWFORD, JOHN. "Success and Failure in the Poetry of Edwin
   Arlington Robinson." Rendezvous: Journal of Arts and Letters, 5 (Spring), 27-29.
       Robinson considered the individual responsible for his
   own failure in such characters as Avon and Cavender. He
   had a balanced view of life in that he saw success beyond
   the failure. This co-existence is best expressed by Tim-
   berlake in Matthias at the Door.

3 CROWLEY, JOHN W. "E. A. Robinson and Henry Cabot Lodge." The
   New England Quarterly, 43 (March), 115-24.
       Henry Cabot Lodge was a man of letters as well as a poli-
   tician. His correspondence with Robinson reveals his critical gifts and his concern about his son George who could
   not succeed as a poet. [Fifteen letters from and to Robinson, housed at the Massachusetts Historical Society, are
   here printed.]

4 DONALDSON, SCOTT. "Books: Amplification." Harper's Magazine,
   241 (September), 9.
       [Letter to the editor objecting to Irving Howe's saying
   that Robinson's centennial was not observed.]

5 HEALY, MARY K. Robinson and Frost. Aspects of English. New
   York: Holt, Rinehart and Winston, pp. 1-31.
       [Biographical introduction and detailed study questions
   for brief selection of Robinson's poems.]

6 HOWE, IRVING. "Tribute to an American Poet." Harper's Magazine, 240 (June), 103-108.
       Robinson "grows through re-reading." He will never be as
   popular as Frost, but some poems are better than Frost's,
   especially "The Clerks," "The Pity of the Leaves," "Eros
   Turannos," "Isaac and Archibald," and the Arthurian poems.
   [Reprinted in 1973.B6.]

1970

7   LEARY, LEWIS. "Robinson, Edwin Arlington," in Articles on
    American Literature 1950-1967. Durham, N.C.: Duke Univer-
    sity Press, pp. 467-70.
       [Bibliography of seventy-six serial articles on Robin-
    son.]

8   MILES, JOSEPHINE. "Robinson's Inner Fire," in Edwin Arlington
    Robinson: A Collection of Critical Essays. Edited by
    Francis Murphy. Twentieth Century Views. Englewood Cliffs,
    New Jersey: Prentice-Hall, pp. 110-16.
       Robinson's theme and subject matter are traditionally ro-
    mantic, but his dry tone and habit of understatement anti-
    cipate much of current poetry.

9   MORAN, RONALD. "Lorraine and the Sirens: Courtesans in Two
    Poems by E. A. Robinson," in Essays in Honor of Esmond Lin-
    worth Marilla. Edited by Thomas Austin Kirby and William
    John Olive. Baton Rouge: Louisiana State University
    Press, pp. 312-19.
       "The Growth of 'Lorraine'" and "Veteran Sirens" are both
    poems dealing with problems of prostitutes, in spite of
    dissenting views by other critics.

10 NILON, CHARLES H. Bibliography of Bibliographies in American
    Literature. New York and London: R. R. Bowker Company,
    pp. 235-37.
       [A list of twenty-four bibliographical aids.]

11 REEVES, PASCHAL. "Edwin Arlington Robinson's Letters to Edith
    Brower." Georgia Review, 24 (Summer), 238-39.
       This book is for specialists, but it does provide insight
    into the life and times of a major author.

12 THOMPSON, LAWRANCE. Robert Frost: The Years of Triumph,
    1915-38. New York: Holt, Rinehart and Winston, pp. 43-46,
    380-91, 418-22, 666-68, and passim.
       [Report of uneasy relationship between Robinson and Frost,
    who was offended when Robinson was introduced to him as
    America's "greatest poet," and whose celebrated preface to
    King Jasper does not mention the poem introduced.]

13 THOMPSON, W. R. "Broceliande: E. A. Robinson's Palace of
    Art." The New England Quarterly, 43 (June), 231-49.
       An examination of symbol and structure in Merlin reveals
    that Robinson is making a parallel of the myth and the 1917
    world crisis. Merlin represents reason while Vivian stands
    for imagination.

14   TURNER, STEVEN. "Robinson's 'Richard Cory.'" The Explicator,
        28 (May), Item 73.
            Morris (1965.B11) is wrong in emphasizing the Anglicisms
        in this poem. They are puns: soul (sole), head (crown),
        finery (in fine).

15   WHITE, WILLIAM. "Remember E. A. Robinson." Literary Sketches,
        10 (September), 8-9.
            England has not shared with the United States the in-
        creased attention to Robinson; a new edition of The Concise
        Cambridge History of English Literature barely mentions him.

16   WOLF, H. R.   "E. A. Robinson and the Integration of Self," in
        Modern American Poetry: Essays in Criticism. Edited by
        Jerome Mazzaro. New York: David McKay, pp. 49-60.
            [Psychoanalytic approach to Robinson's character sketches,
        emphasizing the "telic disorganization" of the personali-
        ties. Special attention to "Mr. Flood's Party," the Annan-
        dale poems, "Aunt Imogen" and "The Gift of God."]

1971 A BOOKS

1   GREBANIER, BERNARD. "Foreword," in Edwin Arlington Robinson:
        A Centenary Memoir-Anthology. Edited by Bernard Grebanier.
        South Brunswick and New York: A. S. Barnes for Poetry So-
        ciety of America, pp. 9-25.
            [Biographical sketch, with brief descriptions of each
        volume of Robinson's poetry and an overview of the criti-
        cism. Considerable attention to Robinson's relationship
        with Frost.]

2   WHITE, WILLIAM. Edwin Arlington Robinson: A Supplementary
        Bibliography. The Serif Series: Bibliographies and Check-
        lists, No. 17. Kent, Ohio: Kent State University Press,
        168 pp.
            [Additions, corrections, and supplement to Hogan's bib-
        liography (1936.A4), listing all primary and secondary ma-
        terials on Robinson through 1970. Includes masters as well
        as doctors theses, reviews of books about Robinson, and
        thirteen items by Robinson hitherto uncollected.]

1971 B SHORTER WRITINGS

1   BLOOM, HAROLD. "Bacchus and Merlin: The Dialectic of Roman-
        tic Poetry in America." Southern Review, 7 (January), 140-
        75; and in The Ringers in the Tower: Studies in the Roman-
        tic Tradition. Chicago: University of Chicago Press,
        pp. 291-321.

1971

[An examination of the first books of Emerson, Robinson, Hart Crane, and Alvin Feinman, with four pages devoted to The Torrent and the Night Before.] Robinson was "nearly a great poet," but American romanticism "demands the exuberance of a Whitman."

2   BONE, ESTHER. "Robinson's Matthias at the Door: A New Variant." Serif, 8 (June), 31.
     [One paragraph describing an edition of this poem at Kent State unlike the description of the editions in Hogan's bibliography.]

3   BRAITHWAITE, WILLIAM STANLEY. "William Stanley Braithwaite Remembers E. A. Robinson." New Letters, 38 (Fall), 53-64.
     [Reminiscence of conversations, drinks, and a party in Lucius Beebe's rooms with Robinson, written by a book reviewer who was one of his earliest supporters and admirers. Several factual inaccuracies in essay.]

4   BRASHER, THOMAS L. "Robinson's 'Mr. Flood's Party.'" The Explicator, 29 (February), 45.
     Ownbey's comment on this poem (1950.B6) doesn't consider Browning's Roland sufficiently, for there are more parallels with "Childe Roand to the Dark Town Came" than with Chanson de Roland.

5   CARY, RICHARD. "Additions to the Robinson Collection." Colby Library Quarterly, 9:377-82.
     [A bibliography of Robinson books, manuscripts, and association items acquired by the Colby College Library since 1969.]

6   DUNN, N. E. "'Wreck and Yesterday,'" The Meaning of Failure in Lancelot." Colby Library Quarterly, 9 (September), 349-56.
     An autocratic society is inadequate for the fulfillment of man's psychological and spiritual nature. Robinson suggests that a new social structure, such as a democracy, is required.

7   GRIFFITH, B. W. "A Note on Robinson's Use of Turannos." Concerning Poetry, 4 (Spring), 39.
     "Turannos" means "unconstitutional ruler," a person who achieves power without having it as a birthright. The husband is perhaps impotent or homosexual.

8   GRIMSHAW, JAMES. "Robinson's 'Lost Anchors.'" The Explicator, 30 (December), 36.

A Christian interpretation is possible here, with the
fisherman representing Jesus and the mother in the last
line Mary. Robinson may be making a claim for a re-vital-
ized religion here.

9   HARKEY, J. H. "Mr. Flood's Two Moons." <u>Mark Twain Journal</u>,
15 (Summer), 20-21.
    Having had only three drinks, Mr. Flood is probably not
drunk. Perhaps the second moon he sees is a memory of
another harvest moon.

10   MacKILLOP, I. D. "Robinson's Accomplishment." <u>Essays in
Criticism</u>, 21 (July), 297-308.
    [Essay-review of anthologies edited by Davis, Dickey, and
Murphy, who is criticized. Explications of "The Unforgiv-
en," "A Man in Our Town," and "Mr. Flood's Party," concentrating on the tensions of the idiosyncratic character and
the "makeshift communal identities" of the collective narrator.]

11   MONTEIRO, GEORGE. "Addendum to Hogan's Robinson." <u>Papers of
the Bibliographical Society of America</u>, 65 (Autumn), 414.
    [Citation of newspaper publication of "The Garden,"
called "God's Garden" in Robinson's first book.]

12   PERRINE, LAURENCE. "Robinson's 'The Tree in Pamela's Garden.'"
<u>The Explicator</u>, 30 (November), 18.
    One coherent explanation of this sonnet is that Pamela is
having a secret love affair.

13   RAFFEL, BURTON. <u>Introduction to Poetry</u>. New York: New American Library, pp. 116-17.
    ["For Calderon" cited as an example of "fake drama."]

14   REXROTH, KENNETH. <u>American Poetry in the Twentieth Century</u>.
New York: Herder and Herder, pp. 30-31.
    Robinson is closer to the nineteenth century tradition
than the modern movement in poetry. His irony is similar to
that of the Georgian poets.

15   RICHARDS, B. F. "'No, There is not a Dawn....'" <u>Colby Library Quarterly</u>, 9 (September), 367-74.
    The speaker in "Luke Havergal" is probably his alter ego.
The "she" of the poem may be love, the soul of man, or creative power.

16   RIESE, TEUT A. "Geschichtsverständnis und Geschichtsdichtung
in Amerika des 20. Jahrhunderts," in <u>Amerikanische Literatur</u>

1971

im 20. Jahrhundert/American Literature in the Twentieth
Century. Edited by Alfred Weber and Dietmar Haack. Got-
tingen: Vandenhoeck & Ruprecht, pp. 73-91.
[Explication of "Ben Jonson," in which Robinson deals
with "the existential problem of the writer," in comparison
with the uses of history in the work of Henry Adams and
Styron's Nat Turner. (Summary in English, pp. 89-91.)]

17   SAMPLEY, A. M. "The Power or the Glory: The Dilemma of E. A.
Robinson." Colby Library Quarterly, 9 (September), 357-66.
Robinson never resolved the problem of "whether the individual should follow his inner direction or the regime
enforced by society." "Captain Craig" and Tristram are his
clearest statements in favor of the individual; most of the
other poems lean in the other direction.

18   SLETHAUG, G. E. "The King in Robinson's 'Old King Cole.'"
English Record, 21 (Fall), 45-46.
The protagonist is similar to the one in The House of
Seven Gables: a man of arrogance who is really powerless
to change the encroaching order.

19   WHITE, HILDA. "Edwin Arlington Robinson," in Portraits of
Eight New England Authors. Garden City, New York: Double-
day, pp. 177-205.
[Biographical sketch based on the Hagedorn and Smith biographies emphasizing Robinson's social ineptness and devotion to his craft.]

20   WHITE, WILLIAM. "Robinson in Leary's Articles...1950-1967."
Colby Library Quarterly, 9 (September), 374-75.
[Bibliographer White (1971.A2) notes the errors and omis-
sions of bibliographer Leary (1970.B7).]

1972 A BOOKS

1   SUNDERMEIER, MICHAEL WILLIAM. "A Concordance to the Poetry of
Edwin Arlington Robinson." Ph.D. thesis, University of Neb-
raska, 781 pp.
[Based principally on the 1937 Collected Poems, this concordance indexes main words and includes appendices that
index words from two uncollected poems, proper names, foreign phrases, et cetera. DAI 33:1744A.]

1972 B SHORTER WRITINGS

1   CARY, RICHARD. "Mowry Saben about Edwin Arlington Robinson."
    Colby Library Quarterly, 9 (March), 482-97.
    [Discussion of one of Robinson's most flamboyant college
    friends who later wrote several articles and letters about
    Robinson, indicating that he admired him enormously as a
    poet and a man, but disagreed with him philosophically.]

2   DAVIS, ROYAL G. "Edwin Arlington Robinson, Congregationalist."
    The Congregationalist, 132 (April), 11-12.
    Robinson's mother was a loyal church worker and he at-
    tended the Congregational church school in Gardiner when he
    was growing up. He reflects this background in his champi-
    onship of the eccentric individual and his attack on mate-
    rialistic values.

3   DICKEY, JAMES. "Edwin Arlington Robinson: The Many Truths,"
    in Modern American Poetry: Essays in Criticism. Edited
    by Guy Owen. Deland, Florida: Everett/Edwards, pp. 1-19.
    [Reprint of 1965.A1, 1968.B7, and 1970.A3.]

4   DONALDSON, SCOTT. Poet in America: Winfield Townley Scott.
    Austin: University of Texas Press, pp. 93-97 and passim.
    [Scattered references to the relationship between Scott
    and Robinson, whose work influenced the younger poet.]

5   EVANS, OLIVER HOUSTON. "The Sonnet in America." Ph.D. thesis,
    Purdue University, 187 pp.
    [Robinson, who expanded the subject matter and tone of
    the sonnet, is one of fourteen American sonnet writers
    studied. DAI 33:5121A.]

6   FISH, R. S. "The Tempering of Faith in E. A. Robinson's 'The
    Man Against the Sky.'" Colby Library Quarterly, 9 (March),
    456-68.
    [Explication of "The Man Against the Sky" as a dramatic
    rather than didactic poem.]

7   HAAS, RICHARD. "Oral Interpretation as Discovery Through Per-
    sona." Oral English, 1 (Autumn), 13-14.
    [Explication of "Richard Cory" with particular attention
    to the diction.]

8   JOYNER, NANCY. "E. A. Robinson's Concessions to the Critics."
    Research Studies, 40 (March), 48-53.
    Robinson removed some poems from subsequent publications,
    made substantial revisions in "Captain Craig" and Avon's

Harvest, and even alternated volumes of short and long poems
in his early years in an effort to please his critics.

9   ____. "Robinson's Poets." Colby Library Quarterly, 9 (March),
       441-55.
            While Robinson's poems about actual poets and the generic
       poet are full of high seriousness, he treats imaginary po-
       ets satirically in "Captain Craig" and Amaranth.

10   LIE, ULF. "A Poetry of Attitudes: The Speaker Personae in
      E. A. Robinson's Early Dramatic Poetry," in Americana-
      Norvegica, Vol. 4. Edited by Britta Seyersted. Oslo:
      Universitetsforlaget, pp. 193-210.
            An examination of poems with speakers written from 1902
      to 1916 reveals that Robinson's method stayed essentially
      the same with varying success: an objective description of
      the event, the introduction of other attitudes revealing
      the speaker's bias, and the use of symbols. "Eros Turannos,"
      by using more dramatic details, is superior to "Luke Haver-
      gal," although the procedures are similar.

11   MARCUS, MORDECAI. "E. A. Robinson's 'Flammonde': Toward Some
      Essential Clarifications." The Markham Review, 3 (October),
      77-80.
            Flammonde is a psychologically more complex character
      than has previously been suggested because he is presented
      both as a Christ-like and Satan-like figure.

12   MORRIS, CELIA. "Robinson's Camelot: Renunciation as Drama."
      Colby Library Quarterly, 9 (March), 468-81.
            [Analysis of Merlin, with some commentary on Lancelot, as
      a vehicle for expressing Robinson's pessimistic views about
      human nature.]

13   PERRINE, LAURENCE. "The Sources of Robinson's Merlin." Ameri-
      can Literature, 44 (May), 313-21.
            Robinson did not use Malory's Morte D'Arthur for his Mer-
      lin, but a popularization of the Vulgate Merlin, S. Hum-
      phreys Gurteen's The Arthurian Epic (1895), which he borrowed
      from Louis Ledoux in 1916. Robinson's Merlin resembles
      Gurteen's summary of the Vulgate version in setting, char-
      acter, plot, and theme.

14   SCHOLNICK, R. J. "The Shadowed Years: Mrs. Richards, Mr.
      Stedman, and Robinson." Colby Library Quarterly, 9 (June),
      510-31.
            Laura Richards encouraged the friendship between Robinson
      and Clarence Stedman, who was a friend and literary advisor

to him during Robinson's difficult early years in New York.
[Five letters to Stedman from Richards printed.]

15 SWEET, C. A. "A Re-Examination of 'Richard Cory.'" Colby Library Quarterly, 9 (September), 579-82.
     The narrator in "Richard Cory" is unreliable; it is the townspeople, rather than Cory, who have erected the barrier.

16 TSCHUMI, RAYMOND. Thought in Twentieth Century English Poetry. New York: Octagon Books, pp. 269-70.
     Robinson and Jeffers are the best of Emerson's followers.
     [Symbolism in Merlin analyzed.]

17 VEZA, LAURETTE. La Poésie Américaine de 1910 a 1940. Publications de la Sorbonne. Paris: Didier, pp. 54-60.
     [Discussion of world view, with particular attention to Dionysus in Doubt and Matthias at the Door, which is compared to the work of Jeffers.]

1973 A BOOKS

1 WILSON, WILLIAM J. "Existentialistic Implications in Edwin Arlington Robinson's Pessimism." Ph.D. thesis, University of Nebraska-Lincoln, 166 pp.
    Ninety-eight of Robinson's 208 poems are pessimistic, an attitude that ties him to existentialism. Critics support and explications of individual poems reinforce this view, especially regarding Robinson's "futility-in-ignorance" theme. [DAI 34:7793A-7794A.]

1973 B SHORTER WRITINGS

1 BAKER, CARLOS. "Robinson's Stoical Romanticism: 1890-1897." The New England Quarterly, 46 (March), 3-16.
    Keats and Wordsworth, as well as other romantics to a lesser extent, were significant influences on Robinson's attitude and style.

2 BROOKS, CLEANTH, R. W. B. LEWIS, and ROBERT PENN WARREN. "Edwin Arlington Robinson," in their edition of American Literature: The Makers and the Making, Vol. 2. New York: St. Martin's Press, pp. 1829-45.
    [Overview of career and assessment of poems in anthology.]
    "Robinson was a superior poet but an unlucky one." His most remarkable voice is narrative, for he lacks sufficient vocabulary or enough literary background for his philosophical poems.

1973

3   CARRUTH, HAYDEN. "The New England Tradition," in Regional
    Perspective: An Examination of America's Literary Heri-
    tage. Edited by John Gordon Burke. Chicago: American
    Library Association, pp. 26-32.
        Robinson's vacillation between optimism and pessimism,
    his ambiguity and understatement, and his "serious humor"
    are part of his New England background. [Analysis of "The
    Torrent."]

4   DAVIDSON, MARSHALL B., et al., eds. The American Heritage
    History of the Writers' America. New York: American Heri-
    tage Publishing Company, pp. 286-88.
        [Robinson is discussed as a representative New England
    poet.]

5   DUNN, N. E. "Riddling Leaves: Robinson's 'Luke Havergal.'"
    Colby Library Quarterly, 10 (March), 17-25.
        A possible allusion to Vergil's Aeneid, Book VI, suggests
    that the "she" in "Luke Havergal" is comparable to the
    Cumaen Sibyl.

6   FRENCH, ROBERTS W. "On Teaching 'Richard Cory.'" English Rec-
    ord, 23 (Fall), 11-14.
        [Essay on pedagogy, emphasizing the importance of the
    teacher's not anticipating student response in such poems
    as "Richard Cory."]

7   HOWE, IRVING. "A Grave and Solitary Voice: An Appreciation
    of Edwin Arlington Robinson," in The Critical Point: On
    Literature and Culture. New York: Horizon Press, pp. 96-
    108.
        [Reprint of 1970.B6.]

8   LIM, SHIRLEY G. L. "The Changing Craft: Essays on E. C. Sted-
    man, T. B. Aldrich, G. C. Lodge, Trumbull Stickney, W. V.
    Moody, and E. A. Robinson." Ph.D. thesis, Brandeis Univer-
    sity University, 201 pp.
        [An examination of traditional and modern aspects of Rob-
    inson's poetry, demonstrating how in his attitude, diction,
    and subject matter he brought a new dimension to tradition-
    al forms. DAI 34:6648A]

9   UNTERMEYER, LOUIS. "Edwin Arlington Robinson: A Reappraisal,"
    in Literary Lectures Presented at the Library of Congress.
    Washington, D.C.: The Library of Congress, pp. 527-51.
        [Reprint of 1963.A1.]

1974 A BOOKS

1 CARY, RICHARD. Early Reception of Edwin Arlington Robinson:
   The First Twenty Years. Waterville, Me.: Colby College
   Press, 321 pp.
   [Study of Robinson's critical reception which includes
   introductory material dealing with the poet's life and
   times and presents a chapter each on the seven volumes of
   poetry he published between 1896 and 1916. These chapters
   include a discussion of the genesis of the work, a reprint
   of every known notice of the work, and detailed annotation
   of the reviews. Annotated checklist of new bibliographical
   material here in 1974.B4.]

2 MANHEIMER, JOAN. "A Study of the Speaker's Voice in the Poetry
   of Edwin Arlington Robinson." Ph.D. thesis, Brandeis University, 249 pp.
   Robinson's speakers provide mediation between the ex-
   tremes of communal and individual, eccentric values. He
   portrays three major types through a variety of syntactical
   constructions and analogies. Similar to a Greek chorus,
   they are crucially ignorant of the dramatic situation and
   are consequently unable to change it. [DAI 35:1110A.]

1974 B SHORTER WRITINGS

1 BAKER, CARLOS. "'The Jug Makes the Paradise': New Light on
   Eben Flood." Colby Library Quarterly, 10 (June), 327-36.
   Since the publication of "Mr. Flood's Party" coincides
   with the Volstead Act, the jug may contain hard cider in-
   stead of whiskey. The poem is possibly modeled on James
   Kirke Paulding's "The Old Man's Carousel."

2 BOOTH, EARL W. "New England Quartet: E. A. Robinson, Robert
   Frost, Charles Ives and Carl Ruggles." Ph.D. thesis, Uni-
   versity of Utah, 211 pp.
   Robinson was not so successful as Frost in capturing the
   New England diction and landscape. His contributions are
   his psychological acuity and his transcendentalism.

3 BRADLEY, SCULLEY, et.al. "Edwin Arlington Robinson," in their
   edition of The American Tradition in Literature. Fourth
   edition. Vol. 2. New York: Grosset and Dunlap; distrib-
   uted by W. W. Norton, pp. 857-84.
   [Introductory sketch, brief bibliography, and explanatory
   notes of individual poems.]

1974

4   CARY, RICHARD. "Additions to the Robinson Collection: II."
    Colby Library Quarterly, 10 (June), 385-88.
        [Bibliography of Robinson books, manuscripts and associa-
    tion items added to the Colby College Library collection
    since 1971.]

5   _____. "'The Clam-Digger: Capitol Island': A Robinson Son-
    net Recovered." Colby Library Quarterly, 10 (December),
    505-511.
        Internal and circumstantial evidence indicates that this
    poem, published in The Reporter's Monthly, April 26, 1890,
    was written by Robinson.

6   _____. "The First Publication of E. A. Robinson's Poem
    'Broadway.'" American Literature, 46 (March), 83.
        Unknown by Robinson, or later by bibliographers, this
    poem was first published in the New York Evening Sun on
    November 15, 1918.

7   _____. "The First Twenty Years of Edwin Arlington Robinson
    Criticism: A Supplementary Annotated Checklist." Resources
    for American Literary Study, 4 (Autumn), 184-204.
        [Annotations of ninety articles on Robinson from 1896-
    1916 which do not appear in the Hogan or White bibliogra-
    phies. See 1974.A1.]

8   _____. "Robinson's Friend Arthur Davis Variell." Colby Li-
    brary Quarterly, 10 (June), 372-85.
        [Account of association between Robinson and boyhood
    friend who later became a physician and world traveller.
    Summary of Robinson's letters to Variell from 1921 to 1929.]

9   CLARK, GORDON. "E. A. Robinson (Some Maine Sources)." Maine
    Edition: Maine's Poetry Magazine (June), pp. 4-7.
        Blair Hill, an area between Head Tide and Gardiner, Maine,
    is the location of many of Robinson's poems, most notably
    "Isaac and Archibald" and "Stafford's Cabin."

10 COX, DON R. "The Vision of Robinson's Merlin." Colby Library
    Quarterly, 10 (December), 495-504.
        Central to the theme in Merlin is the protagonist's vi-
    sion: an understanding that Change ranks with God and Fate
    as prime forces in Camelot. In Robinson's poem Merlin is
    able to leave Broceliande of his own volition, unlike his
    prototypes in Malory and Tennyson.

11 McFARLAND, RONALD E. "Robinson's 'Luke Havergal.'" Colby Li-
    brary Quarterly, 10 (June), 365-72.

198

The Prodigal Son of Luke 15 and Dante's <u>Divine Comedy</u> are likely sources for this poem. If so, Luke Havergal is a penitent sinner rather than an incipient suicide, and the "she" of the poem is Beatrice.

12   MILLER, JOHN H. "The Structure of E. A. Robinson's 'The Torrent and the Night Before.'" <u>Colby Library Quarterly</u>, 10 (June), 347-64.
      Unlike later volumes, Robinson's first book is organized according to theme. It consists of an introductory four sonnets, sections on art, death, light, and living in this world, and a final section consisting of "The Night Before," which serves as a summary of these themes.

13   MONTEIRO, GEORGE. "'The President and the Poet': Robinson, Roosevelt, and <u>The Touchstone</u>." <u>Colby Library Quarterly</u>, 10 (December), 512-15.
      [Facsimile of a satiric account of Roosevelt's patronage of Robinson and a parody of "Richard Cory" titled "John Rockefeller," both from the January, 1909, issue of <u>The Touchstone</u>, a short-lived journal from Chicago.]

14   PERRINE, LAURENCE. "The Sources of Robinson's Arthurian Poems and His Opinions of Other Treatments." <u>Colby Library Quarterly</u>, 10 (June), 336-46.
      [Documented evidence of thirteen influences on Robinson's treatment of the Arthurian poems.]

15   SANBORN, JOHN N. "Juxtaposition as Structure in 'The Man Against the Sky.'" <u>Colby Library Quarterly</u>, 10 (December), 486-94.
      Rather than using an Aristotelian structure in this poem, Robinson employs the juxtaposition of opposites, a device used by Ovid, Chaucer, Milton and Blake. This contrapuntal technique produces an existential effect, although the poem is finally more hopeful than despairing.

16   STAUFFER, DONALD BARLOW. <u>A Short History of American Poetry</u>. New York: E. P. Dutton, pp. 222-28 and passim.
      Robinson is a major American poet because of his short character sketches and some of his poems of middle length. He resembles Hawthorne most among New England writers, but is in Emerson's poetic tradition. "Whereas Whitman was a poet of the soul, Robinson was a poet of the mind."

17   TUERK, RICHARD. "Robinson's 'Lost Anchors.'" <u>The Explicator</u>, 32 (January), Item 37.
      The use of several Biblical allusions suggests that Robinson's theme in this poem is loss of faith.

1975

1975 A BOOKS

1 CARY, RICHARD. "Introduction" and "Notes," in <u>Uncollected Poems and Prose of Edwin Arlington Robinson</u>. Edited by Richard Cary. Waterville, Me.: Colby College Press, pp. ix-xviii; 167-205.
   [Explanation of the sources and background material concerning the poems, essays, and scattered "briefs" gleaned from letters, interviews, and reminiscences that have not previously been collected.]

2 MULLIGAN, LOUISE. "Mythology and Autobiography in E. A. Robinson's <u>Tristram</u>." Ph.D. thesis, University of Massachusetts, 231 pp.
   Robinson made significant changes in the Tristan legends in his treatment of the story, making it closer to his own involvement in a triangular situation. <u>Tristram</u> therefore has autobiographical implications that have heretofore been slighted. [<u>DAI</u> 32:6102A.]

1975 B SHORTER WORKS

1 INSDORF, ANNETTE LILLIAN. "An American Strain: Connecting Art and Experience." Ph.D. thesis, Yale University, 250 pp.
   [An examination of Robinson's "American aesthetic" along with that of John Dewey, Walt Whitman, E. E. Cummings, and James Agee. <u>DAI</u> 33:3714A.]

2 KART, LAWRENCE. "Richard Cory: Artist Without an Art." <u>Colby Library Quarterly</u>, 11 (September), 160-61.
   In support of Kavka's view (1975.B2), Richard Cory might have been driven to suicide because as an artist he lacked a creative outlet or audience response.

3 KAVKA, JEROME. "Richard Cory's Suicide: A Psychoanalyst's View." <u>Colby Library Quarterly</u>, 11 (September), 150-59.
   Richard Cory may be a victim of "Narcissistic Personality Disorder," the possible cause of Robinson's brothers' early deaths. Robinson may have been saved from a similar fate through his creative ability.

4 MONTEIRO, GEORGE. "Addenda to the Bibliographies of...Robinson [and others]." <u>Paper of the Bibliographical Society of America</u>, 69 (Spring), 175.
   [Confused correction of 1929.B68.]

1976

5   MORRIS, CELIA. "E. A. Robinson and 'The Golden Horoscope of
     Imperfection.'" Colby Library Quarterly, 11 (June), 88-97.
        Profound compassion and unflinching judgment are combined
     in Robinson's treatment of characters in "his best long po-
     ems," Merlin and Lancelot. [Discussion of interrelation-
     ships and moral responsibilities of Lancelot, Guinevere,
     and Arthur.]

6   PISANTI, TOMMASO. "Robinson e la Poesia Americana." Nuova
     Antologia, 524 (June), 239-44.
        [Assessment and overview of career, stressing Robinson's
     unique position in American letters and his profundity.]

7   SIMON, MYRON. The Georgian Poetic. Berkeley: University of
     California Press, pp. 84-85.
        Frost and Robinson were the only American contemporaries
     the Georgians admired.

1976 A BOOKS - NONE

1976 B SHORTER WRITINGS

1   BEDELL, R. MEREDITH. "Perception, Action, and Life in The Man
     Against the Sky." Colby Library Quarterly, 11 (March), 29-
     37.
        The short poems dealing with individuals in The Man
     Against the Sky support the optimistic and existential at-
     titude posited in the eponymous poem. [Special attention
     to "The Gift of God."]

2   DAVIS, WILLIAM V. "'Enduring to the End:' Edwin Arlington
     Robinson's 'Mr. Flood's Party.'" Colby Library Quarterly,
     11 (March), 50-51.
        The double allusion to Burns' poem, "Auld Lang Syne,"
     may be ironically related to two Biblical passages that are
     opposite to the "cup of kindness."

3   MILLER, MICHAEL G. "Miniver Grows Lean." Colby Library Quar-
     terly, 11 (September), 149-50.
        Perhaps Miniver was tubercular, since he "coughed" and
     "grew lean."

4   PERKINS, DAVID. "The Beginnings of the Modern Movement in
     America," in A History of Modern Poetry: From the 1890's
     to the High Modernist Mode. Cambridge: Harvard University
     Press, Belknap Press, pp. 120-31.
        Robinson was America's leading poet at the turn of the

1976

century, but only "about forty pages...are likely to last."
The narratives are not read because there has not been an
audience for long narratives since the romantic period, and
his didactic poems are weak. [Explication of "Richard Cory."]

5 PYE, JOHN WILLIAM. "Edwin Arlington Robinson, Otto Dalstrom,
    and the Nobel Prize." Trinity Reporter, 7 (November), 29-
    31.
       Robinson was appreciative but modest in his letters to
    Otto Dalstrom, a Swedish friend of Joseph Louis French who
    worked intermittently from 1921 to 1928 in trying to get
    the Nobel Prize for him.

6 SHINN, THELMA J. "The Art of a Verse Novelist: Approaching
    Robinson's Late Narratives Through James's The Art of the
    Novel." Colby Library Quarterly, 11 (June), 91-100.
       Robinson follows James' principles in "thematic concerns,
    psychological approach, exploration of the real and roman-
    tic, characterization, and dramatic structure" in the late
    narratives. For both writers imagery is subordinated to
    dramatic purpose.

7 VINCENT, SYBIL KORFF. "Flat Breasted Miracles: Realistic
    Treatment of the Woman's Problem in the Poetry of Edwin
    Arlington Robinson." The Markham Review, 6 (Fall), 14-15.
       Lines from numerous poems indicate that Robinson held a
    sympathetic but unsentimental view of women which tran-
    scends the superficial advocacy of social change and makes
    him "the representative poet of nineteenth century American
    Realism."

Index

A NOTE ON THE INDEX

Included in the index are authors of articles and books about Robinson, titles of books devoted exclusively to Robinson, and selected subject heads. Titles of individual essays in serials or books are not included. The subject headings, all of which are alphabetized under Robinson, are listed below:

Associations with,
 People
 Places
Attitudes toward,
 Capitalism
 Communism
 Materialism
 Moral problems
 Music
 Other writers
 Patriotism
 Religion
Bibliographies of
Collections of
Comparisons to
Concordance
Critical reception of
Criticism, general
 Aesthetic theory
 Arthurian legend
 Autobiographical
  material
 Biblical influence
 Characterization
 Classical influence
 Existentialism
 Historical figures,
  portrayal of
 Humor

Idealism
Imagery
Irony
Narrative technique
Naturalism
New England, influence of
Philosophical studies
Poems of, later rejected
Prose
Psychological studies
Puritanism
Realism
Romanticism
Style (diction and verse
 form)
Symbolism
Textual studies
Transcendentalism
Women, portrayal of
World view
Criticism, individual works
Dissertations about
Explicator articles about
Interviews with
Library of
Life and Letters of
Obituaries of
Poems about

G

H

Radenzel, Edward, 1932.B40
Raffel, Burton, 1971.B13
Ramos, Jose Antonio, 1935.B62
Ranck, Edwin Carty, 1913.B3;
     1919.B5-B6; 1921.B20-B21;
     1922.B29; 1927.B56; 1929.B59;
     1930.B32; 1931.B16; 1932.B41;
     1933.B20; 1934.B27; 1935.B63
Randall, David A., 1969.B40
Ransom, Ellene, 1934.B28
Ransom, John Crowe, 1936.B20;
     1947.B11
Raven, A. A., 1944.B7
Read, Arthur M., II, 1968.B15
Redlich, Rosemarie, 1952.B4
Redman, Ben Ray, 1923.B27;
     1925.B23; 1926.A1; 1927.B57;
     1929.B60; 1930.B33; 1932.B42
Reed, Edward Bliss, 1917.B11-
     B12; 1920.B21; 1926.B7
Reese, Lizette Woodworth,
     1929.B61-B62
Reeves, Paschal, 1970.B11
Reichert, Victor Emanuel,
     1934.B29; 1966.A5
Reid, Dorothy E., 1930.B34
Reilly, Joseph J., 1922.B30
Rein, David N., 1963.B12
Rexroth, Kenneth, 1971.B14
Richards, B. F., 1971.B15
Richards, Laura E., 1924.B17;
     1931.B17; 1935.B64; 1936.A5,
     B21
Rickert, Edith, 1929.B53
Ridge, Lola, 1920.B22; 1923.B28;
     1926.B8; 1927.B58
Riese, Teut A., 1971.B16
Ritchey, John, 1940.B24
Rittenhouse, Jessie B., 1926.B9;
     1934.B30; 1941.B5
Robbins, Howard Chandler,
     1936.B23
Robinson, Corinne Roosevelt,
     1919.B4
Robinson, Edwin Arlington:
--Associations with, People,
     Aiken, Conrad, 1969.B1
     Barbe, Waitman, 1960.B7
     Barstow, James, 1964.B7

Bates, Esther Willard,
     1944.A2
Beebe, Lucius, 1933.B2;
     1969.B1; 1971.B3
Blair, Arthur, 1941.B4
Braithwaite, William Stanley,
     1971.B3
Brower, Edith, 1943.B4;
     1968.A1
Brown, Rollo Walter, 1938.B3
Burnham, George, 1942.B1
Burton, Richard, 1938.B4
Cohen, Morris, 1959.B3
Dalstrom, Otto, 1976.B5
French, Joseph Lewis,
     1938.A1; 1965.A4; 1976.B5
Frost, Robert, 1935.A2;
     1939.B9; 1964.B4; 1966.B17;
     1970.B12; 1971.A1
Hardy, Thomas, 1938.B31
Literary Guild, 1928.B3;
     1929.B73; 1936.B33
Lodge, Henry Cabot, 1970.B3
Louis, Alfred H., 1915.B1;
     1928.B20; 1938.A1; 1943.B12;
     1956.B3
MacDowell, Mrs. Edward,
     1938.B18
Mason, Daniel Gregory,
     1937.B11-B12
Maynard, Theodore, 1938.B21
Monroe, Harriet, 1962.B13
Moody, Harriet Converse,
     1947.B7
Moody, William Vaughan,
     1902.B3; 1951.B7; 1960.B2;
     1962.B3
Moore, E. G., 1934.B23
Neihardt, John G., 1938.B23
Neilson, William Allen,
     1954.B6
Peabody, Josephine Preston,
     1969.B3
Richards, Laura E., 1931.B17;
     1936.A5; 1967.A4; 1972.B14
Robinson, H. Dean, 1934.B24
Robinson, Barbara, 1960.B5
Robinson, Marie, 1960.B5
Robinson, Ruth, 1960.B5

Roosevelt, Kermit, 1946.B12
Roosevelt, Theodore, 1905.B1-
    B2; 1943.B13; 1946.B12;
    1958.B5; 1974.B13
Saben, Mowry, 1972.B1
Schmitt, Howard George,
    1943.A2, B9
Schumann, Alanson Tucker,
    1934.B22; 1955.A1; 1969.B24
Scott, Winfield Townley,
    1956.B5; 1961.B5; 1972.B4
Stedman, Clarence, 1931.B11;
    1942.B14; 1972.B14
Van Doren, Carl, 1936.B33
Variell, Arthur Davis,
    1963.B4; 1974.B8
Walsh, William Thomas,
    1942.B10
--Association with, Places
    Harvard, 1938.B16; 1940.A3;
    1941.B7; 1949.B12
    MacDowell Colony (Peterbor-
    ough), 1938.A1, B18;
    1949.B4; 1964.B10
    Maine, Gardiner and Environs,
    1930.B36; 1933.B17;
    1935.B71, B76; 1936.A5;
    1939.B3; 1940.B15, B17-B19;
    1941.B4; 1952.B4; 1969.B51;
    1974.B9
    New York City, 1923.B5;
    1931.B11; 1934.B30;
    1938.A1, B25
--Attitudes toward,
    Capitalism, 1935.B33;
    1936.B4; 1970.A2
    Communism, 1935.B33
    Materialism, 1942.B7;
    1959.B4; 1968.B5; 1969.A3,
    B13
    Moral Problems, 1938.B6;
    1962.B14; 1963.B13;
    1969.B39; 1971.B7
    Music, 1935.B37; 1949.B9,
    B12; 1962.B6
    Other writers, 1916.B13;
    1920.B13; 1927.B29;
    1929.B22; 1933.B22;
    1936.B16, B34; 1938.A1,
    B16; 1940.A3; 1941.B7;

    1959.B3; 1963.B3; 1969.B3;
    1974.B14; 1975.A1
    Patriotism, 1943.B4; 1952.B2
    Religion, 1922.B16; 1929.B30;
    1935.B25; 1938.B21, B24;
    1942.B10; 1943.B1; 1948.B14,
    B16; 1949.B8; 1953.A1;
    1969.B12, B14; 1970.B1;
    1972.B2
--Bibliographies of, 1923.B2, B21;
    1924.B8; 1931.A1; 1936.A1, A4,
    B11; 1937.A1; 1940.B21;
    1941.B2; 1944.A1; 1948.B11;
    1954.B5, B8; 1962.B12;
    1963.A1, B15; 1965.B17;
    1967.A1; 1969.B8, B15-B18,
    B52; 1970.A4, B7, B10;
    1971.A2; 1974.B4, B7; 1975.B4
--Collections of, 1936.A1, B9;
    1938.B8; 1940.B16; 1942.B2;
    1948.A1, B11, B20; 1949.B13;
    1950.B9; 1951.B1; 1963.B4;
    1967.B3; 1969.B15-B18;
    1970.A4; 1971.B5; 1974.B4
--Comparisons to,
    Adams, Henry, 1955.B3; 1971.B16
    Andreyev, Leonid N., 1929.B29
    Aristotle, 1924.B10
    Arnold, Matthew, 1922.B17;
    1929.B31; 1969.B23
    Browning, Robert, 1897.B8;
    1902.B1; 1903.B1-B2;
    1916.B12; 1919.B4; 1920.B6,
    B11; 1921.B1, B6; 1922.B1,
    B8, B16, B35; 1925.B9, B21,
    B26; 1926.B5, B10-B11;
    1927.B63; 1929.B29-B30, B41,
    B63; 1930.B1, B9; 1932.B25,
    B38-B39, B46; 1934.B16, B31;
    1935.B48; 1936.B30; 1937.B8,
    B10; 1938.B12; 1940.B32;
    1949.B5; 1952.B1; 1962.B8;
    1963.B5; 1971.B4
    Burns, Robert, 1976.B2
    Chekov, Anton, 1924.B10
    Clough, Arthur Hugh, 1923.B3
    Crabbe, George, 1920.B11;
    1922.B1
    Crane, Hart, 1971.B1
    Cunningham, V. J., 1965.B5
    Dante, Alighieri, 1934.B35;
    1974.B11

Vincent, Sybil Korff, 1976.B7
Vinson, Esther, 1935.B76

W

W., W., 1921.B24
Wagenknecht, Edward, 1958.B5
Wager, Willis, 1968.B17
Waggoner, Hyatt Howe, 1940.B29;
     1950.B8; 1952.B6; 1968.B18;
     1969.A4; 1970.A3
Walcutt, Charles Child, 1966.B18
Waldo, Fulleton, 1921.B25
Walker, Helen, 1922.B33
Walsh, William Thomas, 1925.B34;
     1942.B10
Walton, Eda Lou, 1930.B42;
     1931.B23; 1933.B30; 1934.B37-
     B38; 1935.B77-B78
Ward, A. C., 1932.B50
Warren, Austin, 1966.B19
Warren, Robert Penn, 1960.B1;
     1973.B2
Wasserstrom, William, 1963.B9
Wearing, Thomas, 1942.B11
Weaver, John D., 1940.B30
Weaver, Raymond M., 1920.B28
Weber, Alfred, 1971.B17
Weber, Carl J., 1935.B79-B80;
     1936.B34; 1938.B30-B31;
     1940.B31; 1941.B9; 1942.B12-
     B13; 1943.A2, B13-B14;
     1944.B8; 1947.B13-B14;
     1948.B19-B20; 1949.B13-B14;
     1950.B9; 1954.B9; 1956.B6
Weeks, Edward A., 1924.B21
Weeks, Lewis E., Jr., 1965.B16;
     1969.A4, B51
Weirick, Bruce, 1924.B22
Wellman, Manly Wade, 1963.B16
Wells, Henry W., 1940.B32;
     1943.B15
Westbrook, Perry D., 1951.B10
Wheelock, John Hall, 1938.B32
Where the Light Falls: A Por-
     trait of Edwin Arlington Rob-
     inson, 1965.A4
Whicher, George F., 1948.B21;
     1951.B11
Whicher, Stephen, 1961.B8
Whipple, Leon, 1927.B67

Whipple, T. K., 1928.B19;
     1929.B74
White, Gertrude M., 1966.B20
White, Hilda, 1971.B19
White, Newman I., 1922.B34;
     1931.B24
White, William, 1947.B15;
     1956.B7; 1965.B17; 1966.B21-
     B22; 1969.B52-B53; 1970.B15;
     1971.A2, B20
Whitney, Emmie B., 1931.B25
Widdemer, Margaret, 1964.B10
Wilder, Amos N., 1940.B33
Wilder, Thornton, 1931.B26
Wilkinson, Marguerite, 1919.B9;
     1920.B29; 1921.B26; 1927.B68
Williams, Alice Meacham, 1942.B14
Williams, M. L., 1934.B39
Williams, Stanley T., 1948.B22
Williams, William Carlos,
     1948.B23
Williams-Ellis, Amabel, 1924.B23
Wilson, Edmund, Jr., 1923.B34;
     1927.B69; 1952.B7
Wilson, James Southall, 1925.B35;
     1941.B10
Wilson, William J., 1973.A1
Winters, Yvor, 1922.B35; 1945.B6;
     1946.A1; 1969.A4; 1970.A3
Wisehart, Marion K., 1928.B20
Wolf, H. R., 1970.B16
Wood, Clement, 1920.B30; 1925.B36
Woodall, Allen E., 1937.B17
Wright, Celeste Turner, 1953.B2
Wright, Elizabeth, 1963.B17

Y

Young, Stark, 1917.B15

Z

Zabel, Morton Dauwen, 1935.B81;
     1937.B18-B19; 1965.A1;
     1970.A3
Zardoya, Concha, 1956.B8
Zaturenska, Marya, 1944.B3;
     1946.B8
Zietlow, Paul Nathan, 1965.A5;
     1967.B16
Ziff, Larzer, 1966.B23
Zillman, Lawrence John, 1966.B24

DATE DUE
